D1707709

Mapping World Literature

CONTINUUM LITERARY STUDIES SERIES

Also available in the series:

Mapping World Literature
International Canonization and
Transnational Literatures

Mads Rosendahl Thomsen

continuum

Continuum International Publishing Group

The Tower Building   80 Maiden Lane, Suite 704
11 York Road   New York
London SE1 7NX   NY 10038

British Library Cataloguing-in-Publication Data
A catalogue record for this book is available from the British Library.

ISBN: 978-1- 84706-123-2 (hardback)

Library of Congress Cataloguing-in-Publication Data
A catalog record for the book is available from the Library of Congress.

Typeset by Newgen Imaging Systems Pvt Ltd, Chennai, India
Printed and bound in Great Britain by Biddles, Kings Lynn, Norfolk

Contents

Acknowledgements

I would like to thank the Carlsberg Foundation, whose support for three years was all-important, the Institute for Aesthetic Studies at the University of Aarhus, where colleagues and students have been a great inspiration, the University of Aarhus' Research Foundation, and the Department of Comparative Literature at Stanford University, for letting me present my work at an early stage. Many thanks as well to Haun Saussy, who generously translated Georg Brandes' essay and endured three unusually cold weeks in Aarhus in March 2006, and to Hans Ulrich Gumbrecht for insisting on reading my manuscript and for always being hospitable at Stanford University. I am also grateful for the exchanges I have had with Jørn Erslev Andersen, David Damrosch, Søren Frank, Svend Erik Larsen, Franco Moretti, Peter Simonsen, and Richard Weisberg. At various points in the process, I have benefited from the advice of Russell Berman, George Bloom, Theo D'haen, Amir Eshel, Ursula Heise, Erik Granly Jensen, Jessie Labov, and Bruce Robbins. Special thanks to my copyeditor, Michaela Scioscia, and to my editors at Continuum, Colleen Coalter and Anna Sandeman. My gratitude also extends to the late Richard Rorty who spent an afternoon with me in May of 2004, in Hamburg, listening to my ideas. Most of all, thanks to my wife Lene, and our sons Marcus and Jonathan for their presence and love.

Introduction

The term *world literature* has received a significant renewed interest in the past decade, perhaps more than anything as the companion to the central keyword of the times, globalization. As most people have experienced in one way or another, globalization is no illusion, but real, and propelled by strong forces – particularly those of economics and the media – and for better and for worse. Globalization is not creating a uniform change around the globe, especially not within the domain that has been loosely termed cultural globalization, where it generates new diversity when global tendencies are expressed as local manifestations. The same logic applies to world literature, which will always be a world literature as seen from a particular place, even though some aspects are shared.

World literature has been put on the agenda, as more than a few scholars have set out to rejuvenate the term Johann Wolfgang von Goethe first introduced in 1827. At least four major publishing houses – Norton, Bedford, Longman and HarperCollins – have published large anthologies of world literature (Caws and Prendergast, 1997; Damrosch, 2003; Davis, et al., 2003; Lawall and Mack, 2003), and a number of noteworthy scholars, such as David Damrosch, Franco Moretti, Christopher Prendergast, Pascale Casanova and Haun Saussy, have published works on the subject (Casanova, 2004; Damrosch, 2003; Moretti, 2000; Prendergast, 2004 and 2007; Saussy, 2006). At universities, departments are being merged, or they collaborate in joint courses. This is not least the case with English departments, where the boundaries between British, American and Post-Colonial literature are undergoing a profound shift towards integration. National curricula are being scrutinized and adapted to a situation in which knowledge about the world is as important as knowledge about the nation. It is also very telling that the American Comparative Literature Association's decennial report from 1995 was focused on multiculturalism, but did not mention world literature, whereas world literature is the pivotal concept in the report of 2006, just as the Modern Language Association (MLA) is publishing a comprehensive instruction for teaching world literature (Bernheimer, 1995; Damrosch, 2008; Saussy, 2006).

Above all, it is difficult at present to give convincing arguments as to why anybody should be interested in studying the literature of just one nation, not only because of the attractiveness of reading works from diverse cultures, but also because the traditional trinity of history, language and literature that provides the basis for many studies seems to be untenable. At the same time, there are few ready answers at hand, regarding how the literary studies should adapt to this new situation. The interest in world literature may be seen as an attempt to determine such answers.

The concept of world literature is notoriously difficult to define. It obviously refers to a way of approaching literature that may exclude works by Martians and other extraterrestrials, but which, in principle, is open to all kinds of literature. This is the not-very-ambitious way in which the term has often been used, as a simple gesture towards an all-inclusiveness that contrasts strongly with another influential, but also simple, idea, namely that *world literature* is the best of the world's literature. As such, the term itself does not state whether it encompasses all the literature of the world, or only a certain kind of literature that stands out due to its formal qualities, thematic universality or some combination thereof. Some might ask if world literature is like world music, blending various local expressions into a new kind of literature that cannot be referred back to a single nation, although local and national traces can be found in it. The ideas of transnational or postnational literature are also akin to this, and although these are too narrow to cover the idea of world literature, this raises questions about whether the distinction between national and international is tenable.[1]

Any approach to world literature must also take into account that the historical development of literature has varied around the globe. Some literatures are old, but have had limited exposure to foreign literatures, while others have been perpetually impacted and changed by outside influences. Other literatures are very young, with mostly oral traditions preceding them. However, the important thing is that, no matter which definition one prefers, *the literature of the world will always be too broad to comprehend.* One cannot have world literature as a whole, in the same way that the world cannot be perceived as a whole. It can be mapped and navigated in order to address its complexity, and what is interesting is *the way in which this complexity is transformed into forms of coherence.*[2]

The focus of this study is world literature as seen in the Western world, because the interest lies not so much in working with an ideal variety of works from all over the world, but, more realistically, to ask questions about how world literature is structured and evolving in the Western world. The intent of this book is to present ideas for analyses of this transformation, and its relationship to the *international canonization* of works and authors. The main arguments can be summarized in the following points:

- World literature is a paradigm that encompasses both the study of internationally canonized literature and the ambition to investigate and to be interested in all kinds of literature.
- The history of international canonization in world literature is marked by considerable discontinuities: temporal sub-centres that blossom, isolated canonical writers and new epochs that change the canon. The continuity is located in the dominant centres of distribution and valuation.

- The importance of formal and thematic properties to international canonization has been underestimated and understudied, especially as national canonization has a different logic and different values than international canonization. World literature is consequently not a reflection of national literatures.
- The international canons consist of several constellations of works that share properties of formal and thematic character, where canonized works can bring attention to less canonized, but affiliated, works, and draw them into the scene of world literature. By studying such constellations, a challenging and realistic mapping of world literature is possible. There has been too much antiquarian criticism, in the sense used by Friedrich Nietzsche, of world literature, and too little critical thought based on the mapping of social selection combined with a textual approach that seeks constellations across time and space.
- It is only within the last decades that the concept of culture has gradually been more and more widely defined as non-essentialist, hybrid and contingent, something that has not been reflected in the practice of literary history, but which in all likelihood is one of the main reasons behind the renewed interest in world literature.
- The immense complexity of world literature does not pose a problem different to that with which other paradigms, such as comparative literature and post-colonialism have been confronted, but which they in turn have neglected, in terms of reflecting on the form of reduction of complexity they make. World literature is an emerging paradigm that works as a supplement to comparative literature and post-colonial studies, as, due to its overwhelming amount of subject matter, its complexity is bound to be taken seriously.
- The idea of globalization and the accompanying changes in geopolitics, media, economy and cultural identity, have only within the past decade and a half propelled the idea of world literature into a new era. This change also results in a significant change in the lengthy history of world literature.

Four chapters investigate these points, the first two dealing with principal aspects of world literature as an object of study, and the uses of international canonization. This is followed by two chapters addressing identity, and formal and thematic properties of transnational literatures.

Chapter 1 describes the paradigm of world literature with respect to its relations to cultural globalization, its history as a concept, and, in particular, to its relations to two dominant paradigms in the study of literature: comparative literature and post-colonialism. This is followed by an inquiry into an important aspect which has not been given much critical attention, namely the temporal differentiations in the idea of world literature. It makes a considerable difference whether one is interested in the extensive history of literature, in the contemporary scene of world literature, or in the changes that globalization may bring about in the future literary system, and all three aspects should be given their due when discussing world literature.

Chapter 2 traces the focal points in the historical canonization of world literature. The canon of internationally dispersed literature is more stable than is often presented, but at the same time it also displays a historical variability of its centres. By tracing such centres, the foundations are laid for further investigations into the patterns of the formal and thematic properties of world literature, which are facilitated by the relatively easy task of indicating which works have been internationally circulated and canonized beyond their own time. Jorge Luis Borges is, in this context, taken as one example of an author who wrote in the space between world literature and his own national culture, and stands as an example of one of the nationally isolated but internationally canonized authors in world literature.

Chapters 3 and 4 combine studies, in particular those of literary phenomena, with discussions of methods for analyses of world literature with regard to thoroughly international literatures. In Chapter 3, literature written by migrants is at the centre of a discussion of formal innovation and cultural appreciation. Since both modernist and contemporary literature have received significant contributions by migrant writers, a survey of their achievements, both in terms of their international impact and their formal inventions, is also informative with respect to processes of international canonization. Moreover, migrant writers provide a historical trace of the development of the ideas of culture, identity, nationalism and cosmopolitanism, which are brought up in a discussion of the contributions to this debate by Pierre Bourdieu, Ulrich Beck and Homi Bhabha.

Chapter 4 discusses fiction that addresses the denial of individuals' right to live, whether this happens through genocide, war or natural disasters. The chapter explores how the theme has had a great impact on its reception, and addresses the aesthetics of this literature, as expressed in five theses that seek to explain why this subject stands out in the international literary culture.

The Conclusion argues that the search for constellations in world literature is a mode of analysis that investigates ways in which very different texts share features that make them stand out on the literary canopy. The concept and use of constellations of works is central to this approach to world literature, namely by seeing patterns in world literature through the shared properties of works written, perhaps, far apart in time and place.

World literature only makes sense if one recognizes that each reader brings his or her own history to it, and that history has to present a coherence which is both shared with the literary community, and unique to the reader. Constellations can bridge genres and, most importantly, they can attach less canonized works to the more canonized. Thus, constellations balance a sense of the identity of the literary system's selections with a methodological curiosity that suggests answers as to why we read texts written by strangers.

Chapter 1

World literature: history, concept, paradigm

Any discourse involving world literature is easily made difficult and complex by introducing numerous counterexamples and arguments that easily blur the precision of the concept. World literature has been variously treated as too antiquarian, too idealistic and almost void of any methodical ideas for handling what is obviously too much for any individual or group, even, to master. Nevertheless, world literature is worth taking seriously as a challenge to research and teaching, not only because it has a resource-filled history, or because history has reached an era of intensified cultural globalization and therefore is ready for world literature, but because it is an emergent field of its own that takes seriously both cultural globalization and literature that can be characterized as transnational. World literature in this sense acknowledges the existence of a world literary system, which is arguably a more realistic way to describe the history of the world's literature than the prevailing national and comparative paradigms.

Cultural globalization is a remarkable and sometimes intimidating phenomenon that involves a number of uncertainties: Will the singular qualities of local cultures be erased by waves of influence, propelled by strong economic interests and media? Will everything have an American flavour to it (Beck, 2003)? A more optimistic prophesy is that everyone will gain something in diversity, as is already very visible in eating habits, where pizza, kebab, sushi and burgers, have, within decades, become popular meals in large parts of the world, changing local habits everywhere. The optimistic attitude would also project more shared references across cultures, to Shakespeare, haiku and soccer alike, and those hybrid constructions will add to this diversity, as, for example, in literature by bicultural authors. The sociologist Urs Stäheli has pointed out the paradox in the critique of cultural globalization that cultural globalization is presented both as the levelling of all local differences and as providing the potential for local cultural products to be appreciated globally, which is seen as a positive effect (Stäheli, 2000). Both positions should be taken seriously. Some of these effects are not new from a qualitative point of view, but are salient due to economic factors, media portrayal and simply because the idea of being globalized works as a catalyst.

Global changes in the economy are producing changes in the global cultural landscape, and there will be an increasing number of translations of Western literature into Chinese, Korean, Hindi and Russian, which will be more important than ever, due to their potential mass audiences. It will be interesting to see what these cultures want – or do not want – from the West, and how that will influence, for example, the compilation of future anthologies, just as the cultural export from East to West will, in the future, be on a larger scale. The power of the book markets to shape or influence literary production and literary history is a force to be reckoned with, and alongside globalization it will take on new forms.[1]

The question of what this does to people's identities is often brought up in this line of thought, while at the same time the whole idea of what identity is has also been changed in the past decades, from an idea of essentialism to one of more contingent construction. Richard Rorty has, in various articles, defended a kind of ethnocentrism, basically arguing that people cannot and should not try to deny who they are and how they have become who they are. This is not particularly controversial; what is more debatable is how one should respond to a changing world, and what ideals for self-creation one should have. Rorty did not have a ready answer for everyone, but he opted for the rationality of expressing irony towards cultural fundamentalism, and of being curious about other cultures, and, under the current historic circumstances, towards people who have experiences of living between cultures (Rorty, 1998: 200–201).[2]

Ulrich Beck has argued a bit differently for the combination of cosmopolitanism and provincialism, saying that there should be a mixture of elements:

> [L]ocal, national, ethnic, religious *and* cosmopolitan cultures and traditions interpenetrate, interconnect and intermingle – cosmopolitanism without provincialism is empty, provincialism without cosmopolitanism is blind. (Beck, 2006: 7)

Much in line with Beck, Kwame Anthony Appiah has coined the term 'rooted cosmopolitanism', which also opts for a balance between local and global influences on people's identities, rather than submitting to either the essentialist ideas of identity rooted in a specific culture, or the idea of identity as something that can simply be chosen at will (Appiah, 2004: 213).

World literature could also be seen as an antidote to the kind of provincialism Milan Kundera observes:

> How to define provincialism? As the inability (or the refusal) to see one's own culture in the *large context*. There are two kinds of provincialism: of large nations and of small ones. The large nations resist the Goethean idea of 'world literature' because their own literature seems to them sufficiently rich that they need take no interest in what people write elsewhere. . . . Small nations are reticent toward the *large context* for the exact opposite reasons: they hold world culture in high esteem but feel it to be something alien, a sky above their heads, distant, inaccessible, an ideal reality with little connection to their national literature. (Kundera, 2007: 37–38)

This chiasmic relationship between the local and the global which Kundera and many others promote is a reasonably realistic and sympathetic description, but it does not mean that there will emerge a new global literary community that will solve every problem concerning peoples' identities and the negative effects of globalization. It should instead lead to the investigation of some of the key aspects of the conditions surrounding reading more globally, as well presenting ideas for tackling the obstacles intrinsic to world literature.

A number of these obstacles are easy to identify. Some of them can be turned around to be productive; others are symptomatic of the way in which literary communities develop, for better or worse. Four of the most important ones will be dealt with here, as they apply to most of the strategies for interpreting and working with world literature as set forth in the rest of this book: the relatively closed history of the Western canon, the linguistic barriers and the dominance of English, the importance of cultural contexts to literature, and the existing interests in promoting national identity.

The closed history of the Western canon can be observed in the extent to which works from outside of Europe and North America that have been internationally canonized are involved with Western culture and literature. A list of canonical authors from places other than Europe and North America in the twentieth century would typically include authors like Jorge Luis Borges, Octavio Paz, Gabriel García Márquez, Pablo Neruda, Mario Vargas Llosa and other internationally oriented writers whose mother tongue is Spanish, as well as a number of Commonwealth writers, about whose long-term canonicity it is probably too early to say too much now, such as Nadine Gordimer, Salman Rushdie, Ben Okri, J. M. Coetzee and V. S. Naipaul. What is remarkable is that all these writers are involved with Western culture and literature to a degree that the idea of a voice that reflects a pure and authentic culture does not make much sense, since it is rather the relationship between the local and the global that is interesting in these authorships. It is also important to note that the authorships are mostly contemporary and therefore it is likely that not all will continue to be considered as part of an international canon.

Moreover, it is significant how few authors from China, Japan, non-English-speaking India or non-Commonwealth Africa have made their way into the Western world's circulation of literature. Even more significant is the fact that the Chinese writers who have recently made an impact, most notably Nobel laureate Gao Xingjian, are exiled writers who originally studied Western culture and literature in China.

This is a pattern that indicates, regardless of one's opinion of the matter, how differences have to be mediated, perhaps much more than one likes to think, when employing notions of genuinely foreign voices and experiences. These voices could have entered the international canons, they do exist, but they have had few chances to make an impact.

Going back in time in literary history, it is obvious that there are very few non-Western writers who have received considerable attention in the West. This tendency only stands out more strongly when anthologies of world literature frequently prefer to print philosophical and religious texts, such as Chinese philosophy or Indian religious poetry, rather than fiction, which would be more consistent with the traditional selection of Western texts. It may be the right choice for a number of reasons, both in terms of what is interesting and what appears as understandable to today's readers, yet it also emphasizes how relatively insular the Western conception of world literature is. It is likely that the idea of world literature as being open to everything is too idealistic with respect to what can, or in practice will be understood and enjoyed by non-specialists. A mixture of the strange and the familiar, which is what David Damrosch has proposed with respect to the development of one's own identity, is perhaps the best that can be hoped for (Damrosch, 2003: 133).

Fortunately, there are texts that defy the general tendencies, such as *The Epic of Gilgamesh*, written more than 3,500 years ago by a Babylonian poet in what is now Iraq. The epic poem was lost for more than 2,000 years, but was rediscovered in the 1850s by archaeologists. The poem is written in Sumerian, which makes it impossible to read in the original for most people, but there have been numerous interpretations of it since it was found, two of which were made just within the last decade, proving that it is a living text in world literature.[3]

The Epic of Gilgamesh tells the story of a Babylonian hero's quest for glory and his attempts to escape death, and the theme of longing for immortality gives it universal appeal. At the same time it combines a fascinating universe of tyrannical powers, women of the demimonde, and mythical figures, with a lucid poetic phrasing that also observes an impressive economy of narration. Being a literary work of a high standard in its own right, *The Epic of Gilgamesh* also fascinates by giving access to a society that is no more, but whose complexity, and both joys and sorrows of daily life shine through, as in the conclusion, when Gilgamesh, disappointed by not being granted immortality or eternal youth, finds some consolation in the beauty of the dynamic and complex society he rules:

> When at last they arrived, Gilgamesh said to / Urshanabi, 'This is / the wall of Uruk, which no city / on earth can equal. / See how its ramparts gleam like copper in the sun. / Climb the stone staircase, more ancient than the mind can imagine, / approach the Eanna Temple, sacred to Ishtar, / a temple that no king has equalled in size or beauty, / walk on the wall of Uruk, follow its course / around the city, inspect its mighty foundations, / examine its brickwork, how masterfully it is built, / observe the land it encloses: the palm trees, the gardens, / the orchards, the glorious palaces and temples, the shops / and marketplaces, the houses, the public squares.' (Mitchell, 2004: 198–199)

The Epic of Gilgamesh is an almost unique case in international canonization, because it is a work that is generally recognized as world literature without being supported by the reception of a living literary culture, but always read in translation. The epic is often read in scholarly contexts, and it is questionable whether the work would be a part of world literature, if it had not been for an academic interest in presenting a text that is both a cultural and a religious document, as well as an aesthetic achievement, whereas its impact on the general reading public is easier to overlook. It does, however, prove that the Western canon can be opened, and not only by contemporary literature.

With regard to linguistic barriers, it is obvious that many works must be translated in order for people from other countries to be able to read them, still a very important factor, despite all the talk about the hegemonic role of English. Even if English is the Latin of our age, many languages and literatures thrive well, demonstrated by the fact that works are being translated in large numbers and that translations are even important to the distribution of best-selling books originally written in English.

The rapid translation of works is not a new phenomenon, but goes back to the nineteenth century (Moretti, 1998: 187), although a rather recent trend is that of works being translated into several languages before being published in the original language, making it possible to simultaneously release a work in multiple languages around the world. Besides the adventures of a certain Harry Potter, this has happened with works by Salman Rushdie and Don DeLillo, while both Paul Auster and Gabriel García Márquez have had works published in translation before the original work was published (Auster, 2003; DeLillo, 2001; Márquez, 1988; Rushdie, 1999).[4] In the latter type of case, Auster gave permission for early release in translation to add to the diversity of languages by giving the translation a headstart, and making it available to devoted readers, who otherwise would read the often less expensive English original. While the simultaneous release is a marketing and sales tool, it does have the aspect of helping to sustain diversity, although the dominance of English is clear, as it is often the original language of simultaneously translated literature.

As mentioned earlier, it will be particularly interesting to observe how the increasingly globalized and economically influential Asian cultures will translate works in the future. If culture follows the money, as F. Scott Fitzgerald once stated,[5] it will be important to determine what kind of Western literature Indian, Chinese and Japanese people will make part of their culture through translations or curricula.

Traditionally, French literary culture has been at the forefront with regard to diversity in translation, but translations into English are also of a diverse character and of growing importance. Yet as Erich Auerbach suggested as early as 1952, the success of the English language could potentially both realize the idea of a world literature, in the sense of a literature that is accessible to almost all the world, and at same time destroy the idea of world literature, in the sense of silencing the diverse concerto of all the world's different literatures, with their specific expressions through their own languages (Auerbach, 1992: 84).

Many years before Auerbach, Thomas De Quincey sketched a similar development, even though it could be argued that he ultimately is more wrong than
right:

> ... through the English colonies – African, Canadian, Indian, Australian – the English
> language (and, therefore, the English literature) is running forward towards its
> ultimate mission of eating up, like Aaron's rod, all other languages. Even the German
> and the Spanish will inevitably sink before it; perhaps, within 100 or 150 years. In
> the recesses of California, in the vast solitudes of Australia, *The Churchyard amongst
> the Mountains*, from Wordsworth's 'Excursion,' and many a scene of his shorter
> poems, will be read, even as now Shakespeare is read among the forests of Canada.
> (De Quincey, 1854: 254)[6]

The risk of world literature becoming world literature in English could be seen
as immanent, particularly in those educational systems in which anthologies
play a big role, and American and English publishers dominate the textbook
market. The dominance of English could be seen as a threat to the literary
experience and the diversity of language. Something is changed, and often lost,
when read in translation. Yet, the range of literatures also needs a common language in order to be truly diverse when it comes to experiencing literature that
otherwise would be available only to specialists, since only few, if any, master
more than a handful of languages.

This raises the question of the extent to which the original language is important to the experience of literature.[7] It is important, given that language is the
medium of literature and thus the medium of the writer, but nevertheless it
is apparent that literature can be translated. The sense of place, of historical
situations, of certain emotions, of the uses of genres and techniques, are also
parts of the literary experience that are not necessarily lost in translation. The
question of cultural context is thus somewhat separate from that of linguistic
understanding, but just as important.

The extent to which Western readers enjoy the strangeness of a tale from
medieval China, or whether Asian or African readers appreciate the finer details
of Don DeLillo's description of the Bronx, remains an open question. In some
cases they probably do, in others not, but there is little doubt that cultural contexts and the way that literary works handle them and present a mixture of the
strange and familiar, is crucial to the appreciation and, ultimately, the success
of a foreign work. Translations are not sufficient in themselves, as has been witnessed over the years in the many failed attempts to introduce foreign writers
into various literary cultures. For contemporary literature, though, these things
will change to some degree, as cultural references are increasingly shared
throughout a wide variety of facets of life.

Finally, world literature is always balancing between idealism and realism: the
idealism of a world of unlimited cultural exchange and diversity with respect
for differences, and the harsh realism of what is actually being translated, sold,

read and taught around the world. There are interests at stake that move in directions that oppose cultural exchange, such as nations' interests in supporting their own literature. However, these same nations also have an interest in supporting translations of foreign literature. From an institutional viewpoint, some of the most important rationales for engaging with world literature at this time are laden both with values and with a more calculating, cool rationality that just happen to go together. Primarily, there is a demand within the educational systems for giving people both a general *Bildung* and more specific competences that enable them to understand others within the increasingly globalizing world. In line with this, the striving for diversity that is inherent in world literature can be seen as rational, as it seeks to create the largest possible reservoir for addressing new situations (Gumbrecht, 1997: 423).

These obstacles to the impact and diversity of world literature – the closed history of the Western canon, the barriers set up by the knowledge of language and culture, and the complicated interests in maintaining a national identity while being open to the world – spell out the realities that challenge the idealism of world literature.

The concept of world literature between idealism and realism

The history of the concept of world literature is marked by widely different uses and nuances, determined by historical circumstances (Birus, 2000; McInturff, 2003; Schrimpf, 1968). It begins with Goethe, who in 1827, five years before his death, talked about the idea of *Weltliteratur* to Johann Peter Eckermann:

> [W]e Germans are very likely to fall too easily into this pedantic conceit, when we do not look beyond the narrow circle that surrounds us. I therefore like to look about me in foreign nations, and advise everyone to do the same. National literature is now rather an unmeaning term; the epoch of World-literature is at hand, and everyone must strive to hasten its approach. But, while we thus value what is foreign, we must not bind ourselves to some particular thing, and regard it as a model. We must not give this value to the Chinese, or the Serbian, or Calderon, or the *Nibelungen*; but, if we really want a pattern, we must always return to the ancient Greeks, in whose works the beauty of mankind is constantly represented. All the rest we must look at only historically; appropriating to ourselves what is good, so far as it goes. (Eckermann, 1998: 165–166)

In hindsight, Goethe's hope for a future wherein the national literatures would not be dominant, and works would be received around the globe, was too optimistic. National literature *did* mean a lot in the period to follow, as it still does for many good reasons, such as familiarity with language and context. Like most people who have written on the idea of world literature, the central question for Goethe is thus not a life and death battle between national or local literatures on the one side, and world or global literature on the other. The relation is seen as symbiotic, but asymmetrical at the time when national literatures were dominant.

An interesting detail of the quote is that Goethe at once projects the idea that world literature will triumph, while also urging others to work for this project to arrive sooner. It is a situation which is also applicable in today's world, where it could be argued that globalization will work as an irresistible force in the long run, and that the hastening of the new age's arrival need not be of great concern. Again, this also reproduces the split between idealism and realism when addressing this topic, and ultimately there is a belief expressed in Goethe's words, that there is literature that has a universal appeal, and which will benefit all cultures.

Goethe never wrote on the subject of world literature himself, or defined the concept at length, but as George Steiner notes, Goethe translated, although often second-hand, from more than eighteen languages from early on in his childhood to his last years, thereby demonstrating a sustained interest behind the later reflections on world literature (Steiner, 1995: 4). Despite the brevity of his mention of world literature, its influence has been enormous, and in his fragmentary ponderings of the concept, Goethe touches upon a number of issues that are still important and often unresolved. Examples of these include whether there is a universal human drive to create literature, and whether the status of classical literature shifts when world literature is taken seriously, and seen in a historical perspective in which the traditions of China and India are given their due.

At the same time, Goethe is hard on German literature and its contributions:

> German poetry . . . really provides nothing but the expressions, sighs and interjections of well-meaning individuals. Each person makes his appearance in accordance with his nature and education. Hardly anything attains to a universal, lofty level. Least of all does one find situations common to the domestic, urban or rural sphere. As far as Church and State are concerned, nothing is to be seen. (Birus, 2000)

The attempt to define world literature could be seen as a longing for a larger context that takes his authorship out of its German confines and into a sphere that needed to be defined in order to be discovered, and to see the writer's work not as borrowing from other literature, but as belonging to it. The same problem is reiterated in Modernism by James Joyce and T. S. Eliot, their relation to Dante demonstrating the ongoing struggle to define the context between nation and world, and the striving to find a 'lofty' and universal context.

Where Goethe's idea of world literature can be seen as leaning clearly to the idealistic side, Karl Marx and Friedrich Engels' more than rudimentary mention

of world literature in *The Communist Manifesto* from 1848 takes a realistic or cynical standpoint, wherein world literature is seen as a consequence of the
globalizing economy:

> The bourgeoisie has through its exploitation of the world market given a cosmopoli-
> tan character to production and consumption in every country. To the great chagrin
> of reactionaries, it has drawn from under the feet of industry the national ground
> on which it stood. All old-established national industries have been destroyed or are
> daily being destroyed. . . . In place of the old local and national seclusion and self-
> sufficiency, we have intercourse in every direction, universal inter-dependence of
> nations. And as in material, so also in intellectual production. The intellectual creations
> of individual nations become common property. National one-sidedness and narrow-
> mindedness become more and more impossible, and from the numerous national and
> local literatures there arises a world literature. (Marx and Engels, 1967: 136–137)

Literature is seen as one commodity among many others, and thus bound to be
produced and distributed rationally in the global economy. Besides being a
commodity, world literature would, according to Marx and Engels, also work as
an ideological instrument that would connect people and make them aware of
their interdependence. The world literature of Marx and Engels is thus a Janus-
faced phenomenon.

These two positions, the idealistic vision of the symphony of the masterpieces
from different nations and the more cynical vision of global distribution of
books as commodities, are still very relevant positions that have to be addressed
today. The case can be made for both, in terms of how literature is studied and
taught, and this is one of the main reasons that the subject of world literature is
so difficult to define and delineate.

Historically, there are also a number of positions that take a different path in
defining world literature. The Danish literary historian Georg Brandes is very
pragmatic in his 1899 essay 'World literature', in which he tries to specify which
kinds of works generate universal interest. Most biographies cannot be classified as world literature, Brandes argues, because they are closely related to a
specific historical context, whereas other works of non-fiction, like the works of
Charles Darwin, count as world literature due to their universal subject. Brandes'
stance leans towards that of Goethe, but his most valuable contribution is the
spirited differentiation of modes and genres that takes into account which
works have actually made an impact outside of their original context. Goethe's
idealism and orientation towards the future are balanced by Brandes' more
realistic analysis of valuable literature, and, in effect, the principles behind this
are those which have defined selections of world literature.

A similar distinction was made by Richard Moulton in 1911, where he discerns between universal literature and world literature:

> I take a distinction between Universal Literature and World Literature. Universal
> Literature can only mean the sum total of all literatures. World Literature, as I use this

term, is this Universal Literature seen in perspective from a given point of view, presumably the national standpoint of the observer. (Moulton, 1911: 6; see also McInturff, 2003: 232–233)

Moulton states the obvious but very important idea of universal literature as a construction or an abstraction; whereas world literature brings a perspective to this overwhelming mass of literature, and thus makes it visible and understandable. The consequence of this view is that world literature is a network of related views on the totality of the literature of the world. Some views may be more influential than others, but all conceptions of the literature of the world contribute to the communication about it, and thus help shape conceptions others can adopt, modify or question. It is still possible to see the major tendencies produced by various perspectives, not least through the selection of authorships or genres, as Brandes suggests, and these perspectives are coloured by their local outlook, which add to the complexity of the field, and produce different connections that might be inconceivable to others.

A different notion of world literature developed vis-à-vis the idea of designating single works to the realm of world literature. A nation's entire literature could be conceived of as a world literature, insofar as it has proven to be dominant. In particular French, German and English literature were thought of as world literatures that influenced those of other nations, whereas the literature of the USA was, by many, not considered a world literature until the 1920s. In today's circulation of books, old and new, it is more relevant than ever to keep in mind that some literary scenes and their authors are favoured because of their sheer magnitude, and the history of the literature. Whereas French was once very important, with Paris as the literary capital of the world, this has shifted to the English speaking cultures, albeit with some loss of the diversity that characterized the French scene (Schiffrin, 2000: 7 and 49).

After the Second World War Erich Auerbach, who had immigrated to the USA after writing *Mimesis* in Turkey during the war, argued, as mentioned previously, that the future of world literature was at a crossroads because of the growing influence of English. He reformulated the idea that world literature is both about differences and unity, by stating that a future dominance of English in the literary world would both create an effective world literature because it would be in one language, and at the same time destroy the idea of world literature by erasing the vital differences that arise from different literatures (Auerbach, 1992: 84–91). Auerbach was probably not correct with regard to his own time, but there are signs that suggest that his observations are more relevant today, as is the case with the influence exercised by the American best-seller lists on the translation of literature in other countries. Auerbach was also observant with regard to the challenge of providing a perspective on world literature that could overcome the problems of complexity, cultural and linguistic capabilities, the lack of contextual knowledge and of one's own historical past, without being reductive.

In the 1960s and onwards, the French literary historian René Étiemble argued that world literature had to include literature from everywhere literature was written. Étiemble's call for more attention to overlooked and new literatures is even more idealistic than Goethe's original idea of a world literature, which also had a strong emphasis on the quality of the literature (Étiemble, 1974). Étiemble's position is anthropological and encyclopaedic in its ambitions, and stands in a sharp contrast to the market. He emphasizes diversity in reading, whereas markets tend to produce unification and standardization. Then again, literary criticism also produces unification through selection and, eventually, canonization. Thus, the question is whether literary history should be about the documentation of works produced or appreciated critically. This will always be negotiated, but it could be argued that Étiemble pushed the idea of universal literature too far towards anthropological recording, rather than critical selection. A similar position was taken by Soviet scholars in the 1960s and 1970s, but with little international impact, in the climate of the Cold War (Møller, 1989).

As mentioned in the introduction, the term 'world literature' was not given widespread *critical* interest until the late 1990s or even the early 2000s. World literature did exist as a field to be studied, as world literature in contrast to national literature, but there was little interest in the methodological consequences of the subject. This changed in the new millennium, when David Damrosch, along with Franco Moretti and Pascale Casanova made some of the most interesting and bold redefinitions of world literature (Apter, 2006; Casanova, 2004; Kadir, 2004; Moretti, 2000; Prendergast, 2004).

At the beginning of his book *What Is World Literature?*, Damrosch tentatively defines world literature as all works that circulate beyond their 'culture of origin,' (Damrosch, 2003: 4) and, in line with Auerbach, he stresses that international circulation and an impact on other cultures is essential (Auerbach, 1992: 83; Damrosch, 2003: 16). He also discerns between commonly held views on world literature as meaning either classics, a canonical body of works or simply works that provide a window on other cultures, without seeing any reason to choose one over the other. In keeping with this pluralistic vein, at the end of the book he does not give a single definition of world literature, but puts forth three more or less controversial definitions that complement one another.

Damrosch's first definition of world literature is that it is a refraction of national literature, meaning that the idea of world literature as something that is not connected to the local roots of the literatures is absurd (Damrosch, 2003: 281–288). It also confirms that world literature is a field of its own, a certain space where literatures meet and bring with them, not complete representations of the literary traditions from which they come, but fragments of it:

> This refraction, moreover, is double in nature: works become world literature by being received *into* the space of a foreign culture, a space defined in many ways by the host

culture's national tradition and the present needs of its own writers. Even a single work of world literature is the locus of a negotiation between two different cultures. (Damrosch, 2003: 283)

The second definition is that world literature is literature that gains in translation (Damrosch, 2003: 288–297). This does not mean that the translation is better than the original, but that the whole corpus of original and translations is of greater value than the original, both in terms of artistic value and cultural impact. Damrosch thus takes a side in the question of whether a work of literature can be called world literature without being translated and received outside of its original context, and it is clear that he opts for the importance of what actually happens with works, rather than praising the potential of the overlooked. Books must prove their worth to translators, critics and readers from other cultures.

The third definition is probably the most important, stating that world literature is not so much a list of works in a giant corpus of world literature, but rather an approach to literature. World literature is '*not a set canon of texts but a mode of reading, a detached engagement with a world beyond our own*' (Damrosch, 2003: 297; italics in the original). There is a minor contradiction between this definition and the second, which actually separates some works from others: those which do not gain in translation or are not translated. The important point though, is that world literature should not be conceived of as something that can be mastered, but rather as an open field in which unknown works can be introduced, and bring new light to the already known.

The last two definitions are somewhat controversial because they could give rise to the idea that they are born as much out of the overwhelming complexity of the field, rather than an idealistic vision of world literature. This is not a problem as such – idealism is not better, per se, than realism – but it could be stated more directly that complexity, rather than essence, defines the subject. Reduced linguistic capacities, a reduced need for knowledge of context due to the excessive complexity of the subject matter of world literature, and an overreliance on canonical lists are potential negative aspects of world literature.

Franco Moretti differs from Damrosch in his approach to world literature in several ways. He does not define world literature as a set of works, but rather as a problem in the study of literature across borders, regardless of whether the individual works have been received by other cultures. He is much more focused on the spread of genres throughout the world, whereas Damrosch's focus is on the apprehension of world literature by the reader of today. Moretti's emphasis is thus on research, where Damrosch's is on didactics; this has profound consequences, mainly in that Moretti is interested in describing how genres diversify as they are imported by other literatures (Moretti, 2000). In contrast, Damrosch does not so much present a programme for describing influences, as one for new ways of reading works whose interrelationships have already been established.

Moretti's approach is closely connected to his main area of research, the novel, which, unlike other genres, is also a commercial genre in which the process of selection is not carried out primarily by critics and professors, which adds another layer to the process of selection that is lacking particularly in those genres that precede the birth of the modern novel. Moretti comes close to claiming that his model is universal, with regard to those parts of literature that can truly be called world literature:

> I would imagine literary movements to depend on three broad variables – a genre's potential market, its overall formalization and its use of language – and to range from the rapid wave-like diffusion of forms with a large market, rigid formulas and simplified style (say, adventure novels), to the relative stasis of those characterized by a small market, deliberate singularity and linguistic density (say, experimental poetry). Within this matrix, novels would be representative, not of the *entire* system, but of its most mobile strata, and by concentrating only on them we would probably overstate the mobility of world literature. (Moretti, 2003: 74)

Moretti is aware of the limitations of his model, but sacrifices parts of literature to better study the major trends. Where Damrosch has an eye for the strange and unique, Moretti focuses on what belongs to a larger stream in literary history.

A third important contribution to the theory of world literature has been made by Pascale Casanova who, in her foreword to the English edition of her book, *The World Republic of Letters*, makes a distinction between world literature as a collection of texts, and the international literary field, which is at the centre of attention of her analysis (Casanova, 2004: xi). This concept is inspired by Pierre Bourdieu's notion of a field of cultural goods which has a dynamic structure with various positions that can be held by agents in the literary field: writers, critics, publishers, etc. Whereas Bourdieu in his analysis is almost always focused on a field limited by national borders, Casanova takes Bourdieu's basic model, and claims that there is a more or less autonomous international literary field, stating that a sort of consensus has evolved gradually since the sixteenth century, regarding what is valuable world literature. Casanova has coined the concept 'the Greenwich Meridian of Literature,' which is a clever metaphor borrowed from the synchronization of the clocks of the world, which run differently, but are all set by the same standard. In contrast to Franco Moretti, she is very observant of the feedback from the peripheral literatures and the ways in which they function within the world system (Casanova, 2004: 175–179). Thus, Casanova combines descriptions of the harsh reality of who is being circulated internationally, with an understanding of the disadvantages faced by writers from smaller nations on the international stage, or as she puts it, the position of the writer in the field of world letters must be understood in connection with his or her own literary position in world literature, as she thus attempts to make Bourdieu's theory work in two contexts:

> At the same time, each writer's position must necessarily be a double one, twice defined: each writer is situated once according to the position he or she occupies in a national space, and then once again according to the place that this occupies within the world space. This dual position, inextricably national and international, explains why – contrary to what economistic views of globalization would have us believe – international struggles take place and have their effects principally within national spaces; battles over the definition of literature, over technical or formal transformations and innovations, on the whole have national literary space as their arena. (Casanova, 2005: 81)

Casanova's heroes are the writers who change the system from the periphery, while she acknowledges at the same time that they are dependent on the centres of the international literary space. However, she often falls short of understanding the canonization of works in connection with a more specific analysis of the aesthetic strategies and properties of the works that become internationally canonized.

In *What Is World Literature?* Damrosch does not discuss canonization, but he later argues that the internationalization of literary studies has led to a situation that can be described somewhat paradoxically as post-canonical and hypercanonical. Damrosch argues that canons do not present themselves with the same validity as they did decades ago, especially not in the field of world literature, where the dominance of old colonial powers is regarded with some scepticism. Instead, a common basis for conversation on the emergent canons of theory and critical thinking has been generated, with names like Michel Foucault, Judith Butler and Edward W. Said as examples of prolific figures who have been associated with all kinds of literature (Damrosch, 2006: 44). But the result of these multiplying ways of approaching literature has also resulted in a concentration on fewer works. The top of the canonical lists has become even more canonical, giving more credit to Wordsworth, Joyce and Rushdie, as Damrosch demonstrates in the case of romantic, modernist and post-colonial writing, whereas those authors who were considered to have a stable presence in the canons, even if they were not considered to be among the very best, are now more invisible than ever. Damrosch instead projects a new structure for the canon of world literature, in which the binary division of major and minor authors, and the whole concept of masterpieces will be replaced by a more dynamic system:

> In place of this older, two-tiered model, our new system has three levels: a *hypercanon*, a *counter-canon*, and a *shadow canon*. The hypercanon is populated by the older 'major'

authors who have held their own or even gained ground over the past twenty years. The counter-canon is composed of the subaltern and contestatory voices of writers in less commonly-taught languages and in minor literatures within great-power languages. Many, even most, of the old 'major' authors coexist quite comfortably with these new arrivals to the neighborhood, very few of whom have yet accumulated anything like their fund of cultural capital. Far from being threatened by these unfamiliar neighbors, the old major authors gain new vitality from association with them, and only rarely do they need to admit one of them directly into their club. (Damrosch, 2006: 45)

Damrosch thus warns of the problems of the hypercanon that may lead to a simplified version of the literary past, but this conflicts with the ambition to read more diversely, which to non-specialists would mean that some of the Romantic poets, to use one of Damrosch's examples, would have to be less exposed in order to make room for others. Furthermore, while he addresses the need for greater diversity in the future, by opening up the shadow canon and counter-canon, this would also mean that some of the former hypercanonical authors would be put more in the shadow as the result of a long and complex process of selection.

Canonical lists are also about counting, and about believing whether canons can be opened and expanded, or whether they are an expression of the level of complexity with which a given culture can cope, in which case something must go, if others are to enter.

The latter view is also held by Harold Bloom, who counts in many different ways (Bloom, 1994). To one: Shakespeare, or two: add Dante, or twenty-six: add a range of writers with a bias towards literature written in English. Or add the long lists in the appendixes of *The Western Canon*, which demonstrate that Bloom is, as would be any person taking on the job of making so comprehensive a list, uninformed about the finer distinctions of many literatures.[8] It also shows that no one can master that much when it comes to world literature, and that one does not want to be stuck with Bloom's canon and have to take it from the top, which would be a bad idea in any case, because the canon is not carved in stone, as difficult as it may be to omit Shakespeare. Reading the world canon could, however, be justified as an approach that is diverse, inquiring and conscious of its incompleteness, as well of the various traditions that make it see what it sees, rather than a task that can be completed, or has a fixed path through the literature of the world.

Both Damrosch, to some degree, and, more outspokenly, Moretti, avoid the optimistic and not very original idea of just bringing in more to read, or of not trying to establish any master canon. Bloom also knows that his canon is idiosyncratic and thus not a real canon, insofar as a canon is the expression of something beyond the individual. Instead, Damrosch argues that there will be a core canon, but this will mix with less canonical works to form sub-canons for groups of people interested in a particular form of literature (Damrosch,

2003: 281). It can also be formulated as a way of mingling hypercanonical and counter-canonical works to the benefit of both:

> So, for example, I wanted to start by giving some sense of the range of ways that realism was dealing with issues of gender in the 1890s, as Joyce approached the period of writing *Dubliners*, and so I assigned three works: Ibsen's *Doll's House*, which Joyce knew intimately, and then short stories by two writers he didn't know at all: Rabindranath Tagore and Higuchi Ichiyo. / Such conjunctions enable us to avoid an either/or choice between well-grounded but restricted influence study and an ungrounded, universalizing juxtaposition of radically unconnected works . . . (Damrosch, 2006: 50–51)

Ultimately, Damrosch's position is to take the selections of which canons are an expression seriously, without being controlled by them, but rather to open up to a way of studying and teaching literature that shows lines of concordance and conflict between cultures.

The approaches of Moretti, Damrosch and Casanova to world literature obviously differ in several aspects. One of the most important differences is that Moretti is oriented towards research, whereas Damrosch is more focused on the teaching of world literature, while Casanova can be said to embrace a wider field of the sociology of criticism. Ideally, these dimensions would be connected, but in practice there may be many good reasons for thinking of these as domains that cannot be fully integrated, due to the complexity of the subject and the purposes of the different activities, yet they will also always influence one another.

A second difference can be found in the fundamental unit of analysis that also guides the interests of their work. Where Damrosch shows his most profound interest in the single text and its conditions for being understood by other cultures, Moretti is first and foremost interested in the evolution of genres and the ways in which local differences shape the techniques of certain genres. Casanova, due to her sociological approach, takes the most interest in the ways in which the international literary field or literary system is construed and changed.

The third important difference follows logically from the others, that is, in the way that historical time is approached. With his interest in canonization and anthologies, Damrosch is mostly retrospective in his work, unlike Moretti, who reconstructs the evolution of literature based more on a prospective outlook on the development of genres, rather than the selections of the literary system, while Casanova is mostly focused on the contemporary organization of the literary field, rather than other historical periods.

All in all, this adds up to three very different takes on world literature, which complement one another, and provide a basis for locating the blind spots in analyses involving a single approach. Yet the fundamental differences of approach could also be combined differently, as in a retrospective systemic analysis of the evolution of the international canons, which is predominant in this book.

Contested paradigms

World literature may be developing into a paradigm of its own, but it may also be seen as a subdivision within both of the two dominant frames of reference for studying literature – comparative literature and post-colonialism – that complements them. While there are many good things to be said about these – that is the reason for their becoming paradigms with significant institutional support – it is also possible to note some problems they encounter when addressing cultural globalization and the literature of the world, both with respect to giving a realistic account of the literary system, and of discovering new works, and, particularly new connections between works.

Comparative literature came into being at a time when national literatures were much more important and dominant than they are today.[9] The basic idea was to compare the literatures, rather than the individual works, of different nations, in order to determine both the specific nature of the literature and the nature of the culture and nation from which it arose. Over the years, this approach has been abandoned for an increasing emphasis on individual works. More importantly, comparative literature has also been the context in which most new theories of literature and criticism have been developed, to such a degree that, in the 1980s, theory might seem to have been its main object. That notion proved not to be valid, but comparative literature remains a successful inventor and integrator of ideas for research and criticism. This success and all-inclusiveness have also led to a blurring of the paradigm's identity (Étiemble, 1963). The new interest in world literature can be seen as a reaction to both the theory-heavy years and to some of the aspects that comparative literature seems to overlook.

The case 'against' comparative literature, when it comes to globalization, can be broken down to five central points: 1) the loss of curiosity, 2) the decline of linguistic skills among scholars, 3) the emphasis on theory, 4) its fuzzy identity due to its success in including new ideas, and 5) the legacy of depending on the nation as a frame of reference.

1. Comparative literature should ideally be about world literature, but in practice it is mostly about Western literature. Arguments can always be made about how big a share Western literature should take up, and how much bias regionalism might reasonably count for, but even then, the fact remains that comparative literature seems to have lost most of its curiosity with respect to the literatures of the world. One reason could be that specialists appear to take care of this aspect, but that is a poor argument, and contrary to the idea of comparative literature, which should be more inclusive.

2. The decline in linguistic skills is, in part, an explanation of the loss of curiosity. Comparative literature has always prided itself in reading literature in its original form, but this also imposes a limit to the literatures which can be addressed. In older reports on the state of comparative literature it is suggested that people must know four or five languages, one of which should be non-Indo-European (see also Damrosch, 2003: 281). The decay of linguistic and cultural skills was already noted by Erich Auerbach, who, in his 1952 essay, complains that a knowledge of Greek, Latin and the Bible had broken down almost everywhere, while he simultaneously claims that there is no reason to teach contemporary literature, because the students can easily understand that themselves (Auerbach, 1992: 89–90). In the present system of education there is rarely time for people to learn more than two or three foreign languages, and even if they did, this would represent only a fraction of the world's languages, and thus be insufficient for truly studying world literature, much less passing the knowledge on to others. World literature in translation is therefore a must, although the skills of specialists, and by extension, their collaborative work is still critical, in some form. The dominance of English in the process of globalization has probably done much to work against the need for diverse linguistic skills. David Damrosch also addresses this tendency in *What Is World Literature?*, and while regretting the state of the linguistic competences, he also comes up with an interesting solution by suggesting, as mentioned earlier, that world literature is literature that gains in translation, which is understood as adding to the value of the original, rather than replacing it (Damrosch, 2003: 288). He thus opens the door for a break with the notion of having to read in the original, without completely relinquishing the idea.

3. The change in linguistic skills is just one of several that have altered the object of comparative literature; another is the emphasis on theory, which, in the 1980s, emerged almost as a field of its own. What was once considered secondary had become a primary subject in its own right. Since then, theory as such has, unsurprisingly, shown itself to not be such an interesting field after all, but it left comparative literature with a fuzzy identity. The interest in world literature and those who have promoted it, particularly Auerbach, can be seen as a return to some of the values that once fuelled the comparative project, namely the interest in the aesthetic and historic complexity of eminent works.

4. Still, comparative literature is *under-theorized* when it comes to addressing those situations in which there is just too much to be read, such as is the case whenever world literature is invoked. Opting for the canon is a poor solution, as is the specialized reading within the confines of the national literatures. Franco Moretti has variously called for, and suggested models of study that establish a certain distance from the texts, in order to facilitate working with more texts from very different contexts (Moretti, 2000: 58).

In a somewhat provocative manner that goes against the grain of the core identity of the discipline, Moretti calls this 'distant reading', but one could also say that he suggests focused readings, wherein certain features are examined across a range of works, in order to find patterns in literary history.

5. Finally, comparative literature has never reflected thoroughly on its own heritage, from being nation-bound, to de facto working with a comparison of texts that have become internationally canonized. As a result, there is a need for a theory and history of the global space of literature and culture. The idea of national literatures is strong, despite anything that globalization may do to the notion of national identity, not least because markets, education, and in some cases, languages, still have a solid national base. Hence, the idea of world literature still seems based on a concerto of national literatures, even in those cases of writers who are very international in their own outlook as well as in their reception, because there is no tradition of thinking about authors as belonging to a subsystem within the literary world which is independent of nations.

However, there are groups of writers and works which could be said to form subsystems that are transnational. Three very different examples are much in evidence: Holocaust writers, migrant writers and instantly translated authors. The former two will be addressed in Chapters 3 and 4. The interesting aspect of instantly translated authors such as those mentioned earlier – Rushdie, DeLillo, Auster, García Márquez – is that their works appear simultaneously in several languages, which does not allow literary criticism to have an impact prior to a work deemed worthy of translation or not. This rapid process is mostly motivated by marketing, which can launch a work in a number of countries at once, thus making the sheer volume of published editions an event in itself. To what literary culture do such writers belong, when they become detached from the literary culture and criticism to which they once belonged? Have they not been transformed from being writers belonging to a nation, to writers belonging more to the world, thus transcending the comparative aspect of comparative literature?

World literature does not act in opposition to comparative literature, but is instead a correction of the way it is going. Haun Saussy notes very tellingly, in his contribution to the American Comparative Literature Association's decennial report, that world literature is an important project within comparative literature, but not as a project that is owned exclusively by comparative literature. It is not, moreover, a project whose success is a given:

Rey Chow observes that the integration of non-Western texts into the Comparative Literature canon may just mean confronting a new class of 'Eurocentric' specialists in remote cultures; there is no guarantee that exposure to the alien canon will teach anyone to see it as the locals see it. Chow fires a preliminary shot across the bow of the heirs of 'the great Orientalists, sinologists, Indologists, and so forth,' thus raising the question of what kinds of expertise will be considered valuable in the new comparative literature: will departments of world cultural studies have to cultivate their own specialists, uninfected by the Eurocentric virus? (Saussy, 2006: 22)

Like comparative literature, post-colonialism is a success insofar as it has become institutionalized, at least in English departments, both as a field of study and as a mode of practicing literary studies. It covers diverse underlying notions and ideas, but is also a label that has detached itself from its origins, and lives a life of its own, so to speak, beyond what its discursive originators, including Edward W. Said, Homi Bhabha and Gayatri Chakravorty Spivak may have intended (Bhabha, 1994; Boehmer, 1996; Said, 1978; Spivak, 1999; Young, 2001). Most importantly, post-colonialism covers a field of literature that comparative literature and its canons have had little eye for.

The theoretical groundings of post-colonialism are suited to the globalizing world, at least those parts of it that emphasize a complex, hybrid construction of identity, and recognize the many influences upon which all literature draws. Post-colonialism also contains a strong tradition of criticism of the international system, both in its political and economical dimensions. Nevertheless, there are also several points of critique that can be aimed at post-colonialism's attitude towards a global conception of the literary system. These are related to the timeliness of national literature as a project, of the preference for the authentic and unique, and for the lack of interest in the literature of the traditional centres of world literature. Post-colonialism is, as already noted, a very diverse field with conflicting viewpoints, and therefore the critique does not apply to the whole paradigm and institutional network as such, but to some significant aspects of it.

1. Post-colonial literature is mostly attached to young nations that were in the process of establishing their own identities. That there has been, and still is, a national or local project connected to this, is only a logical consequence. However, in the globalizing world, where the media penetrate local cultures more than ever, and people migrate in large numbers, mingling their cultures with others, taking part in building a national identity becomes a more complex project, especially when it is being communicated to a world engaged in discovering more and more cosmopolitan dimensions to life.

2. The dichotomy between authenticity and hybridity marks one of the most intriguing conflicts in post-colonial criticism. Critics such as Homi Bhabha have emphasized the hybrid character of contemporary identity, whereas others, among them Elleke Boehmer, have made the case for authenticity, whether it is with regard to a particular voice or experience (Boehmer, 1996: 233–243). Both sides obviously have something going for them, but the

selection of emphasis makes a world of difference. Proponents of the ideology of the hybrid would write off the idea of authenticity as both platonic and romanticist, whereas those who argue for the authentic would claim that there is no metaphysics involved here, but a cluster of specific events and habits attached to a people and a nation, and perhaps also a language, whose sum is more unique than hybrid. Yet, on the scene of world literature, there has been much more attention drawn to the hybrid, migrant writers (see also Mishra and Hodge, 2005: 383).

3. Another general critique of the post-colonial paradigm is that it has not come up with particularly convincing ideas and methods for dealing with the literature of the traditional centres of literature, the old colonizers. The lack of interest in seeing post-colonial literature as part of the same system as the literature of the West, as well as literature from the West that could qualify as post-colonial literature, remains a problem, by creating an irrational divide between the objects of comparative literature and post-colonial studies. This has consequently also led prominent figures such as Gayatri Spivak to emphasize studies of world literature in a global context as a more viable way out of the Eurocentric comparative literature, while warning against the monolingual triumph of English (Spivak, 2005: 19–21). She also identifies the problematic status of the nation in comparative literature, and suggests focusing more on cross-disciplinary area studies (Spivak, 2005: 34–35). The increasing attention on area studies can be seen in a series of literary histories published under the auspices of the International Comparative Literature Association (ICLA), for example, on the literary culture of Latin America (Valdés and Kadir, 2004).

The introduction of the post-colonial discourse to French criticism is an interesting exemplification of a changed world. French literary culture has a long tradition of translating literatures of the world, as well as of having writers with a colonial background making their mark on French literature. The introduction of the post-colonial paradigm came in the mid-1990s, more than a decade after post-colonialism had been firmly established in English and American critique. What is interesting is that things had changed by then, since globalization was the accompanying discourse that altered the way in which post-colonialism was received. Now, it was not seen so much as a programme of overcoming the colonial past, but rather as a way of being in the world, and post-colonialism has not been particularly influential in France.[10]

Finally, as mentioned earlier, it is hard to overlook the fact that the most significant thinker related to the post-colonial discourse, Edward W. Said, was at the same time a strong proponent of world literature. He translated Auerbach on world literature, and kept returning to the idea of it (Said, 2000: 454). Was this the paradigm for which he really hoped, rather than the establishment and fortification of a dichotomy between centre and periphery?

World literature: from object to paradigm

World literature used to be thought of as an object, a set of works, an idea of things of universal interest or as the sum total of all the literature in the world, but as has been shown, until recently there have been few serious attempts to transform this overwhelming and diffuse object into a paradigm for the study of world literature. The traditional approaches to world literature have either been one of antiquarian listings, side by side with the many literatures of the world, a valuable thing to a certain degree, but not very useful, due to its lack of a point of view, or a monumental hypercanonical approach that left little room for relating the highly exposed with the overlooked.

Bearing in mind the critique of comparative literature and post-colonialism presented above, world literature as a paradigm combines, first and foremost, a primary curiosity with a realistic observation of circulation and critical valuation, that will mix and balance the particulars with the main streams. World literature takes a global approach to literature, and sees the literatures of the world as belonging to one system. The individual works and authors within this are what matters, not the identities of different subsystems of the literary communities, and this approach is thus suitable for establishing meetings between scholars of minor or marginalized languages.[11]

Besides being thought of as an object, rather than a paradigm, world literature is usually envisioned in spatial terms, but there are important temporal dimensions to world literature that affect the ways in which world literature can be comprehended. The spatial terms are typically the regional and the worldly, the national and the international, 'the West and the rest', etc. The often unobserved temporal dimensions of the concept, and the field of study that follows with it, are even more important, however, since they lead to very different ideas of world literature, and present alternate conditions for research, criticism and teaching. In the following sections, the past, present and future inherent to the idea of world literature will be discerned among as leading to a discussion of the epistemological consequences that follow from this. A more detailed set of defining properties of world literature as a paradigm should be a by-product of this.

The long history of world literature is mostly a history of literature in the Western tradition, going back to the antique classics. It is dominated by an effective canon, which makes it impossible to put Ben Jonson ahead of William Shakespeare; a canon which is both a reflection of a certain historical power, and a reflection of a long and diverse process of selection. Thus, one intriguing question is 'Would Shakespeare still have been as pivotal, had he not been English?' There is no definite answer to this, but it should at least be remembered that English was not the dominant language of his time, making this historical development even more complex, although no one seems to have presented a body of work with a universal appeal equal to that of Shakespeare.[12]

The argument of the advantages of a dominant culture can also be turned around by pointing to the fact that, even though their positions are of a different nature, Søren Kierkegaard still became Kierkegaard, and Hans Christian Andersen became a part of children's literary heritage around the world, despite writing in Danish, just as an exiled Irishman, a German-speaking Jew from Prague and a blind Argentinean have become household names in the literature of the twentieth century. It is hard to say what can be attributed to the structures of the literary field, and what should be called literary genius. For better or worse, the canon of world literature is also a history of literary structures and of a varied selection by many readers and critics, who, in different ways have determined that Shakespeare comes before Jonson and every other Renaissance dramatist.

One may dream of changing things, of promoting counter-canon to hypercanon, but even the most influential critics have realized that their personal preferences cannot in themselves change the canon, and that diffusion of power is basically a good thing, because it keeps idiosyncrasies out of the system, as the process of change is a reflection of a complex web of selections in many contexts. Taking that into account, there are likely and unlikely expansions and revisions of the canon, but generally, large revisions are unlikely as time goes by. Even though literary critics enjoy the idea of the overlooked masterpiece or the writer who is brought back from oblivion, it is rare to be canonically included in the long run, if there has not been an initial and more or less continuous interest in the works of an author. In a global perspective, however, this also means that some works that have been sustained in a national canon have the potential to become more widely known outside of the borders of their place of origin.

The long history of world literature favours Western literature partly because of the long tradition of cultural exchange between Western nations, which established a literary community able to evolve an idea of 'the valuable' in world literature. The great traditions of China and India, both in terms of the magnitude of the countries compared with the many states of Europe, and with the stability of their art systems and canon, have paradoxically somewhat hindered their presence in world literature.

An interesting and often overlooked case of international canonization concerns foreign literature that stands out as canonical in a local or national literary culture. A significant example is that Montaigne, Cervantes and Shakespeare all have a significant place in literatures around the world. In Danish literary culture, this is documented by new translations of these authors within the past decade; there have been two competing translations of *Don Quixote*. In contrast to this, there are no Danish works from the fifteenth and sixteenth centuries with a similar position, almost all of these being unnoticed by other than specialists.[13] The strong presence of foreign works thus blurs the distinction between a national and an international canon, and paves the way for changes to come.

What kinds of changes might then be projected into the longer history of world literature? One change might be the inclusion of more canonical philosophy, and other texts that are not fiction, in the Western sense of the word. The reasons are numerous. First, it seems easier to anthologize philosophical and other non-fiction from a number of literatures, in particular Chinese and Indian. Second, there will most likely be a preference for texts that very clearly take up basic and timeless existential questions about what a human being is, and how life should be lived, from an ethical and aesthetic standpoint, rather than texts that deal with the specific conditions and norms of a certain period in history. Third, this tendency towards non-fiction will also have an impact on the anthologizing of Western texts, opening up to the inclusion of philosophical writings, letters and other non-fiction, even in those instances in which fiction is available.

The important point, however, is that there will always be an effective canon which is developed and sustained by the selections of many readers and institutions. This is a process that has no determining centre, but which is part of an ongoing conversation about what should be appreciated and valued. The rationales may be very diverse, spanning from aesthetic bliss to the importance of cultural memory of what is both known and different with respect to eras and cultures, but these will be rationales which themselves can be deduced from the effective canon of world literature.

In the social construction of world literature, one of the interesting questions concerning the world literature of the past is: who reads it? Is there a bias towards the schools, universities, etc., while the lay reader is more interested in the literature of the present? This could very well be the case, although universities are not the small and elitist institutions they once were, but rather a segment of mass culture and mass education. This is a point on which David Damrosch's perspective on anthologies and curricula can be said to be of quantitative importance, just as is Franco Moretti's emphasis on the open book market.

Contemporary literature will in some respects always seem inferior when compared with the longer tradition, since a few years cannot yield a body of works comparable to the efforts of centuries. Today's literary scene is a much more complex and uncertain field in which everybody knows that even those who have been saluted for a couple of decades may not be visible to future generations. It is therefore much easier to speak with certainty about the great masterpieces, and be certain that Shakespeare, not Jonson, is the best recommendation to make to others. But contemporary literature has many things in its favour that separates it from the longer tradition, and calls for a different treatment and interest.

First, contemporary literature is important, because it is what is being read. All more or less accurate indicators – book sales and people's personal experiences – indicate that the majority of works being read are contemporary. Literature is a living art, and it is obvious that a huge of number of readers prefer contemporary authors to the classics. If class room reading is not taken into account, contemporary literature, here loosely defined as that of the last 20 or 30 years, would probably make up more than 80 per cent of all that is being read around the world.[14]

It is not just the newness of contemporary literature that makes it different, but also the context in which it is written and received, something which gives it a very interesting edge over the literature of the past. Because of globalization, one can expect many more shared references in contemporary literature with regard to history, media and cultural icons, mixed, as a rule, with local or national references. It can easily be held that writers like the Canadian Douglas Coupland and the Japanese Haruki Murakami have more in common with each other than with the literary traditions in which they grew up, because contemporary music, television and other media have had such a significant influence on their work, both formally and thematically, and these are influences to which many writers of the past did not have access.

The media revolution, propelled by the now only about a decade and a half old emergence of the internet, has been enormous, and provides access to global information. The effects of outsourcing and movement of production, by mobile telephony, cheaper air travel and so on, only enhance the sense of globalization. It can certainly be argued that this development is only new in its extent, not in its nature, but even then one must take into account that changes in quantity can reach a threshold where a change of quality sets in.

This is particularly relevant to certain future developments, of which we have only seen the beginning; the advancement of biotechnology presents the most important challenge to one of the traditional topics of literature: what it means to be a human being. Yet, lives are still lived from birth to death, and deaths are as individual as ever. The life story, which according to Georg Lukács is the essential outward form of the novel, has not become less interesting, either in biographies or as a subject of fiction (Lukács, 1971: 77).

Another important aspect of contemporary literature that differs from what has been seen in the longer history of literature, is that everybody has a chance to make a name for themselves without being part of a fixed hierarchy. This sets a completely different agenda when it comes to receiving new works from relatively young literatures. Whereas attempts to promote these literatures, sometimes from a colonial past, can seem like a Sisyphus project, there are numerous examples of contemporary writers from all over the world who have had a broad international reception and recognition. Although everyone has a chance to make a name for themselves on the contemporary scene, and thus define tomorrow's literature, this is true only in principle. In the literary system as it is construed at the moment, the English language is so dominant, as discussed above, that the condition of global success is success in either Great Britain or the USA.

So, what happens if the literary system is shifting towards a preference for the contemporary, not only when it comes to sales, but also as a dominant value? What if the long canon loses its value, precisely because the world has changed?

Antonin Artaud did not dream of a literature for the ages, but one for the present, while Charles Baudelaire was able to appreciate both the classics and the contemporaries because both combined ephemeral and eternal qualities (Baudelaire, 1964; de Man, 1983: 161). Why should the value of intensity here and now be less worthy than the value of a long life outside of the world from which the literature arose, being a literature of the present and for the present? Some of this has already been realized, except in the dominant ideas of what literature is, and should be.

The literature of the future does not yet exist, but projections of what it is about to become have always been important, in the form of dreams and visions, often supported by an overview of the changes in the present world. Some of the changes have been touched upon, above: the continuing development of a more global culture, the trend towards reading an increasingly larger proportion of contemporary literature, towards more interaction of aesthetic fields, towards a bigger role for non-fiction in literature.

In addition to these tendencies, there are external forces, such as the influence of new centres of economic growth, which will change the role of globally marketed literature to an even larger degree. Damrosch has suggested a differentiation between global literature and world literature, in order to distinguish what is merely sold in large numbers around the world from what has a longer and more profound impact (Damrosch, 2003: 25).

The ongoing evolution among electronic media also impacts the conditions of literature. Few would have guessed that television could become a medium in crisis with younger audiences, yet surveys show that a generation of young people born after 1980 feel more at home with the internet and computer games (Jenkins and Thorburn, 2003: 91; McGann, 2001). With the internet, text based media are undergoing a renaissance, multimedia will play a larger role in future reading, and the future of writing and reading looks much better with these newly blended media, as opposed to the once dominant dichotomy of text versus images. Web logs could be a significant mode of expression, and even though much of the writing will probably be very weak, the form may also be close to ideal for future talents to express themselves. A phenomenon like Facebook, wherein people connect with their friends and acquaintances, could be seen as a kind of multimedia novel, in which each person tells about his or her own life, highly conscious of the way that he or she presents it in words and images. This material is then a part of a unique mosaic of contemporary stories that shows up as text, pictures and video, on the screens of tens or hundreds of Facebook friends.

In any case, no one knows, and anyone can make use of today's trends to project the future, and still end up being very mistaken. The important aspect of the future of world literature is the way in which it is being used to make institutional changes in a situation where fields of research are being redefined, and curricula are being determined to some degree by the idea of what will be relevant to the future.

When asking what can be known and what should be known about world literature, it makes a great difference whether these questions are asked of the past, present or future, since the different temporal dimensions of world literature present very different conditions for studying their objects. The spatial differentiation between nation and globe is basically a matter of preference, whereas the temporal dimension sets up boundaries between the kinds of knowledge that can be obtained, and the means and ends should be adjusted to the limits of the temporalities.

It should, for example, be evident that when it comes to the long history of world literature, any study must take notice of the processes of the selection that have taken place over the years, knowing that changes in the canon cannot be commanded, but only suggested, in the hope that others will consider the suggestion being made. The canons can also be seen as *resources for analyses*, since they represent, or are nothing but, selections made by readers and institutions over a long period of time, some of which can be said to be due to institutional inertia, whereas others are of a more complex and overwhelming nature in their depth and breadth. The point is that they represent a sum of choices that could have been very different, but which are as they are. From the complex fields of their own time, over a period where several others have presented themselves as canonical candidates, they have somehow come to occupy a place in literary history. This is a place which cannot be taken for granted, since the canon is ever evolving, and thus dependent on the future choices of institutions and readers. Taking canonicity seriously also means taking the manifold selections of the literary system seriously. The problem with canons is only a problem if there is no culture of criticism that is perpetually seeking, reading and criticizing alternatives.

With contemporary literature things are more blurred and complicated, the more one moves into the present time. It is usually fairly safe to project that books which are not sold, read, translated and written about after a couple of decades, will, barring a small number of exceptions, probably not have a significant place in literary history, but the closer we get to our own time, the more difficult this becomes to determine.

Critical assessment is made in a wide variety of ways, but there has not been the test of time that can sort temporary trends from something lasting, and there has not been time to let widely different kinds of works enter into a conversation across time and continents. Best-seller lists are of little help in projecting what will be lasting, although all historical examples show that some critical mass should not be underrated. Translations do tell a lot about the streams of cultural capital in the present world, and can serve as rules of thumb to map the present reality of the distribution of literature; yet again, they also have a bias towards works that historically have not proven their long-lasting worth. Nevertheless, many things can change within a generation or two, and knowing that should make critics careful in predicting the future canon. Again, one can ask whether a preference for the present, the here and now, is of lesser value than a preference for the works of the past. It is not an either/or matter, and even if the media offer reasons to believe that there is a greater emphasis on contemporary literature, there is an unprecedented level of activity related to history around the globe.

Thus, the critic, teacher, historian and writer, even, operates in two epistemological conditions: one in which the past can be used as a resource, and one where the voices of the same past may not be fully relevant to describing contemporary literature, particularly if one accepts that the cultural and historical environment of today has changed the conditions of being, everywhere. It might very well be that another threshold is needed, as Franco Moretti has suggested; around the year 1800, which marks the before and after of the emergence of international book markets and centres in the international literary system. However, Moretti's argument favours a perspective that is interested in the prospective evolution of literature (or to be more specific, the evolution of the novel), whereas the preference here is directed towards the study of the process of canonization, which is retrospective, and less based on markets than on a mixture of institutions that include criticism, teaching, and the markets alike (Moretti, 2006).

Chapter 2

Shifting focal points in the international canons

The tendency in literary curricula and anthologies towards a more shared, international canon when it comes to literature written before the eighteenth century cannot be explained only by the fact that literary masterpieces that remain vivid today become scarcer even within the greater nations as one goes further back in time.[1] This also corresponds to a period that was not dominated by the nationalistic closure that essentially took place in the middle of the nineteenth century, and is still partly in effect. A reopening of the national canons of this period to include works of world literature was not a given, but was more likely, given that cosmopolitan competences and cultural knowledge are valuable in a globalizing world. Furthermore, although the traditional principal literatures of the English, the French and the German have central positions in world literature, it is also historically evident that new centres have always been able to make their mark, and that the canon is highly influenced by internationalism, either through writers' approaches, or by way of their migrant experiences.

In the following sections, it is suggested that the mapping of major centres and minor, temporary sub-centres of world literature can provide valuable knowledge about the evolution and composition of the world literary system. Four models that can facilitate more refined research in international canonization are presented and discussed, followed by a reflection on the principle of seeking constellations in literary history.

Temporary sub-centres

Any geography needs a model based on a hypothesis of what generates significance. A geography of politics maps nations, while a geography of religion maps the areas of dominance of the major religions, and so on. Sometimes areas do not tell the whole story, and hence demographic geography must represent the numbers of inhabitants in a given area, just as topography must inform about the heights of mountains and the depths of seas. What should a geography of world literature describe? Should it show literary activity?

International canonization? Directions of influence? The sum of production, readers, preferences, translations, critical valuations, etc., provides so many elements that are difficult to bring together without revealing the ways in which they are constructions and simplifications, and that the importance of the various dimensions can never be fully integrated or agreed upon, unlike the simpler set of elements within which other geographies operate (Bradbury, 1996). Even if a geography of literature will always be tentative and illustrative, it may be worth considering as a serious challenge to literary history.

Some models operate with a centre and a periphery, sometimes with a semiperiphery as well, to separate the dominant cultures from the less influential, without denying that their influences can work both ways. This is the case for the models of Franco Moretti, who appears to be the critic who has gone furthest in trying to explore that which spatial models can reveal about literary history:

> What I know about European novels, for instance, suggests that hardly any forms 'of consequence' don't move at all; that movement from one periphery to another (without passing through the centre) is almost unheard of; that movement from the periphery to the centre is less rare, but still quite unusual, while that from the centre to the periphery is by far the most frequent. Do these facts imply that the West has a monopoly over the creation of the forms that count? Of course not. Cultures from the centre have more resources to pour into innovation (literary and otherwise), and are thus more likely to produce it: but a monopoly over creation is a theological attribute, not an historical judgment. The model proposed in 'Conjectures' does not reserve invention to a few cultures and deny it to the others: it specifies *the conditions under which it is more likely to occur*, and the forms it may take. Theories will never abolish inequality: they can only hope to explain it. (Moretti, 2003: 75–77; see also Moretti, 1998)

This model can make a lot of sense, for example when the spread of the modern novel or the sonnet can be traced back to its origin, but the rapid movements of interests in the modern world and temporary centres of focus need to be represented. Such models that make refinements could be constructed in many ways, proving or disproving their worth when applied to the given material, although some models are more significant and important than others. In *Graphs, Maps, Trees*, Moretti makes a particularly interesting study of the shifting dominance of subgenres of the novel in British literature in the nineteenth century (Moretti, 2005: 14–16). Interestingly, Moretti does not pursue this idea of temporal dominance further into the realm of the geography of literature, but leaves it as a study within a single culture.

Taking into the account the importance of literature's development over time, it would make sense to operate with a geographic model of historical world literature based on the idea of centres that have been dominant over time, as well as temporary sub-centres. In this way, the often very dynamic and unpredictable turns in the focal points of literary history can be represented and given due credit. In antiquity, Athens, Alexandria and later Rome, are obvious examples of dominant centres; in modern times Paris, and later, New York fulfil a similar role, albeit in a much more complex and integrated world. It could even be argued that the true dominance of centres is usually confined to small periods of time, whereas in other times a more complex situation exists, especially in periods of transition.

The centre-periphery model does not need more than these centres, but being focused on the production and distribution of books, it belies the reality created by literary history in the long run, which is more influential to history than the way in which some centres dominated a certain period. A concrete example is the blossoming of the Russian novel with Dostoyevsky and Tolstoy from the 1860s to the beginning of the 1880s, which formed a temporal sub-centre of attention in the *history* of world literature. From both before and after those decades highly internationally canonized works emerged from Russia, but not to the extent that took place in this brief period, and which in time has come to represent the utmost the novel had to offer at that point.

With the introduction of temporal sub-centres, the model acknowledges two complementary types of influence on world literature and international canonization: the dominant centres that exercise influence over a long period, both by distributing its authors to other cultures and by adopting others nations' authors into their culture through translation and canonization, and the literatures whose contributions to world literature can be confined to a relatively short period of time or to a limited number of authors, but which create important temporal sub-centres of attention in the history of world literature.

The short history of dominant centres in world literature would take Greek literature as a starting point, from 700 BC until 300 BC, with the Roman Empire as the next dominant centre. In the middle ages, there was no European centre, whereas Arabic and other Middle Eastern literature flourished and participated in securing an invaluable heritage of European literature. There was little interaction between other parts of world, where Chinese and Indian literature had already been established for centuries. With the Renaissance, Italy and the Vatican State became the most important literary centres, until France took a dominant role in Europe during the Enlightenment, although the literatures of Germany and England also developed, to become influential outside of their own borders.

Pascale Casanova goes to great length in *The World Republic of Letters* to show that Paris was the literary capital of the world from the middle of the nineteenth century until recently, a period that, also according to Moretti, marks the real beginning of the international book trade (Casanova, 2004: 164–165). Casanova acknowledges that London and New York have taken over the dominant positions on the literary scene as melting pots in which all kinds of literature are trying to be noticed, and from where distribution of what is valued streams. Due to the more mercantile nature of the publishing houses that dominate the English and American book markets, Casanova is not sure that this is a change for the better, since many French publishing houses are known for their commitment to publishing literature for the few. However, she accepts the reality of a shift in the centre of dominance, although she still makes the case for Paris as an important centre of canonization, just as is Stockholm, because of the Nobel Prize:

> The recent recognition of major writers such as Danilo Kiš (a Serb), Milan Kundera (a Czech), Thomas Bernhard and Elfriede Jelinek (Austrians), Arno Schmidt (a German), Carlos Fuentes (a Mexican), Mario Vargas Llosa (a Peruvian), Gabriel García Márquez (a Colombian), Julio Cortázar (an Argentinian), Antonio Tabucchi (an Italian), Paul Auster (an American), and António Lobo Antunes (a Portuguese) testifies to the con- tinuing power of consecration enjoyed by the Paris authorities. Kiš, more conscious of the general mechanisms and more clear-sighted perhaps with regard to the structural implications of world literary space than earlier generations of writers recognized by Paris, asserted in 1982: 'For here in Paris, you see, at least for me, everything is litera- ture. And Paris, despite everything, still is and will always be the capital of literature.' The evolution of world literary space since then lends support to Kiš's contention that Paris' function of discovery and consecration will survive the decline (real or imag- ined) of French letters. Certainly Paris remains the capital of 'deprived' as well as 'marginal' literatures–written by Catalans, Portuguese, Scandinavians, Japanese, and others – and it may be expected to continue to give literary existence to writers from countries that are the furthest removed from literary centers. (Casanova, 2004: 166)

Casanova thus tries to operate with the idea of two centres of world literature that have different values and outlooks. However, as is evident in the list of authors above, Casanova does not seem to be aware of the Parisian bias towards an author such as Danilo Kiš, who is certainly more recognized in France than in most parts of the world. Such biases exist everywhere, which is why the principle of looking for international canonization in a *variety of contexts* is so important.

The idea of centres is a simplification, and in the twentieth century the situation is more complex, with more evolved literary cultures, and more from which to choose. It is also clear that there have been golden ages within the dif- ferent literatures that determine their position in history. French poetry from 1850–1900 is just one case of an era that lost force, which is why Baudelaire- Rimbaud-Mallarmé is not automatically followed by another name. But while it is not hard to see Paris' influence from the Enlightenment to at least the 1920s, as well as that of Athens and Alexandria in Antiquity, and of New York in our age, it is more intriguing to pinpoint criteria for temporary sub-centres. There are no absolute criteria for selecting these, but a number of indicators can be considered, in order to create a valid tool for further investigation.

First, sub-centres must have exercised an influence on other literatures and ages. Second, they must have a significant number of works incorporated into an internationally sustained canon. Third, their literature must generally be considered to be among the best written in a given period. Fourth, they must have made contributions to the evolution of literature. Finally, all the above must stand out significantly during a given period, in contrast to other periods of the same literature.

Another approach to defining sub-centres would be to find obvious examples based on these criteria, and see what distinguishes them. The examples given here are Russia during 1860–80, Scandinavia during 1880–1900 and Latin America during 1960–80. Other examples might be the Weimar of Goethe and Schiller, Bavaria and Austria in the first decades of the twentieth century or the American literature of the 1920s. The last-mentioned decade, however, marked more a development of a new dominant centre than what could have been a temporal blossoming.

The novels of Fyodor Dostoyevsky and Leo Tolstoy are still regarded as the zenith of Russian literature in the international perspective. Their body of work, the main part of which emerged within the two decades between 1860 and 1880, marked an unprecedented era of influence that also includes the work of Ivan Turgenev. It is difficult to cite other novels from this same period that have a similar place in world literature, perhaps excepting Gustave Flaubert's work.[2] Russian literature has contributed to world literature both before and since, but none of the same depth and breadth: Nikolai Gogol is a name in world literature, but not a very active part of the international canon; the Russian formalists are more canonized as a literary movement than for their poetry; Aleksandr Pushkin belongs mostly to Russia's national canon, whereas the work of Boris Pasternak and Alexander Solzhenitsyn, together with that of other writers who lived under the Communist regime, depended as much on its political importance as on the quality of their writing. Even Anton Chekhov, perhaps more beloved than Tolstoy and Dostoyevsky, does not provide sufficient weight in his authorship to make him an inevitable candidate for an international canon of his time. The same thing cannot be said for Tolstoy and Dostoyevsky, as they drove the epic novel to its limits. Georg Lukács found that Dostoyevsky transcended the genre of the novel, and wrote what he thought would be the epic of a new era (Lukács, 1971: 152). Thus, Tolstoy and Dostoyevsky contributed to the evolution of the novel, by pushing its limits and influencing later writers from other cultures, not least through their sometimes nihilistic spirit.

At the end of the nineteenth century, Scandinavia had a more unified literary community than it has now, due the integration of book markets and newspaper reviews, and the last two decades of the nineteenth century also stand out for the way in which Scandinavia exercised an influence on European literature, possibly for the first time in any significant and multifaceted way. Prior to that period, Scandinavia was heavily influenced by German literature, but that was a one-way influence. At the end of the century, Henrik Ibsen became a noteworthy European, and highly canonized for plays such as *A Doll's House*.

His plays are still being performed all over the world, and, as have other dramatists, he benefited from the theatre's ability to make local productions of foreign
texts, rather than mere translations. Ibsen's influence on other writers, not least
his ability to navigate between realism and Modernism, is well-documented, for
example is the case of James Joyce, and Ibsen continues to stand out as one of
the most important modern dramatists (Casanova, 2004: 160; Moi, 2006).

Another Norwegian, Knut Hamsun, wrote some early modernist novels, most
notably *Hunger*, in 1890, and in Sweden August Strindberg made his mark in the
same modernist vein, although with a completely different, intellectually decadent attitude, in contrast to Hamsun's background in rural life (Hamsun, 1967).
In Denmark, Jens Peter Jacobsen gradually became increasingly well-known
internationally, especially in Italy and Germany. A number of internationally
renowned composers, including Arnold Schönberg, set his lines to music, while
Rainer Maria Rilke learned Danish in order to be able to translate Jacobsen's
poetry, and based the protagonist of his novel *The Notebooks of Malte Laurids
Brigge* on Jacobsen (Rilke, 1983).

Finally, it was a Danish literary historian, Georg Brandes, who wrote one of the
first major comparative studies in literary history, *Main Currents in 19th Century
Literature*, and who was crucial to the rediscovery of the work of Friedrich
Nietzsche. Brandes wrote in a letter to the poet Sophus Schandorph in 1888:

> I have been studying philosophy for a long time. I am studying a German philosopher
> who is living in Italy. His ideas and mine agree so completely that I find him excellent,
> the only philosopher alive that I have any use for. We have been in touch with each
> other for a few years. His name sounds strange and he is still unknown. His name
> is Friedrich Nietzsche. But he is a genius. Lately I have cast off one of my snakeskins.
> I have turned from the Englishmen back to the Germans in philosophy. English phi-
> losophy seems to me to have reached its peak. But my friend N. has the future ahead
> of him. (Brandes, 1940: 288)

The influence of Scandinavian literature during this period cannot be embodied in a single formula. One aspect of it is that these writers were modernists
before the Anglo-American Modernism broke through, and in a different, less
reflected, and to outsiders, some might say, more authentic way, than the
modern movement in France. In their influential book on Modernism,
Malcolm Bradbury and James McFarlane thus chose 1880 as their starting
point, in order to include the modern movement in Scandinavia (Bradbury
and McFarlane, 1976).

The basis of a second important explanation is that there was, in Germany in
particular, a perception that the Scandinavian *esprit* was closer to something
authentic and uncorrupted, which was given support by images of a rough and
cold life in an untamed nature. Such perceptions would be misleading when
trying to understand a number of the Scandinavian authors, but this is apart of
their literary legacy. Several of them, most notably Ibsen, are typically labelled

'naturalists,' which combines the idea of the authentic with a philosophical and aesthetic attitude that also had a pendant in the dominant French literary culture. Furthermore, each of these authors contributed writing that stood at the forefront, both formally and thematically, for example Jacobsen's mock heroic novels of disillusion, and Ibsen's call for women's rights, which has left a lasting mark in literary history. That the Nobel Prize was inaugurated at the beginning of the twentieth century, paradoxically, but perhaps also logically, marked the end of a period of Scandinavian influence making Stockholm the literary centre of the world, but only once a year.

The artistic and commercial successes of South American literature in the 1960s and the following decade were so significant, that it very tellingly became known as 'El Boom'. Writers such as Gabriel García Márquez, Mario Vargas Llosa, Carlos Fuentes and, Julio Cortazár all had literary breakthroughs that were both conscious of history and formally at the front of Post-Modern narrative techniques (Bowers, 2004; Zamora, 1995). Whether or not 'magical realism' was an expression coined earlier, most agree on the 1920s (Guenther, 2004: 56–59), the works of South American writers of the 1960s provided a body of literature that made it clear that this was a mode of narration. They freed themselves from the more introverted and less straightforward narrative style of European Modernism, while at the same time connecting with the tradition of fantasy found in the works of Jonathan Swift, among others.

Furthermore, just as the Scandinavian literature of the last decades of the nineteenth century thrived on a sense of Northern authenticity, it would be fair to say that the idea of a Southern authenticity is central to the idea of magical realism, which became the most important label applied to this diverse group of writers, who contributed to world literature and made Spanish literature as a whole stronger, vis-à-vis the traditional dominant languages. In an international perspective, there is little credibility a Central European supernatural perspective on life that can compare to that of the South American.

Other examples of temporary sub-centres in world literature could be found, some with a predominantly regional influence, some with an almost global impact. They complement the models of centre-periphery, and the idea of centres from which new impulses are distributed, and as a consequence the model of temporary sub-centres of world literature enables at least four things: a greater realism in the picture that is given of the world literary system, a better way of describing the evolution of world literature, a means of tracing that which may have been overlooked, and finally, it helps to refine a theory of influence.

The realism of historical world literature is a matter of mapping the preferences of the international literary system as it has evolved, and finding out where the action was, so to speak, or where literary history has found it to be and where literary history left it again. Thus, the success of the Russian novel of the 1860s and 1870s did not produce a lasting effect for the writers who followed.

The Scandinavian literary scene could not sustain its position, and today the excitement over South American literature may have become overshadowed by that of migrant writers. In accepting the temporal nature of such centres of influence on world literature, it is possible to write a more realistic story of discontinued influence in a system of shifting centres.

This also has effects on the way the evolution of world literature can be described, here understood as the way the preferences, the complex of genres, forms and themes that dominate world literature, can be portrayed. Rather than models of centre and periphery that do not take into account the two-way influence of such sub-centres, or models that hypostatize the influence of single authors from small literary cultures, the idea and the reality of sub-centres are better able to explain structural changes in the literary system.

Although the immediate result of searching for sub-centres of literary culture leads to a kind of monumental way of making history, such a mapping also provides an idea of where something undiscovered might be found. In the same way that arguments for the sub-centres, which may be equally based on literary features and sociological arguments, give an idea of why some periods have been influential, they can also serve as the beginning of a search for explanations as to why other periods in the nation's or other nations' literature of the same period did not play the same role, and the answer to questions such as why the Scandinavian influence came to an end, or why French poetry never found another golden age.

Finally, sub-centres provide an argument for the quantitative aspect of influence in literature, since they demonstrate how an influence that has structural effects will be based, more often than not, in a cluster of other works in temporarily dominant or influential literatures. Major centres also have golden ages, as shown by the examples already given, of French poetry from the second half of the nineteenth century, or American literature of the 1920s, but the point is that these centres do not depend on their own literature's golden ages; their function is that of a melting pot and a place where the valuation of works has consequences beyond its own borders.

Becoming a world literature

One of the most astonishing aspects of American literary culture is that not until the 1920s did it break into the English departments at colleges and universities around the country. British literature had dominated up to that point, despite America's more than one hundred and fifty years of national independence, and the literary output of numerous accomplished American authors, which spanned the work of poets such as Emily Dickinson and Walt Whitman, poet and short story writer Edgar Allen Poe and novelists as diverse as Nathaniel

Hawthorne, Herman Melville and Mark Twain. Although this list sounds all too familiar today, to the point of resonating of that which is written in stone, that was not the case at the last turn of the century. Melville was then, if not forgotten, not taken seriously, as he has been since the virtual rediscovery of his authorship in the 1920s, and Dickinson was only a rather recent discovery, going back to the 1890s.

The international breakthrough of American literature in the 1920s is interesting in several aspects, which will be addressed here. First, it is important to establish the magnitude of the international canonization of American literature of the 1920s, in comparison with periods before and after. Second, the synergy that American writers created in this period, in particular with the literary scene in France, is of central importance, also to the nature of canonization within the USA. Third, it can be argued that this period marked a transition from a national literature to a world literature, which has had an effect on the backwards canonization of American literature.

A little publication of recommendations from the German publisher Reclam, *Die Leseliste* from 1994, is very telling, with regard to the impact of American literature from the 1920s on world literature. Out of its approximately six hundred selections from world literature, there are four American works from the 1850s, including Walt Whitman's *Leaves of Grass* and Herman Melville's *Moby Dick*, but then no American works from the next four decades are included, and just one work from each of the first two decades of the twentieth century, respectively Upton Sinclair's *The Jungle*, and Gertrude Stein's *Tender Buttons*. There is just one work included from the 1930s, John Steinbeck's *The Grapes of Wrath*, which stands in sharp contrast to the inclusion of eight works from the 1920s, each work being one whose presence on the list would hard to contest, regardless of whether the perspective is on international canonization or on the general status of literary works and their influence on modern literature: T. S. Eliot's *The Waste Land*, Ezra Pound's *The Cantos*, John Dos Passos' *Manhattan Transfer*, F. Scott Fitzgerald's *The Great Gatsby*, William Faulkner's *The Sound and the Fury* and two works by Ernest Hemingway, *The Sun Also Rises*, and the collection of short stories, *The Killers*. All this does certainly not reveal the entire truth about the other periods, but it tells about the strong impact of a particular decade that has had a lasting effect (Griese, 1994: 171–178).

Interestingly, there is no American novelist of this decade who can claim to be its most important writer. There was no James Joyce, Marcel Proust, Virginia Woolf or Thomas Mann. But there were writers affiliated with the modernist movement on the one hand, and at the same time more accessible than these, in particular Ernest Hemingway and F. Scott Fitzgerald. Both produced a variety of works of varying quality, but they also produced works that were quickly canonized, namely Hemingway's *The Sun Also Rises* and Fitzgerald's *The Great Gatsby*. The case could be made for Hemingway having represented the state of the art with a technique that altered the idea of what realist writing could be, but it would still be difficult to put him ahead of the aforementioned authors, in terms of general international recognition of his artistic achievements.

In the same years, other novelists had more impact on their own time, but have not been able to remain part of the international canon over the years, most notably Theodore Dreiser and Sinclair Lewis, while in contrast to these, others have risen to greater recognition, including William Faulkner and John Steinbeck, whereas John Dos Passos has remained a constant presence over the years.[3]

The dominant American novelists of the period are interesting in their combination of affiliation to influential foreign movements in literature as well as having maintained a status of general popularity, from the popularity of Steinbeck through Hemingway and Fitzgerald, to the more exclusive nature of Faulkner's work. None of them can be said to have dominated the evolution of the novel, but they represent a part of that evolution while having found a particular way of being simultaneously state-of-the-art *and* popular.

An almost opposite case exists when it comes to the American poets of the 1920s. With the possible exception of Germany, no other country can claim to have such a range of important poets making their mark on the 1920s, but they also remain more exclusive and less popular.[4] Besides the expatriates Ezra Pound and T. S. Eliot, the 1920s saw some of the best works by William Carlos Williams, Gertrude Stein and Wallace Stevens, and together these poets comprise a group that has superseded the lasting output of poetry from British, French, Italian and other traditional literatures from the first half of the twentieth century. In addition to this highly canonized group, there is another tier of esteemed writers, among which are Hart Crane and Marianne Moore.[5]

It is also remarkable that, when it comes to formal expression and subsequent international canonization, the contrast between some of the recognized poets of the 1920s who have since faded, such as Edwin Arlington Robinson, who received more prizes for his poetry in the 1920s than any other poet, but is now largely forgotten, is even greater than between that of the novelists of the period. The poets were a much more uncompromising part of the Modernist movement, and they became the dominant figures in the world poetry of the age. However, for all the American writers of the period, the degree to which they thrived on international relations from early on is significant.

The strong ties between Paris – and to a lesser extent, London – and a significant number of American writers pose a problem for literary history, namely, how these influences are to be evaluated, apart from observing that they are evident. Would these authors have produced what they did, if they had not gone overseas or elsewhere? Would they have been canonized to the same extent, if they had not thrived on the attention from the then most dominant literary scene, and the people constituting it? Probably not, but it is not possible to propose counter-factual history with any acceptable certainty, by imagining what it would have been like, had Hemingway stayed in the Mid-West, leaving the fact that the Transatlantic, and particularly, French, connections dominated the generation that broke through in the 1920s.

The interrelationships among these authors were widespread. Ezra Pound and Gertrude Stein stayed in Paris for long periods, and acted as mentors and inspirational figures to their colleagues, most notably T. S. Eliot and Ernest Hemingway. F. Scott Fitzgerald also stayed in Paris, and paid court to James Joyce, and even writers who are generally perceived as having stayed at home had ties to France, including William Carlos Williams, whose *Spring and All* was published in France, and Wallace Stevens, who, for professional reasons, could not leave home for long periods of time, paid great attention to the literary scene in Paris and the heritage of the French symbolists. This connection also evokes an important, earlier transatlantic relationship, that between Edgar Allen Poe and Charles Baudelaire.

William Faulkner is particularly interesting, because he was not part of the French literary scene, and his works could be characterized as regional literature, more Southern than American, if one had to choose only one label. Faulkner was not a very successful author in the 1930s, having published *The Sound and the Fury* in 1929, and continuing to publish other works, but nevertheless finding that publishers did not consider it worthwhile to reprint his work, due to lack of demand, which was also the case when he received the Nobel Prize in 1950. But he had readers in France, some of them very influential, such as Jean-Paul Sartre, who grouped Faulkner along with seminal modernists like Joyce, Proust and Woolf:

> We can find the real reason for their similarities in a widely shared literary preoccupation. Most of the great contemporary writers – Proust, Joyce, Dos Passos, Faulkner, Gide, and Virginia Woolf – have tried, each in his own way, to mutilate time. (Hoffman, 1962: 230)

Above all, the example of the American writers of the 1920s demonstrates how international canonization takes part in sustaining national canonization, just as it is worth remembering that Shakespeare's reputation to some degree also hinges on the interest the German romantics took in him. Perhaps the 1920s marked an internationalization that was quantitatively different, although the basic pattern of synergy and interdependence, which was brought up earlier, is not without precedent.

The 1920s also marked, as noted previously, the moment when, after a gradual opening up of the canon, American universities began to teach American as well as British literature (Renker, 2000: 3). That this decade marks a demarcation between two attitudes towards what could be taught as English literature is, as already mentioned, somewhat astounding, considering that the United States had been a sovereign nation for almost one and half centuries. The 1920s was, therefore, also a decade of late canonization. Herman Melville is probably the most significant rediscovery, although he had to some degree been part of a popular literary culture the whole time, it was not until the 1920s that literary criticism showed a real interest in his works, whereas other writers, such as Walt Whitman and Emily Dickinson saw their positions in literary history being solidified. The point is, therefore, when a nation's literature is established as world literature due to its contemporary literature, its past has a greater chance of being recognized outside of its borders.

All in all, the 1920s transformed the literature of the United States into a world literature based on a synergy between a new generation that found a place that combined the new modes brought in with High Modernism with a more popular bearing, a generation which was as internationally oriented as ever, and a literary environment which had accumulated enough self-confidence to canonize its own literature. That the international community was sometimes mistaken in determining what was lasting and what was soon to be forgotten, such as in the Nobel Prizes given to Sinclair Lewis and Pearl S. Buck, is merely an affirmation of the changes in the longer history of international canonization, and the importance of the longer temporal perspective.

World oriented writers and the lonely canonicals

Works that circulate internationally will always face the challenge of contextual knowledge, which may make reading very difficult or almost impossible for some readers, because they know little about the world being presented to them. Much like the readers, writers operate in a field between experience and imagination, and they must find a way to unite these two domains, especially since literature has never been successfully written in a void, without reference to elements from the world, although the ways in which references to the world are included provide a significant range for authors. Much, if not most, literature has been written about the cultural sphere of the immediate world known to the author, and is often shared by his or her readers, when literature circulates within a nation or bordering cultures. There are, also other historically popular genres, such as fantasy and travel literature, which describe places unknown or unfamiliar to the reader, and where the attraction is the experience of the strange through the eyes of someone akin to the reader.

When it comes to world literature, it is significant how differently the contexts of internationally canonized works function. The great Russian novels of the nineteenth century take place in a thoroughly Russian, albeit internationally oriented, society. Balzac primarily cared for Paris, and Joyce wrote about Dublin. There is a certain paradox in an excess of the local, which will be examined later.

Other authorships truly have a world orientation towards a variety of cultures and histories, and one might suspect that this would make it easier for these to enter other literary cultures, and thus be counted as world literatures. Two such authors are the Argentine Jorge Luis Borges and the Danish Karen Blixen, also known as Isak Dinesen, both of whom came from minor literatures, but very deliberately included in their work both experiences from other cultures and a bricolage of the existing world literature and mythological material.[6] The paradox they reveal is that of having become national emblems through their world orientation.

It does not probably insult any of his compatriot colleagues to claim that Jorge Luis Borges is the only Argentine writer to have gained a lasting prominent position in world literature. Borges himself has come to epitomize an apparently paradoxical position as both a writer who thrives more than any other on the literatures and cultures of the world, while also being a symbol of South American and Argentine spirit, at least outside of Argentina. Borges was aware of different positions and paths he could choose, not least in order to capture and express something uniquely Argentine. In his 1951 essay, 'The Argentine Writer and Tradition', Borges considers the arguments for replacing the Western canon with one that is Argentine, in order to inspire future writers. Borges argues that he prefers to express the specific nature of Argentine culture through that of which he is not conscious, rather than trying to refer explicitly to the Argentine context, which should also be seen as a political response to the Peronist regime:

> We cannot confine ourselves to what is Argentine in order to be Argentine because either it is our inevitable destiny to be Argentine, in which case we will be Argentine whatsoever we do, or being Argentine is a mere affectation, a mask. (Borges, 2000: 427)

Borges makes a series of inspired arguments about how the nature of a given nation or culture can be expressed without alluding to objects that otherwise seem to be integral and defining of the world out of which itcame (Borges, 2000: 423). In the same vein, local references in the works of Argentine writers cannot be that which makes them more or less Argentine.

A more important aspect of the tradition has to do with the relationship of Argentine to Western culture. Here, Borges points to a paradox in the arguments of those who wish to replace the Western tradition with an Argentine tradition, because it would be a denial of the very history from which the nation was born. It would also be a provincial limitation to the possibilities of the contemporary writers, if they were confined to the immediate Argentine context:

> I wish to note another contradiction: the nationalists pretend to venerate the capacities of the Argentine mind but wish to limit the poetic exercise of that mind to a few humble local themes, as if we Argentines could only speak of neighbourhoods and ranches and not of the universe. (Borges, 2000: 424)

Borges' own writing refers to a vast mix of imaginary and real references. He invents a Chinese labyrinth in 'The Garden of Forking Paths', although there

was never a tradition of labyrinths in China, and the reader is always left won-
dering whether references to books, people and places are a product of Borges'
imagination or knowledge, even in stories like 'Tlön, Uqbar, Orbis Tertius',
which is very straightforward in presenting a fictional framework, but also refers
to the known world. Thus, one of the often surprising things about his authorship is the remarkably large number of references that are not fictitious, given
the typically unlikely connections in which they are placed (Balderston, 1986
and 1993). In the end, Borges has proven to be successful in maintaining a
cosmopolitan scope of interest and reference, without surrendering the belief
that he wrote from an Argentine point of view, but which would always be a
point of view that could not be made manifest to him.

Against Borges' standpoint, it could be argued that it apparently does not
matter what a writer does, because he can never escape his roots and will always
express them through his writing. A similar idea can be found in the writings
of Pierre Bourdieu, who introduced the concept of *habitus* as the patterns of
socially coded ways of being in the world, which the individual can never fully
comprehend or fully escape (Bourdieu, 1996: 214–215).[7] Yet the way in which
the writer orients herself or himself does matter, and does make a difference,
this also being an integral part of Borges' argument, because the writing should
be good, as good as possible, and not merely an instrument for an ideological
view on culture. This does not mean that every writer must be as globally oriented as Borges, but that every writer should not limit his curiosity, or censor his
or her work in order to please a specific group.

Borges accordingly entered world literature without being part of a dominant world literature, but by being innovative – the last inventor of a new genre,
as Italo Calvino wrote, on the fictions with their implied references to imaginary work (Calvino, 1996: 50) – and by taking both his curiosity for the world as
well as for being Argentine, seriously.

The Danish baroness Karen Blixen, who in 1934 published her first work,
Seven Gothic Tales, in English, under the pseudonym Isak Dinesen, shared with
Borges, although not to the same degree, the ability to transcend her roots in a
minor literature and become internationally recognized. A telling anecdote
about her status is that Ernest Hemingway, on receiving the news that he had
been awarded the Nobel Prize, reacted by saying that it should have gone to
Karen Blixen, and it probably would have, were it not for a certain resistance to
female authors on the part of the Swedish Academy. In addition to Blixen's
literary accomplishments, her life and work have since been embraced by the
movie industry.[8]

Blixen presents an interesting mixture of an aristocratic, cosmopolitan attitude and a colonial setting in many of her works, based on her experiences
of being a coffee farmer in Kenya for almost two decades, until she returned
to Denmark in 1931. This is particularly noticeable in her second book, *Out of
Africa*, published in 1937.

But the story of her authorship might have been quite different, if the American writer and editor Dorothy Canfield Fisher, who knew Blixen by way of her friendship with one of Blixen's aunts, had not taken interest in Blixen's work, and suggested it to the other members of the Book-of-the-Month Club committee.[9] The selection of *Seven Gothic Tales* was important to both the club and to Blixen. The Book-of-the-Month Club had had a troubled economy in the first years of the depression, and Blixen's work, when published in 1934, sold well and helped to solidify the economy of both author and publisher. Furthermore, the American media found out who was behind the pseudonym 'Isak Dinesen', and the story of a Danish baroness with a past in Africa – bolstered by her aristocratic mien – made her a media celebrity who later appeared publicly with younger figures such as Arthur Miller and Marilyn Monroe.

Meanwhile, Blixen had an immense influence on the literary milieu in Denmark, both as a mentor to young writers and academics, and as one of the founders of the Danish Academy. While one of the most cosmopolitan Danish writers ever, she is also the most highly canonized female writer in Danish literary history. As with Borges, a cosmopolitan attitude helped to produce a paradoxical effect of local recognition.

A cosmopolitan attitude is not a prerequisite to being either internationally or nationally canonized. There are more examples of the opposite being the case, where the quality of the writing and universality of the themes are enough, although even then it is likely that there will be specific features or techniques that compensate for the reader's lack of first-hand experience of the context of a literary work.[10] There is in Balzac and others an excess of the local that creates a paradoxical effect, where the exactness of the references is not of vital importance to the understanding or appreciation of the work, because it has absorbed a certain historical environment, which is used to create a world of its own. Just as Borges' works create what could be called a referential excess, in which the truth or falsehood of the references to all kinds of people and works loses significance, because in his works the references obtain a status of their own, it is telling that several works in the international canon do so likewise, and create what could be called topographical excess.

There are quite a few examples of this: the Dublin of James Joyce's *Ulysses*, the France of Marcel Proust's *À la recherche au temps perdu*, the St. Petersburg and Moscow of Fyodor Dostoyevsky's novels or the England of Thomas Hardy, all create universes that simultaneously depict a historically extant environment, but do so in such a way that the novels can be read for more than their historical accounts. The excess of detail in *Ulysses* is perhaps the best example of this effect, but the same thing could be said for Honoré de Balzac's Paris, and William Faulkner's and Gabriel García Márquez' small towns. It is of course difficult to specify exactly at what point a work shifts from being burdened with a context that is an obstruction to the reader to making use of a context that makes an outside world its own, but what is also remarkable about the above mentioned authors is that they have been propelling the formal evolution of the novel while taking on a specific local context. In a historical perspective, international canonization is thus more dependent on formal innovation; never formal innovation in an empty space, however, but rather, one laden with culture and specific histories.

There will always be contemporary and local literature that is enjoyed by an audience that has a first-hand impression of the literatures' contexts, and they will be written because writers write about what they know. But most of it will not be internationally canonized, since it does not have the specific features and qualities that make it interesting to a foreign audience. That does not mean that local literature is not important, or that it should not be respected; it is just different, and fulfils other functions and desires. Still, there is the importance of international canonization to a sustained national canonization, as shown by the examples of William Faulkner, Karen Blixen and many more. Their places in literary history thrive on their international canonization, which again demonstrates how the national literatures are interconnected.

International canonization has a way of creating clusters that go together as shown above – Tolstoy and Dostoyevsky, Ibsen and Hamsun, Kierkegaard and Andersen, Márquez, Fuentes and Paz, etc. – but then there are those who do not have a highly canonized compatriot who worked within decades of themselves. These could be called the lonely canonicals, although they are only lonely from the perspective of that which has achieved international canonization, but has done so without carrying other writers with them. Jorge Luis Borges is one obvious example, as is the Portuguese Fernando Pessoa and the American Edgar Allan Poe. They are writers who also were very unlike anyone else writing at the same time and place, and thus not particularly representative of a literary milieu, but rather departures from the main currents, yet they are the foremost representatives of their nations' contribution to world literature of their own time.

Two types of lonely canonicals can thus be described: the truly lonely figure, who is different from all others and whose work not makes it unlikely that others might follow him or her onto the international scene as being more of the same. Then there is the writer who, for various reasons, has had an international breakthrough, but cannot be said to be significantly better or different from a range of contemporary countrymen. The first type is often the most interesting from a formal viewpoint, whereas the latter is more interesting from a sociological viewpoint.

Discussions of whether an author belongs to the first or the second category can be enlightening with respect to positioning the writer, both in the international canon and in his or her national canon. Georg Brandes finds, at a time when Søren Kierkegaard was not internationally recognized, that Hans Christian Andersen is a telling example of an author who received world fame even though he:

> does not stand with our greatest; in his own lifetime he was never thought of as belonging to the first or second class. Nor, I might add, even after his death. As a thinker he

was inconsequential and never had an intellectual influence. He was viewed as a gifted, childlike creature, and this estimation was not incorrect. But nonetheless he belongs to world literature, for he wrote fairy tales that made their way everywhere through their general comprehensibility.[11]

Similar discussions could be had about authors like Milan Kundera, who is not the only talented writer of a generation that includes Ivan Klima, or Chinua Achebe, whose debut *Things Fall Apart*, has become a standard in anthologies of world literature and has had the double effect of bringing attention to African literature and of also becoming an icon in world literature that puts other African works in its shadow, or Nobel Prize winner Gao Xingjian, who is one of many Chinese writers who describe the horrors of the Cultural Revolution. In trying to determine the character of the loneliness of the lonely canonicals, much can be learned about the differences in national and international canonization, as well as where it might be fruitful to try to search more broadly for other works and authors, and where it would be unlikely to discover another Borges, who despite the odds, made a difference to world literature.

Modernism as a new antiquity?

A change in the way the past is perceived creates both revivals and oblivion, and, as already noted, the temporal mapping of world literature is just as important as the spatial mapping with which the considerations of sub-centres, world literatures and lonely canonized writers have dealt in the preceding sections. The thesis is that because the 1920s produced more internationally canonized works than any other decade, the literature of that period still defines the literary field and the idea of the potential of literature. In a historical perspective this is not something new. Other periods have had their defining pasts, and changes towards a newly dominant period have often gone hand-in-hand with revolutions in the mediascape.

The notion of antiquity and its functions have, to a high degree, been preserved to designate what we call the Antique, namely Greek culture from the seventh to the third century BC, and its successor, the Roman Empire. However, in *A Farewell to an Idea*, T. J. Clark presents the following provocative thesis that seems particularly apt when applied to the literary community:

> Modernism is our antiquity, in other words; the only one we have; and no doubt the Baku Palace of the Press, if it survives, or the Moltke Museum, if it has not been scrubbed and tweaked into post-modern receptivity (coffee and biscotti and interactive video), is as overgrown and labyrinthine as Shelley's dream of Rome. (Clark, 1993: 3)

The idea is strikingly clear and mind-numbing at the same time. Is it really so, and if so, what does all the preceding period mean to us? Are they just remnants of a past that we can never fully understand, because we have been shaped by Modernism?[12]

The battle for defining the threshold of modernity is an unfinished and often tedious business, but nevertheless very interesting, when it comes to examining Clark's thesis on Modernism as antiquity. Virginia Woolf famously placed the transformation of the human being at somewhere around December 1910, and often 1918 or 1920 are selected as threshold years, because of the enormous influence of the First World War (Woolf, 1991: 421–422). Some literary historians choose to ignore those years as essential threshold years. In *Modern Epic,* Franco Moretti studies literature written from 1800 until now, as being part of the same greater period, whereas Remo Ceserani has argued that the two essential threshold years are 1800, with Romanticism's inauguration of modernity, and the 1950s as the coming into being of the Post-Modern, leaving no special place for Modernism (Ceserani, 1994: 376–377; Moretti, 1996). But threshold years or not, international canonization suggests that the time after the First World War was one of the transitions to a new era.

The 1920s and the years immediately around that decade present a list of artists who are still perceived as artistically purer, more radical and more talented than anyone following them. In conventional wisdom, fair or not, no novelist can match James Joyce or Marcel Proust, no painter is comparable to Pablo Picasso, no modern classical composer has done as much to change music the way Igor Stravinsky and Arnold Schönberg did. They are supplemented by a crowd of figures who share that aura, partly due to their life and work, partly because of the way history has staged them.

T. S. Eliot, Ezra Pound and Gertrude Stein are among the primary exponents of a uncompromising attitude towards literature, both with regard to changing and absorbing tradition. Although less affiliated with the avant-garde, novelists such as Virginia Woolf, Thomas Mann and Robert Musil belong to the same uncompromising vein. Writers such as Robert Walser and Walter Benjamin are also *Schriftstellers,* taken to the extreme. Furthermore, there have never been literary movements like Dada and the French Surrealists that were able to redefine the literary field, and these are supplemented by the Imagists, the Russian Formalists, the Italian Futurists and many other, often short-lived, movements. Together they form a cluster of avant-garde movements the like of which has not been seen since, although the lasting quality of their literary production is not comparable to that of the best poets and novelists of that period. Aside from the above mentioned poets, there were poets like Rainer Maria Rilke, Paul Valéry, William Carlos Williams and Wallace Stevens, who also made their contributions to the decade's substantial output of canonized works, characterized particularly by an aura of uncompromising dedication.

Is the 1920s overrepresented in literary history? The question is probably too simply put. If there were objective standards of what counts as great writing, the 1920s would, in all likelihood, do better than most decades, and should thus be well-represented by canonized works. One argument might be that some works and writers are canonized together with the really important works, but to counter that, it can be argued that the works of Modernism defined a new standard of writing which should canonize them, because it is still the standard to which we return.

It is thus not just the artistic merit, but the extreme nature of the works and the way in which they are perceived later on in literary history that is unique, and makes the case for seeing Modernism, and particularly the literary culture of High Modernism, as a quasi-antiquity to the literary environment of the present day. It may be an over-statement to call Modernism an antiquity, but if that is the case, why do Joyce and Proust remain reference points for the extent to which literature can be pushed?

The aura of being a pure and radical artist is important to the idea of an antiquity.[13] Sophocles, Plato, Dante, Shakespeare, Goethe and a number of other writers who were part of significant movements in history that exercised a lasting influence on their past have been presented as possessed of that uncompromising attitude towards art. In the same way, there is something enchanted about the great projects that took place in the midst of post-First World War nihilism.

Franco Moretti has written that the writers of the 1920s envisioned a new beginning and a glorious future for a literary culture that had set itself free (Moretti, 1983: 209). Joyce, and many with him, thought that *Ulysses* was a way of liberating the novel from the tradition, but was not a masterpiece in itself. Instead, history showed that the literary culture was in fact at its zenith in the 1920s, a perception that remains unchallenged even given the many great works that could be said to belong to Post-Modernism.

The Renaissance introduced the idea of Antiquity as a reference point that could make art and culture move beyond the ideas and habits of the medieval world, and the influence of the antique writers is legendary: Dante would be very different without Virgil, Montaigne drew extensively from the whole range of antique writers, and British Renaissance drama owes a great deal to Greek and Roman theatre. Classical French drama and its foremost representative, Jean Racine, took the ideals of Antiquity furthest, by trying to also obey the formal requirements of antique drama with a strictness that also hindered a genuine evolution of the drama.

The difference in the attitudes of British Renaissance drama and French Classical drama epitomize the conflicting attitudes towards any idea of a privileged reference point in the past. The first sees an ideal that can help shape the art of the present, the other sees a world that produced things the present will never be able to equal, and thus the arts of the present should try to make copies of the works of the antique to the best of their ability. The effect of this difference in attitude was such that French classical drama could never aspire to be a new point of reference, such as the drama of Shakespeare or the poetry of Dante and Petrach have become (Gervinus, 1863: 513). The functions of the antique can thus be conservative and antiquarian, as well as progressive and critical. This is also what was at stake in the quarrel between *Les Anciens et les Modernes.*

Greek antiquity has, for some, remained the ultimate reference point for an authentic way of being and acting in the world. This is clear in many of Goethe's references, and the Romantic poet Friedrich Hölderlin is also a prime example of such an attitude, as is one of his most dedicated readers and an ardent critique of modernity, Martin Heidegger. However, in the two most important Romantic movements, namely in British and German Romanticism, there was also a movement canonizing Shakespeare in particular. To some degree their fascination with the Renaissance ran parallel with the fascination with the antique, but there was still no doubt that they also had to create their own roles, vis-à-vis the idea of the Renaissance.

The relationship between Romanticism and Modernism is perhaps the least sharply defined relationship between two paradigmatic movements in culture, but the parallels and connections are clear enough. There was a period during which the Romantic project did not present itself any longer as something that could be carried out; the mid-nineteenth century can be said to have had the idea of a negative romanticism that was still defined by the paradigms of Romanticism, but as an impossible dream. The idea of modernity also became more developed, but it cannot be said to have had its breakthrough until there was also a rediscovery of the Romantic poets and their ideals. Modernism could thus be said to be a new Romanticism, sharing the ideas of 'making new', and thus the poets of the modern movement were also the ones who contributed to bringing new value to the Romantic writers, some of whom had been marginalized during the nineteenth century.

The story of parallel encounters with the past continued nevertheless: Joyce wrote in the shadows of Homer and Dante alike, and T. S. Eliot undertook large parts of the same tradition in his works, as well as explicitly trying to define a position that was different from that of Romanticism. And perhaps now Modernism is our Antiquity, as the canonical selections quietly argue, but for how long? We may very well be at the end of a period where Modernism holds a special position, and where the intrinsic values of modernist literature will have to give way or to be transformed into something new. The likelihood of this is suggested by the fact that all the other antiquities have also been able to emerge and define their positions in a time of revolution in the mediascape.

It is still an open question whether Post-Modernism signifies a break with Modernism or is a continuation of it, but the important thing in this context is that it has not produced a canon with the same aura as that which came out of Modernism. It may change over time, but for now the standards are still set by the figures of Modernism.

It is striking that these defining periods in history have been accompanied by significant changes or revolutions in their contemporary mediascapes. First, Greek antiquity is only known to us because writing gave future generations access to the theses, plays and poems of the time. The medium of writing itself is deeply embedded as a theme for Plato, who paradoxically argued against writing and for the spoken word, in line with Socrates.

The defining evolution in media from Medieval to Renaissance is the invention of the printing press, which made possible a broader and cheaper distribution of books. The age of Romanticism was also the age of industrialism, where the price of paper fell dramatically, and the capacity of printing presses was enhanced by machine power, which meant that even greater audiences could be reached, which again changed literature and made way for the popularization of the novel (Behrendt, 1998: 92). The change in quantity was also a change in quality.

In the twentieth century the revolutions in media have emerged in a seemingly endless stream, but two of the most significant changes took place at the beginning of the century, namely the capacity to reproduce sound and to capture moving images. The spread of film throughout the world, from its invention in the 1890s, was remarkably rapid, whereas the phonograph and telephone had a slower diffusion, and eventually were supplemented by the radio in the 1920s, which also spread remarkably quickly. This had both a direct influence on the historical avant-gardes, such as the Italian Futurists and their sound poetry, and it more indirectly changed the way writers have treated writing and the book as media, both in terms of exploring ways of including the new forms of representations from other media in literature, and by reacting to other media as competition. The influence of these media on literature has been thoroughly documented by Sara Danius in a study of James Joyce, Marcel Proust, and Thomas Mann (Danius, 2002).

The end of twentieth century saw the next major revolution in media, with the first computers and then the internet, which connected virtually all computers on Earth, gradually leading to computers that mix text, images, sound, and moving pictures, more and more powerfully, in ways that have never been seen before (Manovich, 2001: 19). The internet also revolutionized ways of accessing information, of following local news from a distance, or of quickly obtaining information from all places on Earth. Search engines, most notably Google, not only facilitate this access to information, but have also very concretely influenced the way people think about relationships between concepts, in the way they learn to search by using related keywords, which then generate results based on the ways in which these are represented and interconnected on the internet. Again, literature has responded to the medium both with experiments and with the recognition of the existence of yet another competing medium.[14] The interesting question, however, is whether the revolution in media, which also affects film, television, radio, etc., will change the privileged place in history held by the modernists, and if so, in what way their works will play a role in redefining the historical before and after for the period that we are entering, since participating in their own dissolution as the pivotal reference point has been a common trait of all other antiquities. Concerning the media reality, Andreas Huyssen has noted that the status of literature in society has been changed:

> To celebrate global literature today as a new and expanded form of Goethe's *Weltlitera-tur* ignores the fact that literature as a medium of cultural production no longer occupies the privileged place it once held in Goethe's age. (Huyssen, 2005: 10)

A change in the status of Modernism could also have consequences for the geography of world literature, in that it would be unlikely to reproduce the centres of the past, just as the breaks and connections between Antiquity, Renaissance, Romanticism and Modernism were marked by different geographical centres. It is by no means certain that this is the age of world literature, but there is reason to believe that a literature that embraces globalization and the idea of world literature, as well as the new media reality with which we live, could be the literature that establishes itself as that which makes the literature of Modernism seem less like our Antiquity. It might also be a literature written by a number of writers who are aware of their roots, but who are also conscious of being part of a globalized world, and who write for a much more diverse audience.

A system of perpetual circulation and valuation

In this chapter a series of different perspectives on the mapping world of literature has been presented: ideas of centres, temporary sub-centres, old and emerging world literatures, international canonization without the support of a major national literature, and temporal shifts in the historical horizon. This is part of an attempt to comprehend a vast and changing system of circulation and valuation, rather than an attempt to pin down a definite typology. The different models that have been presented here basically share one aim, namely, to explain why some works have the capacity to interest strangers, while other works do not.

No one would argue that there is a definite or 'right' model for describing international literary history, but that does not set aside questions of more or less realistic models; this will be addressed here in some of the questions that follow from that: What could and should the relationship between realism and construction be, with regard to such models? In the same vein, how does the ambition to design better or more definite models relate to the conviction that one has to select units for analysis? How can the difference in describing dominance and change conflict, and should that be integrated into any literary historical activity? Finally, it is argued that national and international canonization realistically can be seen as separate if connected systems.

The idea of canons is often looked upon with a certain reservation, as selections that have been determined by power relations, as much as by the qualities intrinsic to the works. Both elements certainly play a role, but what is usually overlooked is the immense number of individual selections, by critics, literary historians, writers, teachers and general readers, that combine to make works canonical over the years. Canons are thus both the expression of some sort of realism in a manifold and decentralized process of selection, and they express the harsh realities of unequal opportunities of even being in the range of a wide and differentiated audience, and as such they are supported by a set of historically constructed premises (Bloom, 1994; Carnochan, 1993; Guillory, 1993; von Heydebrand, 1998; Thomsen, 2005a: 139). Constructions, however, are also part of reality and history, and if one agrees with Nietzsche that there should be a mix of the antiquarian, the monumental, and the critical attitudes towards history, then the distinction between realism and construction loses its significance by being transformed into a differentiated strategy for studying history that acknowledges this conflict.

Another way to transform the conflict between realism and construction is to look at the status of models that are used to describe literature, and its history and development. Whenever a model is constructed, it should be able to claim that it tries to reduce complexity without overly distorting reality, but there can still be very different attitudes towards the nature of models. Ideally, progress in literary studies can be made through models that would fit together well, and end up as a unified theory of the field. Yet, the complexity of the subject, the diversity of histories and the plethora of relevant theories and approaches to literature, makes this very unlikely, but it could still be a goal. Another way of tackling this conflict is to relinquish the idea of the perfect model, and accept that literary history itself is an evolutionary system, in which simple facts can be proved, but where the outcome of that which certain perspectives and models reveal about larger parts of history goes beyond true or false, and is subject only to challenge by other descriptions. This is Franco Moretti's perspective, when he opts for a literary history that evolves into 'a long chain of related experiments' (Moretti, 2000: 62).

Moretti's strategy is to select a specific unit of analysis – the spread of the novel, the clue in late nineteenth century crime fiction and so on – and use that as a very limited perspective, but a perspective that makes it possible to compare much larger bodies of works. The argument is built upon experience from history and social sciences:

Writing about comparative social history, Marc Bloch once coined a lovely 'slogan', as he himself called it: 'years of analysis for a day of synthesis'; and if you read Braudel or Wallerstein you immediately see what Bloch had in mind. The text which is strictly Wallerstein's, his 'day of synthesis', occupies one third of a page, one fourth, maybe half; the rest are quotations (fourteen hundred, in the first volume of The Modern

World-System). Years of analysis; other people's analysis, which Wallerstein's page synthesizes into a system. / Now, if we take this model seriously, the study of world literature will somehow have to reproduce this 'page'–which is to say: this relationship between analysis and synthesis–for the literary field. But in that case, literary history will quickly become very different from what it is now: it will become 'second hand': a patchwork of other people's research, without a single direct textual reading. Still ambitious, and actually even more so than before (world literature!); but the ambition is now directly proportional to the distance from the text: the more ambitious the project, the greater must the distance be. (Moretti, 2000: 56)

The risk will always be that the perspective will overlook what is interesting in works that do not possess certain features, and it also runs the risk of being deductive. However, this need not be a major obstacle, since criticism of the outcome of the models, the result of the 'experiments,' can solve such problems and refine the outcome, and eventually also provide feedback to the strategies for analysis.

A more serious problem with regard to the question of realism lies in the balance between the dominant and the emerging changes, and the role criticism should play in this. That changes occur is not problematic, but the blind spot in studies that rely on the canon is that they tend to fortify the established works, if they are not aware of the critical role and sense of marginal or rival works that such studies should also include. This is what David Damrosch urges, to balance with his concepts of hypercanon and counter-canon (Damrosch, 2006: 44).

Finally, it is useful to consider national and international canonization as two very different systems that operate from different criteria, as pointed out by Pascale Casanova (Casanova, 2005: 71–72). Most literatures have nationally canonized works which have had little impact on the international scene, even if they have been translated to some extent. Other authors find that their status is greater abroad, than at home,[15] but, as has been argued, in the long run there seems to be an effect on national canonization arising from international canonization.

The contemporary 'middle-brow' novel, together with less ambitious genres such as the crime novel, have dominated the cultural exchange of literature for a long time, whereas translations of classics or emerging canonical works do not appear to take up as much space, in comparison; however, these novels are usually forgotten after a decade or two, and new works emerge. One of the best examples of this is the canonization of Georges Perec, who now stands out as the most important French writer of the 1970s, something that would have seemed unlikely to most observers in the early 1980s.

Anthologies of world literature have such a widespread impact within the educational system that they deserve special attention as a particular genre of literary history. As mentioned in the introduction, several major publishers have taken an interest in compiling quite comprehensive anthologies of world literature, each comprising up to six volumes and several thousand pages. If an anthology is successful, it will have a great influence on the fate of certain texts' long-term place in literary history, such as is the case with Chinua Achebe's *Things Fall Apart*. Apart from all the criteria faced by writers of literary history, editors of anthologies must pick representative texts, both with regard to length and to the pedagogical challenges that accompany the texts. With regard to length, excerpts can be used to make texts available, and as such are not too problematic – even though most anthologies also boast that they contain unabridged works, thus acknowledging the problems associated with excerpts – whereas the problem of what can be taught is more complex. A short story from *Dubliners* is, in many respects not unwisely, likely to be favoured over an excerpt from *Ulysses* or *Finnegans Wake*, although those stories would not themselves have made James Joyce canonical. In other cases, things go well together: Joseph Conrad's *Heart of Darkness* is canonical in its own right, short for a novel, offers the intriguing blend of a European voice and a colonial setting, and has been countered by authors such as Achebe.

Anthologies also have the interesting property of mixing highly canonized texts with less known texts, which may then gain in canonical status by their representation in successful anthologies, whose sheer volume can in itself generate a sufficient critical mass for bringing a work into the international canons. However, this does not mean that anything goes in anthologies, but there are important differences in their selection strategies.

In *What Is World Literature?*, David Damrosch identifies two unfortunate strategies for selecting texts that have been common to anthologies of world literature in the past, to look for either the strange or the familiar:

> From Henry Cabot Lodge and Charles Elliot to the HarperCollins and Norton anthologies, world literature has oscillated between extremes of assimilation and discontinuity: either the earlier and distant works reflect a consciousness *just like ours*, or they are unutterably alien, curiosities whose foreignness finally tells us nothing and can only reinforce our sense of separate identity. But why should we have to choose between a self-centred construction of the world and a radically decentred one? Instead, we need more of an elliptical approach, to use the image of the geometric figure that is generated from two foci at once. We never truly cease to be ourselves as we read, and our present concerns and modes of reading will always provide one focus of our understanding, but the literature of other times and eras presents us with another focus as well, and we read in the field of force generated between these two foci. (Damrosch, 2003: 133)

As the general editor of *The Longman Anthology of World Literature*, Damrosch has addressed this problem in praxis by editing his anthology with an emphasis on presenting clusters of texts that have common themes, but originate from different parts of the world. Sections on avant-garde movements, stories inspired by the *Tales of the Thousand and One Nights*, and the conditions of gender and post-colonialism around the world, are balanced by texts and authors which stand alone. Thus, the anthology strikes a compromise between the idea of picking only the best works, and forging the links between the literatures of the world by presenting clusters of texts that have thematic features in common. This stands in contrast to anthologies like *The Norton Anthology of World Masterpieces* and the *HarperCollins World Reader*, which do not present works from different cultures in the same sections, but divide the texts by a more traditional concept of periods and cultures such as 'Poetry and Thought in Early China', 'Medieval India' and 'The Enlightenment in Europe'. Both strategies have their pros and cons. The strategy of blending is more ambitious in its presentation of the idea of world literature as a unified field that can be studied as such, whereas the division into periods and cultures facilitates a greater focus on the depth of a certain period. The latter strategy could seem to be academically more respectable, with its emphasis on a particular period, but that is not necessarily the case, either because the texts have a direct relation to other traditions, or because one holds that the specificity of a culture can only be understood when seen in a constellation of differences.[16]

The conflict between seeing an individual work as nearly unique, or as just a representation of more general properties in a larger system, can always be brought forward. The first position is too involved in the specific history and conditions of a single work or author to determine how it might be related to other works, while the second position tends to reduce historical contingencies to a mere filling in of a larger structure. Nobody defends either position when taken to their extremes, but it is nevertheless almost impossible for literary critics and historians to not have a preference for one or the other.[17] Others acknowledge the need to find methods and frameworks that transcend these positions; among these is Damrosch, who, as mentioned previously, has repeatedly supported Moretti's attempts to use quantifiable research in the study of world literature, not, however, without justly criticizing Moretti's idea of writing literary history without a single direct reading (Damrosch, 2003: 25). The strength of Damrosch's descriptions lies in his three-stringed definition of world literature as a refraction of national literature that circulates in translation, while stressing that world literature must also be a way of studying literature, rather than being a set of works. This conception broadens the field without being merely all-inclusive, but unlike his editorial work, it has weaknesses when it comes to seeing and evaluating patterns that mix descriptions of a quantitative and qualitative nature, rather than singular stories.

But how can one argue for a combined strategy that blends, for example, the positions of Damrosch and Moretti? One of most interesting attempts to find an intellectually respectable intermediate path between the preferences for the singular and the general is Ludwig Wittgenstein's concept of family resemblances. In *Philosophical Investigations*, he describes the notion in a series of examples:

> Consider for example the proceedings that we call 'games'. I mean board-games, card-games, ball-games, Olympic games, and so on. What is common to them all?–

Don't say: 'There must be something common, or they would not be called "games"'–but *look and see* whether there is anything common to all.–For if you look at them you will not see something that is common to *all*, but similarities, relationships, and a whole series of them at that. To repeat: don't think, but look!–Look for example at board-games, with their multifarious relationships. Now pass to card-games; here you find many correspondences with the first group, but many common features drop out, and others appear. (Wittgenstein, 1953: 31e–32e)

In the next paragraph, Wittgenstein sums up the idea:

I can think of no better expression to characterize these similarities than 'family resemblances'; for the various resemblances between members of a family: build, features, colour of eyes, gait, temperament, etc. etc. overlap and criss-cross in the same way.–And I shall say: 'games' form a family. (Wittgenstein, 1953: 32e)

Wittgenstein's proposal is just another model, another metaphor for describing reality, but it carries with it a determination to be both pragmatic and historic in insisting on the knowledge that conventions have instilled in culture, and by not focusing on an idea of a model into which things must fit, but rather to see and accept that there can be important relationships between categories that also differ at points which, in other frameworks, would mark a crucial difference. Some of Wittgenstein's ideas are now deeply rooted in the post-structuralist way of thinking, and his examples are so obvious and pedestrian that they hide the underlying implications for a research programme. For world literature, the implications would be to seek out clusters of works, techniques and genres, which have also had a record of being significant; to find the family resemblances of works that have been internationally canonized for decades, or have been internationally successful in the present.

Harold Bloom has to some degree made practical use of the analytic mode of constellations, both in *The Western Canon* and even more clearly and predominantly in *Genius*, which is organized around ten different thematic clusters that bundle authors from different periods and cultures. He is also very observant of the merciless functions of history, but has his own ideas of the logic of the system:

A pragmatic definition of a genius of language is that she or he is not a producer of period pieces. . . . Time, which destroys us, reduces what is not genius to rubbish. (Bloom, 2002: 813–814)

Although Bloom's rhetoric of the genius is questionable, it would be reasonable to argue that there will always be an ongoing separation of world literature into contemporary and canonical literature. It is a difference that remains and a threshold for texts to pass. Once the broader principles, such as the uncompromising and romantic idea of genius, are abandoned, there is the meticulous work of seeking better descriptions of ever more interesting constellations in 'a series of related experiments'. The different ways of mapping world litera-ture presented in this chapter are thus dependent on the power history gives to or takes from the components of which they consist. Sketches of these have been presented in this chapter in order to exemplify the general strategies and the ways in which formal traits, clusters of writers from unlike contexts and the historical valuation of their works have gone together. In what follows, in Chapters 3 and 4, literature by migrants and the literature concerned with mass killing are analysed as two important constellations in world literature.

Chapter 3

Migrant writers and cosmopolitan culture

The writing of migrants is an understudied but increasingly interesting topic in the history of literature, particularly with regard to the effects it has had on modernist and contemporary literature, and in making transnational literature visible as field to be taken seriously in its own right. The relatively large influence of migrant writers in internationally canonized literature is reflected in the number of Nobel Prize recipients who are migrants, sixteen of the approximately one hundred recipients so far, as well as a number of writers who would have been valid candidates.[1] Migrant literature is literature by authors whose work does not really belong to a specific national literature, or at least they have often been so treated, although there are signs of a change in this approach. This is evident, for instance, in volume thirteen of the *Oxford History of English Literature*, which is devoted to migrant and bicultural writers, and takes up as much space as the volume on post-Second World War British writers; it would be fair to say that they surpass them in international reputation (King, 2004). Some of the best insights into this literature come from the authors themselves, as is documented in *Writing Across Worlds* (King, 1995).

Migrant writers and bicultural writers speak from a place between cultures. They give a foreign voice to local material, and historically they have made seminal contributions to both the formal-inventive and the historical-descriptive aspects of literature. In a special issue of *New Perspectives Quarterly*, the editor comments on the impact of postnational literature that goes beyond the individual writer:

Today, societies have evolved far from the pure ideal of 'heimat,' or homeland. Yet, they are also still far from merging into Teilhard de Chardin's utopian 'noosphere,' in which the intensive communication enabled by technology ties us all together in a common global consciousness. / A wired world with roots in the air instead of the soil does not in and of itself add up to a cosmopolitan culture. Forging such a culture is largely the task of the arts, especially the new genre of post-national literature of which Rushdie's *The Satanic Verses* was an early expression. For all the digital images, satellite signals and instant messages swirling around the vast planetary network, there has so far been precious little advance in the shared understanding which post-national writing can bring. / Post-national literature is a new genre for a new era without boundaries, re-imagining the world and giving voice to the experience we are all living. (Gardels, 2005: 2–3)

Beyond their qualities as individual writers, the visibility of migrant writers in contemporary literary culture and in literary history provides an argument for the existence of transnational literatures that correspond better to the cultural streams of the age than much other literature.

An argument both for and against the importance of the role played by migrant and bicultural writers is that national borders are just one kind of border that inspires and challenges writers. The difference between the country and the city, the province and the capital, are historically significant examples of the importance of migrancy,[2] where cultural differences provide the material and conflicts on which one may write (Williams, 1973). The influence of American writers moving from the Mid-West to the East coast or to Europe is also an example of migrancy, just as many national literatures are filled with examples of how the provincial meets the established world in the capital, as, for example, in the works of Stendhal and Knut Hamsun.

The continuation of this pattern in literary history in the literature of migrant writers is thus not surprising, but nevertheless it is also significant with regard to at least two aspects. First, the differences in culture are typically far greater in migrant literature than in literature that thrives on movements within a nation. Writers who exist between the cultures of separate continents and navigate between languages that perhaps do not even share the same linguistic roots differ significantly from those who ponder the cultural differences within a nation. Second, migrant writers have a more complex relationship to the book markets and literary institutions. Taken as a group, there are many distinct differences in their relations with both national and the world markets, but as individuals they are almost always facing an awkward relationship with the markets, and the national canons and preferences. The theme of belonging, which is often central in their works, is thus also made thematically important by the external conditions of market, critique and the writing of literary history.

In spite of these obstacles, a number of migrant writers are very important to both the literature of Modernism and to contemporary literature. In this chapter, the distinctive traits of both will be analysed and compared with respect to their impact, variety and correspondence to the changes in the world of their times. In a globalizing world, migrant writers are particularly interesting as emblems of the cosmopolitanism lived out by an increasing number of people, no matter whether their own bodies move, or their interaction with the world has changed due to shifts in their own society and the media they use.

In a formal perspective, the voices of migrants, along with literature by minorities and cosmopolitan writers, are an interesting blend of the tacit knowledge of more than one culture, and this produces particular, but not automatically successful, modes of writing from an intermediate perspective. A recent success, commercially and artistically, is the bicultural writer Zadie Smith's novel, *White Teeth*, which is a good example of how a voice that has been developed between cultures can be one of the driving forces of a book. Even more radically,

Sam Selvon's novel *The Lonely Londeners* from 1956 takes advantage of mixing local and foreign voices in the depiction of migrant's diction. More important though, are the ways of presenting the obvious as unlikely and contingent, a trait of migrant literature that adds to cultural understanding by means of the very concrete, sensual experience that can be presented through a voice that is not at home. Again, this is not unique to migrant literature, but the effects are enhanced, both in their importance and in their clarity with regard to the specific historical conditions of today's world.

Migrant writers are a very diverse group, and although their first-hand experiences of different cultures have been important to the international attention accorded to a number of them, there are also many migrants who have not been noticed in wider international circles, but have primarily been noticed in their old or new country, or both. As with any writer of some stature, contingent circumstances may determine whether he or she is internationally recognized, and some writers who are only recognized in their national surroundings may be considered more accomplished than those who have made a name outside of their home base. Some may be more difficult to translate, or less appealing to publishers due to complexity and preferences for local milieus. Then there are writers who are already established in one country, but move – or in many cases, escape – and begin working in their new country, and gradually become more identified with their new country than their original one, as is the case with Milan Kundera, who had already been translated into a number of languages before he moved to France, and gradually took up writing in French, or Vladimir Nabokov, who shifted from writing in Russian to writing in English. More complicated is the history of Gao Xingjian, who was an important playwright in China but who had to re-establish a career after leaving for the West, while remaining dependent on translations of his work, as he continued to write in Chinese.

A critical note on migrant writers has been made by Andrew Smith and Elleke Boehmer, among others, who suggest that there is the risk that the focus on migrant writers by post-colonial criticism will universalize the perspectives and values of a cosmopolitan elite (Smith, 2004: 62).[3] This is an important point, but it fails to explain or recognize why there is an interest in the writing of these particular writers, and in comparing their achievements to other writing. Above all, it is also a critique that may be rooted in a view on culture that is more essentialist than hybrid.[4]

Culture, identity, hybridity

'Culture' can often seem like the golden calf around which the humanities dance while trying to capture its essence. It can both be an objective of the humanities and something inescapable that needs to be reflected in any discipline. As a term, it is one of the most notoriously difficult to define, perhaps only surpassed in complexity by the concept of nature, as Raymond Williams has pointed out (Williams, 1983: 87–89 and 219). Its complexity derives from its being both a very general concept, and having been imported into numerous specialized fields. Everybody has a sense of what 'culture' means, but this may not be compatible with others' idea of it. This depends on the kinds of distinctions one makes in order to separate a certain recurrent phenomenon in the world, and designate it as part of some culture, as well as on the theory of cultures' own reality as structures, organic entities, or as mirages that we use in the same way that physicists might have talked about ether.[5] It is also very closely connected to the idea of both collective and individual identities, and thereby to a central theme in literary criticism and history, not least when it comes to world literature and literature by migrant writers. But for all its complexity, it is possible to note some central changes in the use of the concept of culture over the past decades, regardless of whether the definition is based on a grand scale model of the driving forces of culture, or tries to single out the finer constituent details.

A central idea in this chapter is that there has been a change in the way culture is defined and thought about, which can be summarized as a gradual shift from essentialism to hybridity. This aspect also touches upon the way in which history and culture can be seen as having opposing interests in the specific and the generalized. Following that, three sections each investigate the consequences and importance of modern thinkers' key concepts to understanding the world of today: Pierre Bourdieu and his concept of the field, Ulrich Beck's notion of the cosmopolitan and Homi Bhabha's concept of hybridity. These concepts all relate to the idea of globalized identity to the way identity and strangeness interplay, a theme that will be readdressed at the end of this chapter, through the question of why migrant writers have been particularly important to world literature (Appiah, 2004; Bhabha, 1994: 12; Dharwadker, 2001).

Culture is an almost unavoidable term, no matter how difficult it is to define, yet it has not always been so, as Stephen Greenblatt has pointed out, when, in fact, the academic interest in the term is fairly recent, dating back to the end of the nineteenth century (Greenblatt, 1995: 225). The term's unavoidability is shown in the plethora of buzzwords surrounding the descriptions of culture, the forces that change it, and the levels at which culture should be studied. On a larger scale, there are attempts to define culture through different types of societies, some of which are historically observable, such as the agricultural and the industrial societies, to the newer, less sharply defined attempts to identify the essence of today's world, and thereby describing society as dominated by service, information, knowledge, networks, etc. Some claim that capitalism is still essential, perhaps in a late state, perhaps on the verge of a new order, which in turn might also signal the end of history and the sedimentation of capitalism, as world systems theory and Antonio Negri and Michael Hardt's idea of empire suggests (Fukuyama, 1992; Hardt and Negri, 2000). Others focus, for good reasons, on the threshold between the colonial and post-colonial era.

Culture can also be defined by its ability to defy identification with the dominant idea of national culture as *the* culture, which then can be emphasized by terms such as 'ethnic', 'multicultural' or 'hybrid' societies containing different cultures. Another way of envisioning this is through a number of interweaving levels, which include sub-national levels such as the local or the regional, as well as super-national levels, such as regions, continents, religions and the all-encompassing idea of the global. Then, there are the consequences of, and attitudes towards this situation, in the form of people defined as cosmopolitan, migrant and exiled. All these changes and attempts to best describe change take part in defining the historical situation and in redefining and also blurring the notion of culture.

The economist Jeffrey Sachs has underlined how cautious one should be in trying to predict development based on cultural insights. There is no doubt that local traditions and global cultural phenomena confront each other in many contexts, but it is also evident that cultural traits that are presented as obstacles to a certain kind of modernization have often been overcome (Sachs, 2005: 317). Furthermore, changes in economy and media have a great impact on daily life and outlook. Two global media revolutions that have taken place within the past two decades are the spread of the internet and mobile phones. These are both technologies that radically change the way people communicate, and thus, in one way or another, also influence the culture of which they are part. These have also had a quicker diffusion than the hardware of former media revolutions, and have a very strong presence in people's everyday lives, including the way in which their user interfaces have become a part of a shared means of accessing the world.

Even if culture as a concept is too extensive to synthesize and comprehend abstractly, what is apparent is how the use of the term has changed over the second half of the twentieth century, from being thought of as something with a unique essence that was not subject to larger historical changes, to a concept of culture that, albeit in many forms, emphasizes the hybrid and contingent elements of culture. This can be seen in theory, where Post-Modernism and post-colonialism have, in various ways, tried to devise less essentialist notions of culture, while also being criticized for being too relativistic and unhistorical. There would still remain dominant cultural traits that could hardly be overlooked, as well as the culturally embedded notions of race and gender. However, the basic idea of abandoning the romantic and nationalistic conceptions of culture is the important and defining feature of these contributions (see also Butler, 1995).

Finding a balance between the identity that is post-romantic and non-authentic, and one that is developed dialogically and with the recognition of collective identities, whether national, religious, cultural or so on, is still a key problem, which Kwame Anthony Appiah addresses in *The Ethics of Identity*, and to which he finds no easy solution between his basically liberal standpoint and his political morality (Appiah, 2004: 107–110). By opting for a 'rooted cosmopolitanism', Appiah suggests a compromise between the local and the global, which seems very realistic with regard to the way that many people experience their situation, while at the same time being more than a compromise with which nobody would disagree.

The change from essentialism to hybridity has also made its mark in politics. An interesting and illustrative case is the development of integration politics, which took place in Sweden between the early 1970s and present. In the 1970s many resources were put into helping immigrants to keep their culture intact by supporting their organizations with government money. The idea behind this policy was that cultures were entities. Throughout the 1980s and 1990s, the view on this changed, mainly because of the observation that people living in Sweden became partly Swedish, and thus lived with a dual cultural identity. By providing inducements to stay embedded in the ideas of a particular culture which had been taken out of its original context, more damage than good was often done. At the same time, the political level abandoned the idea of multiculturalism for the ideal of an open societal structure, wherein there would be dominant common elements, for example the Swedish language, but apart from that, a society shaped by a multitude of cultures.[6]

The importance of this shift from essentialism to hybridity, of which the Swedish example is just one illustration, can hardly be underestimated, as it affects a number of important domains that shape the world, from policy-making to the individual's motivation for interacting with the world, and migrating in it. In the social sciences and the humanities, this is reflected in a shift from an interest in anthropology to one in sociology. These are two sciences that, roughly speaking, have historically worked quite differently: anthropology has traditionally been marked by an interest in describing the unique and specialized, whereas sociology works by compiling elements and making them available for comparison. This distinction reflects the difference between essence and hybridity, which created the feedback that facilitated changes in the field of anthropology.

Niklas Luhmann has reflected on the concept of culture, which shifts the focus from the question of essentialism, to the function of culture. First, he does not see culture as the overarching or underlying foundation of society or identity, but that these are instead the roles of social systems of all kinds, from codified human interaction through organizations and symbolic means, to societal functions, such as politics. These systems will perpetually reflect on their own unity and on their relations to their environment. In this respect, Luhmann introduces his notion of culture as that which makes systems overlook or avoid seeking alternatives to their present way of functioning (Luhmann, 1997: 586–594). Culture can therefore be seen in opposition to evolution and to structural changes in the system. This does not disdain culture for its opposition to evolution, since passing over some alternatives can help systems to function better. In contrast to that, an endless search for alternatives can endanger the survival of the system, such as the case could have said to be with experimental literature, or the concept of art in the twentieth century. Culture and evolution are thus two oscillating rationalities within the large number of systems of which society consists. They complement each other, but it is not a given that the ideal balance is maintained at all times. Furthermore, in Luhmann's perspective there is no single privileged position from which culture can be described, not least because the different systems have such differently constructed borders.

There is, however, a weakness to Luhmann's reflections. Systems and cultures describe structures, but not events, which are what make up history. The interests in culture and history intersect, but they are also sharply divided by guiding interests in the fabric of repeating events that define culture and the single events of which history is made. Events are concrete and unique, whereas culture is both derived from these, and also shapes events. An interest in literary history can lead to studies in literary culture and sociology, as well as a desire to link the contents of works to the wider culture surrounding them, whereas an interest in concrete and unique historical moments can be reflected in studies of canonical works, and in concrete series of events of which the biography is one of the most wide-spread genres. That choice, however, can be both one of a more or less subjective interest, and one of epistemological conviction regarding how knowledge about literature can be produced in a meaningful and respectable way. This reformulates the hermeneutic problem of how to understand the parts and the whole, which over time has given rise to meaningful and specific theoretical and analytical problems, such as is the case in world literature, with David Damrosch's close readings, for example, and Franco Moretti's sketches of larger lines. Furthermore, some of the most intriguing attempts at synthesis have been made in the fields between the specific and the general. Examples include Hippolyte Taine's argument in the nineteenth century that there was no document of history which was not also a monument, thereby suggesting that canonical works hold a certain privileged knowledge of history (Taine, 1908: 35).

In contemporary criticism, Stephen Greenblatt and other New Historicists are those who are most notable for their efforts to link together the specific anecdote and the canonical work, claiming thereby to provide insights into distant cultures. Greenblatt confirms his affiliation with the anthropological approach to culture, of which Clifford Geertz is one proponent, by defining culture as:

> a particular network of negotiations for the exchange of material goods, ideas, and – through institutions like enslavement, adoption, or marriage – people. (Greenblatt, 1995: 229)

This preference for the close interweaving of elements, and the sense of detail revealed by thick descriptions could work as arguments for the nationalist perspective. Italian philosopher Giambattista Vico argued that only what man has created could be fully understood, and that this would always leave some mystery in nature (Vico, 2000: xvi). If that logic applies to culture, which is doubtful, given the radical nature of Vico's argument, then a full understanding of a given historic culture would only be comprehensible to those who had a deeply rooted experience of it. But this distance is exactly that which also creates a certain desire among New Historicists to overcome it. This is a challenge that has also been taken up by Pierre Bourdieu, Ulrich Beck and Homi Bhabha, among others.

Bourdieu was generally sceptical about globalization, although he also found ways to downplay its importance, and while certainly not being an anticosmopolitan, he was pessimistic about the development of culture (Leitch, 2001). What is particularly interesting about his work is the way that it argues for a methodological approach to social studies as well as the study of artworks, that has as one of its consequences an emphasis on the importance of local frames of reference, such as those that nations provide in the form of national markets, press, media, educational systems, etc.

Bourdieu's principal argument is that society consists of relatively autonomous fields of economy, art, education, science and so on, that each has a unique structure in which agents must manoeuvre. The positions and the values they express are characterized by great subtlety, and it requires a thorough knowledge of the structure of the field to discern between the different positions. The fields themselves are also historically changeable. Bourdieu argues that a strategy for the analysis of the role played by a certain work of literature must take this into account, and knowledge about the defining positions and specific holders of these positions in the field must be acquired (Bourdieu, 1996: 264–267).

In practice, Bourdieu's theory of the field is always presented with a national framework defining its borders, not only for the practical reasons of restricting research to limited empirical material, but also because the national scene is the dominant one. There is no indication in Bourdieu's writing that this could not, in principle, change, but in practice there are so many institutions to which he ascribes large influence, that the national field still has primacy, because the balance between the national and the international has not yet tipped towards the latter, and the national markets are still more important than the international streams.

In the framework Franco Moretti has put forward with regard to world literature, this argument could both be included and rejected, since, even though national fields of literature differ, they do so as do leaves on a tree which repeat the same structures, such as a certain mode of writing novels, or the idea of writing sonnets, to use two of Moretti's key examples (Moretti, 2000). Still, this argument can also be turned around in Bourdieu's theory, which seems to hold that the finer details are the truly interesting part of culture and works of art, rather than the large and easily seen tendencies, and so it was more a matter of methodical conviction than preference that led Bourdieu to a theory that would emphasize the importance of the national field. This stands in sharp contrast to the view of Niklas Luhmann, who argued that most functional systems in society were not confined to the national borders, and to that of Ulrich Beck, who has continually argued for a cosmopolitan theory of society (Beck, 2004; Luhmann, 1997).

In his own attempts to make close readings, Bourdieu has, in *The Rules of Art*, taken an interest in Gustave Flaubert and William Faulkner, about both of whom Jean-Paul Sartre wrote extensively, and Bourdieu makes explicit references to Sartre's readings. Not surprisingly, Bourdieu tries to find further support for his analysis of literary works by projecting this into an analysis of the content of the works, which claim that the key to understanding them is the stories' portraits of social structure. Flaubert's *Sentimental Education* is a mirror of the social structure at the time of its publication, claims Bourdieu, whereas Faulkner's short story 'A Rose for Emily' shows how human beings live within a social structure and take part in determining how to address this over time (Bourdieu, 1996: 322–329).

There are several interesting differences in the way that Bourdieu reads these two stories. The investigation of Flaubert's work is much more elaborate, because it sets out to show how the novel is realistic with regard to describing a social structure, and although Bourdieu is over-enthusiastic in crediting Flaubert for creating an almost exact mirror of the social structure of nineteenth century Paris, which Bourdieu cannot verify in detail, there are many enlightening concrete observations (Bourdieu, 1996: 3). Faulkner's story is read in a very different way, focusing much more on the principal, philosophical dimensions of the tale, but without the ties to an actual social environment. Such an environment would also be more complicated to reconstruct for someone who lacked any extensive experience with the southern states and their rural side, or who has not done anthropological field studies of this. The interesting thing is that Bourdieu does not reflect on the vast differences in the readings and their contextual foundations. One is highly dependent on an intimate historical and societal knowledge, while the other sees the protagonists in a more universal light. The analysis of Faulkner's story, which was supposed to demonstrate how the social dimension and the idea of what Bourdieu terms the *habitus,* as the meeting place of agents and structure, is relevant to literary analysis, also ultimately undermines the claims that Bourdieu makes in his reading of Flaubert.

Bourdieu thus ends up producing a double standard for the analysis of works, one for those with whose social space one is familiar, and one for those with which one is less familiar. This is a condition faced by everyone interested in world literature, but the problems of contextual knowledge are highlighted, when set against the demands of a theory like Bourdieu's, where the finer details of a local field are put forward as the dominant source of understanding literary works. It might have been interesting if Bourdieu had taken this paradox, embodied by the analyses of Flaubert and Faulkner, seriously, and had developed a theory of cultural interaction and understanding with regard to works of art. However, apart from the important defence of the still vivid national fields, Bourdieu's theoretical framework lends itself to clarifying some important points about canonization and migrant writers.

In particular, Bourdieu's concept of symbolic capital, the way that achievement and reputation can solidify a writer's position in the literary field, is also an important aspect of the interplay between national and international canonization, just as its success on the international market can be decisive to the fate of a book in its national market (Bourdieu, 1996: 255–256).[7] It is also likely that the importance of international recognition to national recognition will continue to be an important factor, particularly when some authors are published in several languages at once.

Bourdieu's use of the metaphor of refraction is also used by David Damrosch in *What Is World Literature?* Bourdieu uses the term to describe the relative autonomy of the literary field and of the individual works of art (Bourdieu, 1992: 182; Bourdieu, 1996: 252–253). This is similar to Luhmann's insistence on the both closed and open natures of social systems, which use elements of their environments, but for their own purposes and with their own logic. Bourdieu emphasizes the double-bind in this, since not only will a work of art make use of the environment, it will also be influenced by it in a way that is not transparent to itself, hence the insistence that Flaubert recreated an image of the social structure, without his being aware of everything in it.

As noted in Chapter 1, Damrosch uses the metaphor of refraction to designate a relationship between national literatures and world literature by saying that 'world literature is an elliptical refraction of national literatures' (Damrosch, 2003: 281). Thereby Damrosch also argues for a particular kind of double-bind, but at the level of the national and international, which in this way are acknowledged to be two distinct fields or systems. It does make a difference whether one finds that there is an international literary system or a field called world literature which has a relative autonomy, or whether there are only local fields that may interact with others, but all are essentially nationally based, and strongly supported by media, schools and book markets, which just happen to look similar from a distance. With Bourdieu's theory, the latter conviction is the most obvious, whereas Damrosch speaks for the former.

The importance of migrants in Bourdieu's perspective, apart from the political struggle to defend illegal immigrants in France[8] in which he is engaged, is that they are writers who must establish themselves in a field where they do not fit in at once. Bourdieu operates with the idea of positions and position-taking in the literary field, which designates a difference between structure and agent

(Bourdieu, 1996: 203–204). The specific structure is different from country to country, but the position in the field sets up a game that everybody has to play, either by trying to occupy an already existent position or by creating a new one. Literary systems make room for certain kinds of books in a literary culture, crime fiction, biographies, romantic novels, etc., but the authors who fulfil the needs change over time.

Migrant writers have been historically good at creating new positions in the literary field, based on their experience as bicultural authors who can provide a different angle on the field, because they bring in an intimate knowledge of other traditions and cultures (see for example Borges, 2000: 427). Creating new positions does not guarantee that they will succeed, but the chance of coming up with something new is enhanced by existing between cultures of which the author can be equally critical. Salman Rushdie is a primary example of this, as are most of the migrant writers mentioned here. As such, Bourdieu's theory provides a convincing part of the explanation regarding the successes of migrant writers.[9]

Bourdieu's work makes an important contribution to the understanding of the literary field; however, with ever more internationally oriented readers, scholars and media, and a more efficient international distribution of books, the conditions may begin to change at pace that was not foreseen in Bourdieu's work and the history it addresses. Yet, a counterargument may be easily raised: why then, is translation still such a big business confined to national literary markets?

In contrast to Bourdieu, Ulrich Beck sees the nation state as a quickly eroding entity, a *zombie* state that is more and more influenced by factors that it cannot control (Beck, 2000). Three of the major risks in today's world are, according to Beck, financial crisis, ecological catastrophes and changes and terrorism. None of these can be controlled effectively by single nations, and in this scenario Beck sees two responses: one that tries to isolate the state, and one that embraces the challenge and tries to convert the nation state into a cosmopolitan state. Beck's contribution to the reflection on globalization should thus be read with some caution, since it also states a political interest in a certain development, although this recommendation is based on an analysis of the challenges in today's world, and the above-mentioned alternatives they present.

Beck has made several important conceptual contributions to the analyses of contemporary society and world order, first by suggesting that the reality of globalization cannot stand alone as an explanation of change, but must be supplemented first and foremost by the idea of risk and of a second modernity, which together lead to the valorization of cosmopolitanism in contrast to not only nationalism, but also multiculturalism and other competing attempts to envision a pluralistic society.

The risk society does not posit that there has ever been a distribution of unequal risk throughout nations and world society, but rather that some of these risks have been intensified along with the emergence of new types of risks that strike classes and groups much more differently, such as the previously mentioned examples of financial crises, ecological threats and terrorism. To that could also be added the risk of job movement, which to some groups, for instance accountants or engineers, was inconceivable a few decades ago. These new risks have also made it clear that societies around the world share a common destiny more than ever before. In past times, isolationism could be a response to global financial crisis, something that would be unthinkable today, just as the territory of the nation state is to a lesser degree than before the only place where the nation's citizens live.

With the concept of a second, reflexive modernity, Beck argues that, whereas the first wave of modernity that took place vis-à-vis the development of the industrial society was occupied with reflecting on tradition, the second modernity is reflecting upon its own modernity and its consequences, while at the same time affirming its fundamental values, in contrast to the idea of post-modernity, which brings Beck in line with Jürgen Habermas and Anthony Giddens. One of Beck's main objections to Post-Modernism is its lack of belief in universals, including the ideas of universal human rights and international law, and he explicitly refers to Post-Modernism as a cosmopolitanism without universals, and therefore an ideology that is politically weak as well as irresponsible, if one accepts the basic premise of the idea of universal risks (Beck, 2004: 92).

From this position of the new conditions of a global risk society, and a confirmation of the universal values in modernity, Beck has gone on to formulate a vision of a contemporary cosmopolitanism which is also highly dependent on the migrations that took place in the second half of the twentieth century. Among numerous works on the globalization and cosmopolitanism, the role of migrants is particularly important in 'The Cosmopolitan Perspective: Sociology of the Second Age of Modernity' and *Cosmopolitan Vision*, in which he focuses both on the concrete consequences of migration as well as outlining a theory of cosmopolitan culture (Beck, 2000 and 2006).

The migration of labour takes place in different ways in the global economy, as the movement of people to places where they do specialized work or can compete with local workers with respect to wages and conditions, as the migration of jobs to new job markets, or simply as the migration of people who hope to find a better future, as suggested by the frequent migrations from South to North. Migration can have both positive and negative effects on a nation, but more often than not it is seen as something negative. This stands in sharp contrast to the desirability of movement of people within the nation, which is strongly needed to keep economies efficient (Beck, 2000: 93–96).

Increased migration has created new and highly interesting diasporas that are no longer regarded as unfortunate in the way they once were, but simply as circumstances which can also benefit nations. The Indian government thus recognizes the contributions made by Indians working abroad, from Sydney to Silicon Valley, as discussed by Beck (Beck, 2004: 101). He sees these migrations and new diasporas as propelling a part of a change in attitude and discursive mode, where nations will change their self-understanding, and embrace the notions of diasporas, cultural blending and hybridity rather than see them as problems to the identity of state and society. This will also change the view on the experience of strangeness, of living between cultures, and not least, the sorrow of displacement (Beck, 2004: 109–110; see also Cohen, 1997). This perspective on things is different from the idea of multiculturalism, which Beck sees as an attack on the individual and its rights to create its own identity, rather than to be attached to a certain culture that is sustained politically, as described in the previous example of the Swedish immigration politics of the 1970s (Beck, 2004: 105). This does not mean that cosmopolitanism does not tolerate anything but the universal; on the contrary, the national and cosmopolitan are seen as being dependent on each other, at least when seen in a pragmatic and historical perspective, because nations face problems that require them to shift towards being more world oriented (Beck, 2004: 97).

However, as mentioned before, Beck does not see the cosmopolitan as something that is a given, there is also the possibility of different kinds of reversals to the process of globalization. He lists a long series of factors that can help to analyse and indicate in which direction this process is heading, in a number of distinct fields. The first is, probably not by chance:

> *Cultural commodities:* developments in the import and export of cultural commodities, transnationalization of the book trade, developments in the import and export of periodicals, in the number and proportion of local and foreign productions in the cinema, in the proportion of local and foreign productions in television, corresponding radio broadcasts and so on. (Beck, 2000: 96)

Beck goes on to mention the status of dual citizenship, the representation of minorities in political forums, linguistic capabilities worldwide and the diversity of languages spoken within communities, including those of foreign students, the development of internationally carried mail, of international tourism and travel in general, the activity level of transnational NGOs, the transnational ways of life in new diaspora communities, the level of transnational news coverage, but also more unfortunate outcomes, such as new levels of transnational organized crime, and the ecological crises that affect more than one nation (Beck, 2000: 96–97; Beck, 2004: 142–143). Most of these factors point to a rise in the level of cosmopolitanism, but they can also be used to give some relative measure of where the effects of cosmopolitanism are strongest, as the parameters are very specific and differentiated.[10]

Beck is first and foremost a sociologist, but his observations on the influence of migrants and his valuation of what exchanges of cultural products signify, emphasize the role of a cosmopolitan idea of literature and of the agents that propel it. In the end, Beck more or less explicitly argues for a cultural politics for the cosmopolitan state, or rather for the state that wants to become cosmopolitan, particularly the European nations that have to address an increased diversification that is seen as much more natural in many other parts of the world.

More than to any other critic, the concepts of hybridity and hybridization can be ascribed to the work of Homi Bhabha, who has made a subtle and multifaceted use of them, both when dealing with changes to local and global culture, and when he addresses single authorships, and he has combined a lucid diagnosis of important tendencies in the cultural field and national identity with a critical definition of hybridity. The precondition of the term is internationalization in a diverse number of spheres, from the lifeworld of migrants to changes in the global economy:

> What is striking about the 'new' internationalism is that the move from the specific to the general, from the material to the metaphoric, is not a smooth passage of transition and transcendence. The 'middle passage' of contemporary culture, as with slavery itself, is a process of displacement and disjunction that does not totalize experience. Increasingly, 'national' cultures are being produced from the perspective of disenfranchised minorities. The most significant effect of this process is not the proliferation of 'alternative histories of the excluded' producing, as some would have it, a pluralist anarchy. What my examples show is the changed basis for making international connections. The currency of critical comparativism, or aesthetic judgement, is no longer the sovereignty of the national culture conceived as Benedict Anderson proposes as an 'imagined community' rooted in a 'homogeneous empty time' of modernity and progress. The great connective narratives of capitalism and class drive the engines of social reproduction, but do not, in themselves, provide a foundational frame for those modes of cultural identification and political affect that form around issues of sexuality, race, feminism, the lifeworld of refugees or migrants, or the deathly social destiny of AIDS. (Bhabha, 1994: 5–6)

The results of this situation are more phenomena that can be described as hybrid, as bearing the trace of more than one culture, and Bhabha attaches a certain value to the moments of hybridity (Bhabha, 1994: 208). It is also significant that Bhabha does not see the hybrid as a third option that resolves the tension between opposing cultures (Bhabha, 1994: 113). There is no depth or truth to hybrid objects, no promise of a truer representation, but rather a subversive nature to them, which is particularly obvious in the meeting of the values and symbols of colonizers and colonized. Bhabha finds support for his analysis in Frantz Fanon's 'On national culture', which also criticizes attempts to conceal the instability of national identity and its dependence on outside elements. Fanon stated, with regard to the situation in the late 1950s, that:

> the building of a nation is of necessity accompanied by the discovery and encouragement of universalizing ideas. (Fanon, 1963: 199)

Moreover, Bhabha draws attention to Julia Kristeva's notion of a double temporality of national identity, one of sedimentation that looks backwards, and one of further identification that looks forwards (Bhabha, 1994: 152–153). These positions, the linking of the national and the universal, and of past and future, also mean that cultural signification is more complex than ever, because it is induced by so many inputs from without, in the form of cultural translations:

> The transnational dimension, of cultural transformation – migration, diaspora, displacement, relocation – makes the process of cultural translation a complex form of signification. The natural(ized), unifying discourse of 'nation', 'peoples', or authentic 'folk' tradition, those embedded myths of culture's particularity, cannot be readily referenced. The great, though unsettling, advantage of this position is that it makes you increasingly aware of the construction of culture and the invention of tradition.
> (Bhabha, 1994: 172)

Even though the concept of the hybrid is convincing and useful, it can be criticized for being both imprecise and immune to critical analyses (Brah and Coombs, 2000). The lack of precision is a consequence of the large clusters of cultural formations to which hybrid objects refer; exactly how different traces of cultures merge, and what form they have is not easy to tell, even if Bhabha can be very specific, for instance showing how Salman Rushdie's *The Satanic Verses* mixes genres and expressions from the Quran with those of the post-war Western novel to negate the idea of authenticity (Bhabha, 1994: 226). Even with such clear oppositions, however, the idea of the hybrid easily establishes a free-floating point of reference that can be impossible to grasp. This may also be an essential part of much of the writing, in particular that of migrants who wish to show how the national cultural goods belong more to the world, than anything, and who want to present new positions that consist of both something recognizable and something alien, yet have an inner logic that is revealed by the fact that it can be perceived as a hybrid, or as a failed hybrid, if there is such a thing. More often than not, the hybrids of literature have been successful, in large part due to their aesthetics.

Modernists

The influence of migrants in literature can be seen in numerous periods in the history of literature. Was not his exile from Florence an essential experience to Dante, without which his work would definitely have been different? Would Rousseau's work have been possible if it had not been written on the dual experiences of the rural Swiss communities, and urban and elitist Paris? The literary historian Georg Brandes argues, in *Main Currents in 19th Century Literature*, that the turbulent years following the French revolution had a decisive effect on European literature, while French intellectuals migrated about

Europe (Brandes, 1901: 194–196). Brandes also argued that this had an effect not only on other literatures, but also on French literature, when the migrants returned with new experiences, and knowledge of other languages and literatures. Consequently, Brandes sees the literature of the migrants as a defining movement in the nineteenth century, propelled by the turmoil of the French revolution, and the importance of the migrant writers and the general spirit of transnational movement is obvious.

A similar importance of migrancy can be found in the literature of Modernism. There was not a wave of migrant authors, but there were still enough and of such importance to literary history that they are hard to overlook. Three key figures of Modernism, James Joyce, T. S. Eliot and Ezra Pound, were all migrants, and without them, the whole idea of linking migrancy and Modernism would not perhaps have been obvious. To these could also be added Joseph Conrad, nor should an important figure, the Rumanian-born Tristan Tzara, a co-founder of Dadaism, be forgotten. In the continuation of the modern movement, seminal writers such as Samuel Beckett and Vladimir Nabokov were also migrants, not only in place, but in language, changing their primary medium of expression from, respectively, English to French, and Russian to English.

In this period, though, the migrant writers who had an impact on the international literary scene were mainly migrants between European and North American cultures, although there are significant cosmopolitan writers who stayed outside of their own continent for longer periods, such as Fernando Pessoa's stay in South Africa, or Jorge Luis Borges' years in Europe.

All these writers are important in their own right, but they are also interesting figures in a time where post-war nationalism and liberal modernization coincided as part of a shifting cultural movement in the world. They advance a cosmopolitan consciousness, not only in the broader culture as such, but also in the arts, being writers in a globalizing world.

It is obvious that the migrant modernists have had a significant impact on world literature, but it is more difficult to assess whether they were statistically unlikely to have been so successful and dominant in literary history. Even though they were few and important, the question of how to evaluate their importance to the international canonization of the period of Modernism remains an open one. Joseph Conrad and James Joyce were migrants, but Marcel Proust was not, and neither were Virginia Woolf, Robert Musil and many other significant novelists. Tristan Tzara was a migrant, but neither Filippo Marinetti nor André Breton, or a number of other avant-garde artists were. Nevertheless, it is difficult to imagine Modernism without the migrants who contributed to it, or to imagine their works without the very different roles played by migrancy and cosmopolitanism. Their contributions on this subject follow.

The migrant experience of Ezra Pound, T. S. Eliot and James Joyce was supplemented by an ambition to contribute to the great literary tradition in which

Dante stood to them all as a pivotal figure, thus also reinforcing the international orientation of the authors. However, migrancy yielded two initially very different responses that were also remarkably paradoxical. One combined a cosmopolitan, liberal approach to the art of literature, with a strong thematic emphasis on the national or regional, while the other combined a conservative, aristocratic attitude that embraced multiculturalism. To the first category belongs Joyce, at least in the thematic material in the larger part of his authorship, together with non-migrants such as Norway's Knut Hamsun and W. B. Yeats. Joyce's use of the Irish context was not outspokenly political beyond his works, whereas both Hamsun and Yeats were engaged in questions of their nation's politics. Nevertheless, they are writers who could be characterized as cosmopolitan regionalists.

T. S. Eliot and Ezra Pound belong to the second category, and they both included an overwhelming number of references to cultural artefacts from all kinds of cultures, but unlike Yeats, they had become migrants and abandoned their native roots. In the most interesting periods of both authors, around 1920, they were both undecided about their place in the world, and afterwards it seems that this helped to provide a vibrant energy in their poetry, whereas Eliot's later commitment to the Church of England and nation distanced him from the paradoxical and undecided position, but also took away an important driving force in his authorship, namely that of not belonging in a world whose order has been splintered. This shift in attitude, along with his status as an almost too highly and rapidly canonized author, which sparked reactions from both poets and critics in decades to come, has somewhat blurred the multicultural aspirations that are particularly evident in *The Waste Land*, with its combination of a vision of a wrecked Europe, combined with references to, and images from a wide range of mythology from around the world.

Pound, even more than Eliot, is the epitome of a poetical strategy of referential inclusiveness, curiosity and subsequent complexity. In his work, particular *The Cantos*, there is a belief in the manifold contributions to human culture from a number of cultures and religions, including the Oriental literatures from which Pound himself had translated extensively. Perhaps unfairly to Walt Whitman's work, he saw his own work in opposition to the idea of a distinct American poetry that would be self-sufficient in its referential outlook.

Joyce's authorship is unique in literary history, with regard to the span of complexity his work presents, from relatively traditional poetry, through highly readable short stories in *Dubliners* and the more complex *Portrait of the Artist as a Young Man*, to the manifold modes in *Ulysses*, and finally, the supremely complex and ultimately incomprehensible *Finnegans Wake*. No other author has produced works that serve as emblems of the limits of literature, while at the same time having produced accessible works that are a legitimate and valuable part of the oeuvre. A key question in this context would be whether *Finnegans Wake* is a shift away from the strategy of making universal works, by creating a referential overload such as the earlier works did, while at the same time, in *Ulysses*, referring to a larger tradition in European literature, and whether *Finnegans Wake* takes up a project that was foreseen in the earlier work, or whether it takes up the strategies earlier pursued by Eliot and Pound to a higher level, by incorporating the languages of the world the work. *Ulysses* responds to the crisis and war in Europe with its expression of collage, which was certainly also important to Eliot and Pound, whereas *Finnegans Wake* takes the collage to another level by leaving the discrete interweaving of local material and an imported narrative for the globalization of language itself. However, seen from the point of influence and canonization, the important point is that history has demonstrated that extreme strategies fail to yield broadly canonized works, by producing literature accessible only to experts, whereas *The Waste Land*, *Ulysses*, *Dubliners*, and a number of Pound's poems have had a more wide-spread influence in international canons, at least in terms of being read and commented.

The trajectory of these writers also confirms the importance of Paris to literary history at this period; that it was the centre to be conquered. This is also evident from the perspective of the avant-gardes who were thriving all over Europe at that time, leading to the Dadaist and Surrealist movements, and of which the most important initiator of the former was also a migrant, Tristan Tzara. He was an accomplished and interesting poet, but this aspect of his work has been overshadowed by his success as a writer of manifestos. The co-founder of Dada, in Zürich in 1916, he later collaborated with French avant-garde poets such as André Breton, Phillipe Sauphault and Louis Aragon, and Tzara was also active in the Surrealist movement from 1930, although not as a leader of the movement.

In his 1922 lecture on Dada, Tzara talks about the meaninglessness of everything, including Dada, and the contingencies of all things, but one given is that diversity makes life interesting:

> What are the Beautiful, the Good, Art, Freedom? Words that have a different meaning for every individual. Words with the pretension of creating agreement among all, and that is why they are written with capital letters. Words which have not the moral value and objective force that people have grown accustomed to finding in them. Their meaning changes from one individual, one epoch, one country to the next. Men are different. It is diversity that makes life interesting. There is no common basis in men's minds. The unconscious is inexhaustible and uncontrollable. Its force surpasses us. It is as mysterious as the last particle of a brain cell. Even if we knew it, we could not reconstruct it. (Tzara, 1982: 246–247)

The manifesto and the lecture themselves are interesting as literary texts, not least because of their canonical status, and for their argument, which essentially wants to put an end to the idea of high art, while using the philosophical grounds of that for the production of exactly that. Nevertheless, the rhetoric of the manifesto is by no means careless, and it exudes enormous energy in its juggling of philosophical concepts and broad statements; statements that in hindsight also bear the marks of the historical setting, and thus further add to the credibility of experiences, alongside the theatrical character of the text.

It is significant that these migrant writers – Joyce, Pound, Eliot, Tzara – were central to the evolution of Modernism after the First World War, perhaps not only because the figure of the outsider belonging nowhere had some attraction in a situation where national identity had been misused, but, more than anything, because they could combine that stance with a leading role in the renewal of artistic expression.

The epoch of Modernism also represented by a series of authors to whom migrant experiences played an important role, although they, for the larger part of their lives, did not live outside of their native lands. Most notable is Jorge Luis Borges and the years he spent in Switzerland during the First World War, Fernando Pessoa's upbringing in South Africa, Giuseppe Ungaretti's childhood in North Africa, and later on, the long periods during which he settled in Paris and Brazil, and Pablo Neruda's dual modes of being a migrant, both as a diplomat from the late 1920s to the middle of the 1930s, and as an exiled writer in the late 1940s to the early 1950s. Particularly important in this aspect, besides their all having been internationally canonized far more than their contemporary compatriots, are the different ways in which migrancy can be said to have had an influence on their writing.

Borges' cosmopolitan perspective and cosmopolitan curiosity have already been addressed to some extent, while Pessoa's multiple pseudonyms can be said to be a variant on the theme of identity in which Borges is also engaged. Ungaretti balances the question of belonging and being of the world through a significant use of a sense of cosmological endlessness in his poetry, whereas Neruda can be said to more romantic and traditional in his later work, but also subtly integrates surrealist strategies.

Even though Borges argued for a cosmopolitan regionalism or patriotism, in his writings the question of identity is also posed as a fundamental problem to the individual, which will never be fully self-transparent and never encompass the magnitude of sensations in one's own lifespan. This desire is played out in fantasies of an all-inclusive vision of the world, such as in 'The Aleph' where a crystal-like object contains a complete vision of the world at all times, from all angles, thus being a profane materialization of God's point of view. In 'Funes the Memorious' the protagonist's capacity to remember everything, in all its details, is presented as a tragedy, because it blocks a direct interaction with the world and the formation of synthesis, which, in Borges' own words, is formulated as 'thinking is forgetting differences', thus identifying the condition of forgetting as a favourable situation, considering the alternative of total recollection. Finally, in the very short fiction 'Borges and I', the non-identity between the younger and the older individual is embedded in an imaginary meeting between the young and the elderly Borges, a theme which is also essential to

'Pierre Menard: Author of *Don Quixote*', where is the contextual circumstances surrounding the text are those that play out the problem of identity and non-identity (Borges, 1999).

The paradox that Borges' fictions want to maintain is that of the simultaneous longing for insight combined with keeping a mystery intact, including the mystery of identity. In a very early essay from 1922, 'The Nothingness of Personality', Borges reviewed a series of Western attempts to negate the possibility of self-identity, and came to the conclusion that no single moment could lead to a perception of the essence of all life's moments (Borges, 2000: 3–6). The only salvation would lie in the mystery, in some epiphany that could conjure up that which is longed for. In the essay, Borges said that he despised all mystification, yet his fictions nonetheless balance very coolly between rational expositions and mysterious conditions, giving a glimpse of what it might be like to have powers that enable one to get a definite grasp on identity, often with both tragic and comic results, leaving the imperfect human being seeming a little less imperfect.

In Fernando Pessoa's work, the absence of a certain identity for the individual is turned into a play with multiple identities, the heteronyms or *noms de plume* Pessoa used in his different, not least stylistically very diverse, works. The playful negation of a stable identity can be seen as a central element of the modernity of Pessoa's work, and one presented with a radicalism matched by few other writers, when he was variously, among the more than seventy heteronyms, Ricardo Reis, Álvaro de Campos, Alberto Caeiro and Fernando Pessoa. This escape from a fixed identity is also a central theme of his poetry, such as in the poem 'If, after I die':

> If, after I die, they should want to write my biography, / There's nothing simpler. / I've just two dates – of my birth, and of my death. In between the one thing and the other all the days are mine. (Monteiro, 1998: 110)

This combination of a seemingly self-effacing attitude and an affection for the freedom of hiding one's identity is recurrent, like the heteronym Bernardo Soares, who lends his voice to *The Book of Disquiet*:

> Caesar defined the entire scope of ambition when he said those words, 'Better to be first in one's village than second in Rome!' I am nothing, neither in a village nor in Rome. At least the shop owner on the corner is respected from the Rua da Assumpção to the Rua da Victoria; he's a one-block Caesar. Am I superior to him? In what? After all, nothingness connotes no superiority, no inferiority, no comparison. (Pessoa, 1991: 65)

Like Borges, Pessoa expresses a complex attitude towards belonging and merely being of the world, where both alternatives can be presented as both desirable and undesirable, thus creating a constant instability in the valuation of identity, which is central to a number of these modernist migrants.

In Giuseppe Ungaretti's poetry, the relation between identity and migration is supplemented by the idea of endlessness, which bears some affinity to Borges' fictions, but is presented in a much more sombre, sometimes religious or cosmological register that does not present itself as fiction, but reality. This endlessness is very explicit in Ungaretti's most famous poem 'Mattina' ('Morning'):

M'illumino / D'immenso[11]

An individual situated in time and space is confronted with the infinity of times and places that the rising evokes. This confrontation with the sublime aspects of history and of the universe is recurrent in central poems by Ungaretti. In one of his most important, 'I Fiumi' ('The Rivers') the individual's own history as a migrant who has lived his life along a number of rivers, the Nile, the Seine, etc., is supplemented by the idea of the historical endlessness of these rivers, all the other histories in which they take part, thus conjuring up imagery that is both frightening and liberating, with regard to what it means to belong:

These are / my rivers // This is the Serchio / where maybe / two millennia of my farming people / and my father and mother / drew their water. (Ungaretti, 2003: 37–38)

The close bond to his family and to the farmers is conjured up and connected through the river, which provides a powerful image of water that silently but strongly, slowly but perpetually, runs through the exact same location and provides the basis of a certain culture. In other poems the identification with other people and a sense of belonging elsewhere is a motif leading to complicated and disparate emotional states, such as in the poem 'Lucca':

The main aim here is to leave. / I sit outside the entrance to the tavern with some people who tell me about California like it's one of their farms. / I'm terrified as I discover myself in their features. / Now I feel it running hot in my veins, the blood of my dead. (Ungaretti, 2003: 69)

Another distinct experience in Ungaretti's poetry is that of being a soldier during the First World War. The modes of belonging are again played out against one another, in a mix of the relations to the immediate group of soldiers of the platoon, the general conditions of all the soldiers from different nations trapped in the hell of war, like the leaves on the trees that are about to fall, as his 'Soldiers' can be paraphrased,[12] and then again, the immense feeling of a cosmological belonging, sometimes evoked by the image of the stars of the sky, as in 'Damnation':

Closed off among things that die / (Even the starry sky will end) / Why do I long for God? (Ungaretti, 2003: 25)

This interweaving of death, the cosmological and the exile, which Ungaretti excels at presenting so compactly, is also apparent in the poetry of Pablo Neruda. Instead of the rivers or the starry sky, it is, in many cases, the ocean that is emblematic of the eternal and endless, such in 'The Poet':

> Estranged to myself, like shadow on water, / that moves through a corridor's fathoms, / I sped through the exile of each man's existence, /this way and that, and so, to habitual loathing; / for I saw that their being was this: to stifle / one half of existence's fullness like fish / in an alien limit of ocean. And there, / in immensity's mire, I encountered their death; / Death grazing the barriers, / Death opening roadways and doorways. (Neruda, 1963: 177)

In addition to the important fact that they became internationally as well as nationally canonized, and had extensive migrant experience, the trait common to Borges, Pessoa, Ungaretti and Neruda is that questions of identity and cosmological experiences go hand in hand with problems of identity in the modern world. What is more, and probably should not be underestimated, is that they came up with strong formal answers to this, as has been shown by Borges' installation of doubles and infinity, Pessoa's multiple egos, Ungaretti's evocation of a cosmological infinity, and to a lesser extent, Neruda's integration of the influences of Surrealism into his more simple and direct style. Their background as cosmopolitans and migrant authors is, in their fiction and poetry, central to presenting a complex and self-experienced account of this problematic relationship to the idea of belonging.

There is an important continuation of the tradition of migrant modernists in internationally canonized literature, in the authorships of Samuel Beckett, Vladimir Nabokov and Paul Celan, in particular, but also a significant change, in that they all began by expressing themselves in a language that, in the case of the first two, was not their mother tongue, whereas Celan's mother tongue was German, although he was a native of Rumania. This stands in contrast to the high modernist and cosmopolitan authors, with the exception of Joseph Conrad. These authors were also at the peak of their writing careers after the Second World War, which gave rise to very different experiences than the First World War.

Beckett is a particularly multifaceted author, who translated his own works into English, including *Waiting for Godot*, and was both a prolific dramatist and novelist at the same time. He had legendarily strong ties to James Joyce, although in many ways he can be said to have pursued a completely different path than that of Joyce, by writing with a minimum of explicit references in his works. Regardless of whether Beckett's tone was so unique that he could write within a space containing few explicit references, or whether he became unique by writing in a particular and original space, it created a mode of writing that was also highly suited to the existential themes of his authorship.

In his dramas, the theme of the universal homelessness of man's existence is also central, but conveyed via absurdist drama, which another migrant, the Rumanian-born Eugene Ionesco, took part in defining, through a series of almost immediately internationally canonized plays. The almost muted tone of the novels is also to be found in the plays, but surrounded by a much more active and dramatic presentation of different characters pitting themselves against one another. However, the fundamental conflicts of living with a personal past and an inherited cultural tradition, with which none of the protagonists feels at home, is prevalent everywhere in his work.

Whereas Beckett broke into the literary scene early on, Nabokov published his first nine novels in Russian, before switching to English in 1941. An aristocrat, he lived in exile following the October Revolution, graduating from Cambridge and living in Berlin for fifteen years, before he once again had to flee with his Jewish wife, first to Paris, and then to the United States. Had it not been for *Lolita*, it is likely that Nabokov would not have been internationally canonized; one indication of this is that his early Russian novels were not translated until the 1960s.

Both Beckett and Nabokov can be said to have taken their writing to the literary centres of the world at a phase where that centre was in transition, and they wrote on the influence of High Modernism while also pushing it to its limits, both with regard to formal experiments and the will to be experimental, while they also pushed borders on the thematic level, most notably in Nabokov's *Lolita*, which continued the tradition of banned books that included *Ulysses*.[13]

An important similarity between Becket and Nabokov is that they were both involved in other media and made use of theatre and film. Where Beckett took part in the productions of his plays, Nabokov himself wrote the screenplay for Stanley Kubrick's adaptation of *Lolita*, and both can be seen as transitional figures from Modernism to Post-Modernism, both in their use of media and in their attitude towards the world. This transition can be described as the overcoming of the tragic loss of coherence which was the modernist experience after the reign of a national romantic world order, followed by the recognition of the world's lack of coherence, but also the playful joy of the absurd and the decadent, which is prevalent in the works of Beckett and Nabokov.

For important reasons, this attitude could not be shared by all, and certainly not by Paul Celan, whose authorship is another that is balanced between oblivion and broad recognition. His obvious qualities as a poet, his life story and central poem, 'Death Fugue', are so intertwined with the Holocaust that his status as a writer is inseparable from this, and makes his status as migrant a less important trait. A Jew born in Rumania, oriented towards the German culture in the Austro-Hungarian Empire, he lost both parents in the Holocaust, and could have shared their fate in the labour camp from which he was liberated by the Russians in 1944. Celan moved westward after the war, first to Vienna, and then to Paris, where he eventually committed suicide in 1970. His is unique as a poetic work from a German-speaking victim of the Holocaust, who had to push the limits of German poetic language, in order to express the most incomprehensible crime in history, most significantly in 'Tenebrae' and 'Death Fugue':

> Black milk of daybreak we drink it at sundown / we drink it at noon in the morning we drink it at night / we drink and we drink it / we dig a grave in the breezes there one lies unconfined / A man lives in the house he plays with the serpents he writes / he writes when dusk falls to Germany your golden hair Marguerite / he writes it and steps out of doors and the stars are flashing / he whistles his pack out / he whistles his Jews out in earth has them dig for a grave / he commands us strike up for the dance. (Celan, 1995: 63)

Apart from its lyric qualities and the profound expression of the tragedy of a people, the poem owes some of its canonicity to Theodor W. Adorno, who had claimed that poetry could not be written after the Holocaust, yet to most readers of the poem, this proves just the opposite (Rosenfeld, 1980, 13–14). Less known, but just as intricately balanced between the desire for silence and its representation of the Holocaust, is 'Tenebrae', which describes an arrival at a concentration camp:

> Near are we, Lord, / near and graspable. // Handled already, Lord, / clawed and clawing as though / the body of each of us were / your body, Lord. // Pray, Lord, / pray to us, / we are near. // Wind-awry we went there, / went there to bend / over hollow and ditch. // To be watered we went there, Lord. // It was blood, it was / what you shed, Lord. // It gleamed. // It cast your image into our eyes, Lord. / Our eyes and mouth are so open and empty, Lord. / We have drunk, Lord. / The blood and the image that was in the blood, Lord. // Pray, Lord. / We are near. (Celan, 1995: 606)

Celan's mixing of religious references with references to the actual execution-ers of the Holocaust provides the poem with a complicated enunciation, where the long historical situation of the Jews being without a country is combined with the concrete situation of being deported and killed, thus intricately blending elements of fatalism and protest into the themes of genocide and migrancy.

The migrant modernists discussed here are strongly canonized internation-ally, and it is evident that they are more part of international canons and circulation of literature than most of their compatriots who did not have migrant experiences, when compared to the second tier of internationally circulated writers of their time. What is more significant and important is that the striving for formal inventions, from Eliot's and Joyce's transformation of the tradition, through the metaphysical endeavours of Borges and the multiple per-sonas of Pessoa, to the muted universe of Beckett, is combined with a profound challenge to the idea of identity that seems to have been the condition of their dominance.

It is also apparent that the exploration of identity and modernity has a more profound resonance in the subject matter of which they write, both in terms of self-experienced transformations and in their intimate knowledge of dissimilar cultures.[14] These traits are also evident in the contemporary migrant authors, albeit in a changed political and cultural environment.

Contemporary

The internationally circulated contemporary literature by migrants comprises a vast body of work, compared to that of modernist migrant writers, and, unlike modernist migrant literature, it encompasses both writers who have migrated within the same larger cultural space, such as the Czech author Milan Kundera, who established himself in France in the 1970s, and writers who have travelled a long distance, such as the Chinese Nobel laureate Gao Xingjian, who, since 1987, has also been based in France. In particular, the large number of bicultural authors who have migrated to former colonizing powers makes this body of work unique in the history of literature.

Besides being numerous and forming a very diverse group, the contemporary migrant writers share the experience of globalization as a process, as well as the evolution in media that enhances the experience by way of faster, longer ranging, and diverse communication, and by being part of the historical processes in which the East-West conflict had a magnitude that globally impacted almost every local conflict in the world. Following the end of the Cold War, globalization has instead become a force that makes its mark on all societies.

It is highly difficult to predict the future canonical status of contemporary writers, and the criteria for the selection of those addressed here derive from their being internationally circulated and critically recognized, rather than forming part of an internationally established canon. Literary history shows that even a Nobel Prize is no guarantee for remaining an active part of the literary system's circulation and memory, whereas almost all books that can be identified as 'middle-brow' have a hard time staying in the canons, unless they are linked to a more profound, new wave in the arts or decisive historic events. Still, it is possible to indicate those migrant writers who have better chances of becoming canonized, in contrast to those who have been minimally translated and given little critical attention.

The internationally circulated contemporary migrants can be divided into three main groups: the post-colonials, the political exiles and the voluntary migrants. The post-colonial migrants and bicultural authors in particular are a Commonwealth phenomenon, with such a large number of influential writers that they have, as mentioned, a volume of their own, in the latest edition of *The Oxford English Literary History* (King, 2004). Writers such as V. S. Naipaul, Salman Rushdie, Ben Okri, Michael Ondaatje and Hanif Kureishi are just a few of the bicultural writers who have had an impact on not only the British literary scene, but on world literature (Sauerberg, 2001). To these should be added other cosmopolitan writers, including Amitav Ghosh, Derek Walcott and Vikram Seth, just as there have been, to a lesser degree, post-colonial migrant writers in France, particularly the Negritude literature, which came into being in the 1930s and 1940s, as a reaction to French colonialism, and which has been influential outside of France, not least since Jean-Paul Sartre wrote about the movement in 1948, and due to the quality of the writing, for example that of Aimé Césaire.

Another important group is that of the politically exiled writers, which again comprises a large number, although fewer than the post-colonial writers, when it comes to international circulation. Among the most prolific over the past decades are Soviet-émigré Aleksander Solzhenitsyn, Milan Kundera, a number of Chinese writers such as Bei Dao, Gao Xingjian and Jung Chang, the Chilean Isabel Allende, and the Bosnian Aleksandar Hemon. These also have all been translated into languages other than that of their adoptive nations.

Finally, there are writers who have migrated of their own free will, as was the case with a number of the modernist migrants such as James Joyce, and is a tradition that has continued after the Second World War with for example W. G. Sebald, who at a young age left Germany for England, and the French author Michel Houellebecq who, before moving to Ireland and later Spain, made migrant desires an integral part of his novels.

In what follows, a critique of migrant and cosmopolitan writers coming from a post-colonial viewpoint will be discussed, leading up to analyses of the decisive traits in four migrant authorships that complement one another with regard to the cultural distances they have overcome and the motivations for their migrancy. They are Milan Kundera, Gao Xingjian, Salman Rushdie and Michel Houellebecq, and by being born roughly a decade apart, in 1929, 1940, 1947 and 1958 respectively, they also represent a gliding change in time and historical outlook. This chronology could be continued with Aleksandar Hemon, born in Bosnia in 1964, and Zadie Smith, born in London in 1975, and even further, with Nigerian-born Helen Oyeyemi, who, in 2004, as an 18-year old, first-year college student, signed a £400,000 contract for her novel *The Icarus Girl*, which was published in 2005. Due to the relative youth of the latter authorships, this study will concentrate on the four first mentioned.

Contemporary migrant literature is not without its sceptics, who see a flip side of the coin. In her comprehensive study *Colonial & Postcolonial Literature*, Elleke Boehmer presents a manifold critique of migrant and cosmopolitan writers. The critique is in many ways well argued, but in the end it comes down to subjective preferences and a political agenda for literary history.

In her critique, Boehmer makes three main arguments. First, she contends that the norms of the cosmopolitan writer in many ways correspond very well to those of the Western world, instead of being true to their origin. Hence, Boehmer opens up an ethical and aesthetic debate between authenticity and hybridity which deems the migrant writers to be less authentic than those who are focused on one cultural context (Boehmer, 1996: 233–243). But one might also hold that it is in the processing of the differences between cultures that the original identity stands out.

Second, it is argued that cosmopolitan and migrant literature also sets the writer free from his or her roots, but as a result he or she also becomes detached from the political engagement which is an important part of much other post-colonial writing. This may be true, and a loss were the writer to serve as nationally based political agent, but it is also hard to see why the individual should not be free to explore the world as an individual. Can the individual be blamed for finding his or her path in life? The questions of individuality and collectivity are at stake here. Moreover, migrant writers, whether voluntarily exiled or not, bring international attention to their nation, and can thus function more effectively as important political agents for issues such as human rights, democracy, development and poverty.

Third, Boehmer points to the way in which the cosmopolitan writer engages and overtakes Western aesthetic norms, and in that way influences the way post-colonial literature is conceived:

> In the Western academy and liberal literary establishments, polycultural 'translated writing', in Rushdie's phrase, is now widely accepted as one of the oppositional, anti-authoritarian literatures or textual strategies of our time. As we saw, it is on occasion described as the fullest expression available of the Bakhtinian dialogic. The novel, in particular, is regarded as polyphonic plurality in its authentic, street-muddied, market-place form. That this should be so is not at all surprising. The minglings of migrant writing accord well with political and critical agendas in Western universities. For example, the literature can be read as endorsing a democratic vision of multicultural mixing and individual self-expression. Its heterogeneity symbolizes the kind of integration which, on a cultural level at least, many critics and opinion-makers seek to promote. It may also be that the notoriety whipped up around Rushdie's work by the 1989 fatwa affair has contributed to the prominence of migrant writing generally. (Boehmer, 1996: 236)

In other words, migrant writing directs attention away from what is more true to a specific place and community, and towards points of view that are more pleasing to Western academics and readers. But even though Boehmer may be partly right about the analysis of why a certain literature has been more success-ful, she seems to be somewhat blinded by a political agenda, rather than maintaining a literary focus. It then becomes a question of how literary history should be written, and essentially lines up the positions of post-colonialism and world literature. There are, moreover, vital questions that Boehmer does not ask: what if the cosmopolitan and migrant literature that has been written is actually of superior quality? Or, at least, if it is given preference, also critically, and is better attuned to describing and confronting the largest shift in cultural horizons in decades? And if one insists on the discourse of authenticity, what if the most authentic voices today are those that are blending all kinds of impressions? These include those of Milan Kundera, Gao Xingjian, Salman Rushdie and Michel Houellebecq as suggested below, although Boehmer's critique certainly also applies to parts of their works.

When Milan Kundera left Czechoslovakia in 1975 to settle permanently in France, he had already established an international reputation, primarily based on his 1967 novel, *The Joke*, about the misfortunes of a young man during communist rule. Kundera himself had a more complicated relationship to that period than most writers. He was twice excluded from the Communist Party, in 1950 and 1970, but he was also a prolific figure in the republic's literary life as author of poetry and plays, as well as being a well-known public figure. Yet, he has been very successful in downplaying this, even though his break with the post-1968 rule and his highly critical novels tell the story of a man who did not fit the system. By not giving interviews since the mid-1980s, and by preventing his early production from being translated, he has effectively made it difficult to access and assess his past. In his writing he has also called for the author's right, much like that of a composer, to determine what parts of his work belong to the oeuvre (Kundera, 1988: 146). That, however, would be a new practice in the literary world, where the tendency has been to include an author's notebooks and diaries in the complete works (Foucault, 1987).

Kundera thus displays a complex, almost paradoxical form of engagement. On the one hand, his novels have always been critical in a very persuasive and intelligent way, mixing sketchy, yet charismatic, characters with essayistic interludes and observations, and they have been critical at all times until the fall of communism, of the lack of freedom, and the illusion that there were things worth giving up for it; in the French part of the authorship, his criticism is directed against the noise, speed and stupidity of modern Western societies. His analyses are original, such as the Oedipus analogy to the leaders of the Communist party who should have behaved, metaphorically, like Oedipus, instead of staying in power, or the coupling of the ideals of the seventeenth century to contemporary ways of living, and his belief in the pluralism and strength of the European tradition and history have had great resonance.

Yet, this insistence on the cultural tradition and having the courage to stand by one's history is negated by both Kundera's concealment of his own past, as well as his meticulous control over his own works and their translations, which in some cases do not aim at concealing the past, but rather at making the works more universally accessible. A peculiar and telling example of a means of overcoming the distances between the local and unfamiliar can be found in the translations for the Czech-French writer. As Peter Bugge has pointed out, Kundera has methodically stipulated the omission of names of specific Czech places in his earliest work, and avoided the many accents in Czech names when his novels have been translated into other European languages. Kundera has not spoken about this, but one could assume that he has done this so as not to confuse his readers with unfamiliar names and places, and thus Prague is the exception to this practice. Bugge comments on this strategy:

> One paradoxical consequence of this was that while Kundera the essayist praised the cultural capacities of the small peoples of Central Europe and lamented the western negligence thereof, his own poetic strategy contributed to this oblivion as it wiped out any trace of what was linguistically, historically or topographically specific in the region . . . (Bugge, 2003: 11)

Kundera's reply to this critique might be that if he had not done this, his books would not have been read so widely, as they truly are, and that would have resulted in even greater oblivion, rather than a Hollywood production of one of his novels, which provides a version of the conditions of the events in 1968. On the other hand, Tolstoy and Dostoyevsky never changed their characters' names in order to adjust to a foreign market.

There is another remarkable shift in Kundera's writings that presents itself as an almost perfect chiasm: up until the mid-1980s, when Kundera stopped giving interviews and thereby stopped being an accessible public figure, he always used fictitious characters and rarely referred to persons who could be taken as more than vague alter egos. In the play *Diderot and His Master*, this changed, and in the novel *Immortality*, and in three later novels, Kundera has used a character named Milan Kundera in his works, often presented as a much less than all-mighty figure, and whose wife Vera also plays an important part. Kundera has thus gone from trying to hide the author's ego behind alter egos, to playing a game where a figure named 'Milan Kundera' effectively blocks the idea of being able to say something serious about its author.

There is an interesting connection between these two themes, namely the riddle of identity and the commitment to history. Kundera has often praised the libertine life of the seventeenth century, just as he has opted for the Epicurean mode of living in peaceful seclusion, but this conflicts with the imperative of engagement. This theme of finding causes worth fighting for, contrasted with the individual's right to live his own life and perhaps even abandoning causes worth fighting for, is a theme that is played out both thematically throughout Kundera's writings, and more subtly in some of the writing strategies that he has chosen over the years.

Kundera is thus a highly complicated figure, definitely successful on the literary scene, politically debatable and one of the most radical novelists when it comes to blending the essayistic and fiction in a highly composed text. In one of his early short stories, 'Edward and God', the themes of engagement, essence and an epicurean desire are presented in a humorous and speculative passage:

> God is essence itself, whereas Edward hadn't found (and since the incidents with the directress and with Alice, a number of years had passed) anything essential in his love

affairs, or in his teaching, or in his thoughts. He was too bright to concede that he saw the essential in the unessential, but he was too weak not to long secretly for the essential. / Ah, ladies and gentlemen, a man lives a sad life when he cannot take anything or anyone seriously! / And that is why Edward longed for God, for God alone is relieved of the distracting obligation of *appearing* and can merely *be*, for He solely constitutes (He Himself, unique and nonexistent) the essential opposite of this unessential (but so much more existent) world. (Kundera, 1987: 240)

The migrant's desire to stand apart is a recurrent theme, regardless of whether it is within the collective of communism or the collective of the celebration of stars and media in the West.

Kundera has also, as touched upon in the introduction, taken part in the discussion of world literature, not least by discussing the interaction between literatures and the differences between contexts and the positions of nations. Kundera discerns between the small and the large context of any work, a more flexible term that can cover the local and the global, as well as the national and the international, before he goes on to define provincialism as the inability or the refusal to see oneself in the larger context. This can be applied both to large nations and literatures, who see themselves as too abundant in works and history to need the larger context, as well as small nations which are aware of the lacunas in their past, but which insist on their own small context out of fear that the larger context would erase the smaller, and thus its specifics:

> There are two basic contexts in which a work of art may be placed: either in the history of its nation (we can call this the *small context*), or else in the supranational history of its art (the *large context*). We are accustomed to seeing music quite naturally in the large context: knowing what language Orlando de Lassus or Bach spoke matters little to a musicologist, but because a novel is bound up with its language, in nearly every university in the world it is studied almost exclusively in the small, national context. (Kundera, 2007: 35)

Kundera also makes the argument that the best interpreters or inheritors of seminal European authors have been foreigners, thereby creating a series of bonds between authors that are more profound than those that exit only within the national literatures:

> And yet Rabelais, ever undervalued by his compatriots, was never better understood than by a Russian, Bakhtin; Dostoyevsky than by a Frenchman, Gide; Ibsen than by an Irishman, Shaw; Joyce than by an Austrian, Broch. The universal importance of the generation of great North Americans – Hemingway, Faulkner, Dos Passos was first brought to light by French writers. . . . These few examples are not bizarre exceptions to the rule; no, they are the rule: geographic distance sets the observer back from the local context and allows him to embrace the *large context* of world literature, the only approach that can bring out a novel's *aesthetic value* – that is to say: the previously

unseen aspects of existence that this particular novel has managed to make clear: the novelty of form it has found. (Kundera, 2007: 36)

Kundera's argument goes hand in hand with Franco Moretti's argument of local voice and foreign form that combines, and which makes its mark by adding something new to literature, just as he dismisses the idea that this model is just an exception rather than the dominating rule.[15] Kundera's material is not all-encompassing, and it is also somewhat biased by his own preferences, but nevertheless it points to a number of connections that make up more than mere coincidences.

Like Kundera, Gao Xingjian was in his mid-forties when he left China for France in 1987, and like Kundera he had been a prolific figure under a strict regime, and eventually could not manoeuvre between the limited right to create freely, and the need to express personal and historical experiences, primarily related to the events of the Cultural Revolution. Gao is one of many Chinese writers who were, early on, through their university education, influenced by Western literature; literature that during the Cultural Revolution was difficult and dangerous to get, keep and read. When Gao was sent for re-education in the countryside, he felt he had to burn a suitcase full of his own manuscripts, and even when the situation lightened in the late 1970s and he could write for the stage, his plays were harshly criticized by the political system. Eventually, Gao left China carrying the manuscript of one of his two great novels, *Soul Mountain* (Gao Xingjian, 2000a).

The Swedish Academy's motivation for giving the Nobel Prize to Gao Xingjian was that he has created:

> an oeuvre of universal validity, bitter insights and linguistic ingenuity, which has opened new paths for the Chinese novel and drama.[16]

The phrase 'universal validity' is an interesting one that would not have been singled out, had Gao Xingjian not come from a non-Western culture; on the other hand, it also states the vision of world literature that lies behind the Nobel Prize.

Again, much like Kundera, Gao's writings establish an eminent juxtaposition of life under a communist regime and in the capitalist West, which again highlights the conflicts of the collective and the individual, the lost utopias and the realities of suppression and indifference. This dual perspective, which is one of the insights that migrant writers possess by definition, is highlighted in *One Man's Bible*, through the very composition of the narrative, which oscillates between a laid-back presentation of life in the present-day West, a life in hotel rooms, with a German girlfriend, and no immediate worries other than those that remembrance presents. This remembrance is the other part of the novel, where the protagonist's life during the Cultural Revolution and its atrocities are unfolded. The dual perspective is most likely an important explanation of the artistic success and general interest in such works, including Kundera's, since they do not simply condemn the past or moralize, but put it into perspective by showing a hope for change, while also criticizing the values of the capitalist societies' unlimited and unheroic individualism.

Gao's novels include more distinctive formal traits that supplement the fundamental feature of presenting a dual perspective. Most significant is the use of a simple, but important, device, where he uses pronouns as the names for his protagonists, such as 'You' and 'He'. Gao finds this so important that he mentioned it in his Nobel Lecture:

> In my fiction I use pronouns instead of the usual characters and also use the pronouns I, you, and he to tell about or to focus on the protagonist. The portrayal of the one character by using different pronouns creates a sense of distance. As this also provides actors on the stage with a broader psychological space I have also introduced the changing of pronouns into my drama. (Gao Xingjian, 2000b)

He further complicates the differences of first and third person narrative in a most elegant way that also includes the second person, the reader:

> It is clear that life naturally ends, and when the end comes, fear vanishes, because fear is itself a manifestation of life. On losing awareness and consciousness, life abruptly ends, and there can be no further thinking and no further meaning. Your affliction had been your search for meaning. When you began discussing the ultimate meaning of human life with the friends of your youth, you had hardly lived. However, it seems that having savored virtually all of the sensations to be experienced in life, you simply laugh at the futility of searching for meaning. It is best just to experience this existence, and moreover, to look after it. (Gao Xingjian, 2002a: 410)

Another important element is the integration of an essayistic element, something which he shares with the other writers discussed this chapter, Kundera, Rushdie and Houellebecq. The reflexive mode is a feature used by range of novelists around the world, although the clear-cut divide between telling and reflection that often can be found in these writers' works is less common to the novel.

Gao's work therefore incorporates a series of distinctive divisions: in the temporal dimension of his narratives and the very different settings in which they take place, in the manner of presenting the protagonists by using pronouns, and in the division between telling and reflecting, all characteristics that make his work stand out as a unique way of presenting migration and remembrance in the light of the distance between both general and political cultures.

Whereas Gao and Kundera had to bridge a linguistic divide, by either trusting translators or by learning to write in another language, this has not been the case with a number of Commonwealth migrant writers, particularly to those who had been educated in England. Salman Rushdie is by far the most widely known migrant writer, and he would probably have been so even without the Fatwa of 1989, which linked his writing and his person to religious, political and despotic dimensions that no one had envisioned would become an international problem. Rushdie also represents all three types of migrant writers described here, being a post-colonial writer focusing on the identity of a new nation, a political writer in a sort of exile, having to live under cover, and a cosmopolitan writer with migrant desires.

Like V. S. Naipaul and many others, Rushdie has a colonial and post-colonial background, being born at the time of India's birth as an independent nation, raised in a cosmopolitan environment in India, but later educated and settled in England. His early authorship deals intensely with the birth of the Indian nation, most notably in *Midnight's Children*. With the Fatwa, Rushdie became a political writer who could not appear publicly for several years, and after that, only as a high security risk. In practice this could be called a de facto exile with personal consequences like those of an actual exile, including the separation from his family. In his later authorship, there has been a turn towards a cosmopolitan joy of not belonging, which has only highlighted the fact that Rushdie has always written about multi-lingual areas like Bombay, London and later on, New York. Jaina C. Sanga has given a precise account of Rushdie's position and project as a migrant writer, claiming that Rushdie's position as a migrant writer can probably best be understood in terms of his occupying an in-between place. She refers to Homi Bhabha's use of 'interstitial space', which is a condition that allows the overlap and displacement of areas of difference, so 'that from the location of inhabiting both worlds, the writing constantly shifts terrain' (Sanga, 2001: 17). To Sanga this means that Rushdie can belong to both worlds, but without belonging fully to either. In writing from such border zones, Rushdie unveils the unequal relationships between peoples, races and languages, and in a sense, Sanga claims, the border becomes the only reliable home, because Rushdie and others who share his circumstances cannot find a place to settle. When the border has become the place where he lives, Rushdie can use his writing to expand the border, and, in Sanga's words, give it an authority of its own:

> It is from such an interstitial position, then, that Rushdie calls for a reconception of history from a postcolonial perspective so as to generate new and alternate sites of representation. Rushdie's stance is that the Western metropolis must contend with its postcolonial history as told by its migrants and incorporate this voice into the national narrative. (Sanga, 2001: 17)

In Sanga's version of the migrant and his position on the border, this is also an epistemologically superior position, being 'reliable', and close to being morally superior, since the migrant is not dependent on a good relationship with a single homeland, but is free to criticize all, from his position in between them.

On the other hand, the position on the border could also be a position from which one does not understand the true substance of things, and where the perpetual journey stands in stark contrast to the lives of those who are part of dominant cultures. These two modes of seeing things are also what separate Elleke Boehmer from proponents of migrant literature, or Pierre Bourdieu from proponents of globalized culture, such as Niklas Luhmann and Ulrich Beck, and this is ultimately a discussion that cannot be solved abstractly, but must be considered in the light of the trajectory of single writers.

Rushdie himself has been very outspoken about his views on migrancy. In *Imaginary Homelands* Rushdie highlights his complex sense of identity with regard to his writing:

> Let me suggest that Indian writers in England have access to a second tradition, quite apart from their own racial history. It is the culture and political history of the phenomenon of migration, displacement, life in a minority group. We can quite legitimately claim as our ancestors the Huguenots, the Irish, the Jews; the past to which we belong is an English past, the history of immigrant Britain. Swift, Conrad, Marx are as much our literary forebears as Tagore or Ram Mohan Roy. (Rushdie, 1991: 20)

In line with this, Rushdie has spoken against the idea of national purity, especially when it comes to India, which to him is far too complex, linguistically, culturally, as well as religiously, to be represented as a unit (Rushdie, 1992: 67).

Mapping the world is a new challenge, which is essentially what Rushdie has taken up in his works, both thematically and through his philosophy of representing, which has been compared to the metaphor of the rhizome used by Gilles Deleuze, which indicates a cartography in which there are no definite centres, only lines in perpetual movement, a view on the world which is not unlike that of Rushdie's friend and travelmate, Bruce Chatwin.[17]

Rushdie achieved a certain notoriety with respect to Indian literature due to his having edited a collection of Indian fiction which only included an absolute minimum of texts not written originally in English (Rushdie and West, 1997). He is biased, when he sees more positives than negatives in the dominance of English in world literature. Nevertheless, he could be right, as well:

> . . . I think that if *all* English literatures could be studied together, a shape would emerge which would truly reflect the new shape of the language in the world, and we could see that Eng. Lit. has never been in better shape, because the world language now also possesses a world literature, which is proliferating in every conceivable direction. (Rushdie, 1992: 70)

Like Edward W. Said, Rushdie sees the transformation from post-colonial literature to world literature as a welcome change, while pointing out that the biggest threat to the local Indian literatures is not English, but Hindi (Rushdie, 1992: 69). It would be unfair to say that Rushdie has simply followed a major trend in his transformation from post-colonialist to cosmopolitan; rather, this tells more about the change in conceptions and of the general tendencies in what defines the conditions of authors and their ability to think about personal and collective identities.

The youngest of the contemporary migrant writers included here is Michel Houellebecq, a recent migrant author who first settled in Ireland, then in Spain, after living most of his life in France. In the past decade his novels have been translated into a number of languages almost immediately after their publication in French, making him the most transnational contemporary French author. His relations to French culture are complex, with an often hate-filled tone and manner, recalling the position of Louis-Ferdinand Céline, and he reveals how French culture has also been transformed by the same commercial trends that influence the rest of the world. The dream of an escape from daily life is a recurrent theme in his work, often in the form of migration, most notably in *Platform*, but also in *The Elementary Particles*, where the camps of new age subcultures serve as a form of migrancy, or as a forlorn alternative to this, they seek refuge in Club Meds, or even go on to reorganize these resorts into quasi-swinger clubs, which only highlights the awkward relations of Western people to their surroundings. In an interview, Houellebecq clearly stated his views on Western culture:

> I don't know anybody who lives in the West without being forced to . . . I love Thailand and often fly there. At the moment I live in Ireland, because I like countries with beautiful landscapes. (Steinfeld, 2001: 100)

Houellebecq's dream of migration is not usually a dream of something better, just an escape from what is false, much like those of Albert Camus' protagonists. A clear difference is that Houellebecq writes about a society which is richer than ever, and in which the many ways of separating oneself from society are not linked to poor living conditions, which have been explored in literature from Dostoyevsky through Hamsun and Kafka to Céline, but take place in a kind of numb comfort, where the experience of hitting rock bottom both emotionally and physically is turned, first and foremost, into a mental void. The extreme position is the migrancy to poorer countries, where the protagonists' currency gives them the opportunity to live luxuriously in a warm climate. That, however, is not the answer, and can even take the form of radical disillusionment as in *Platform*:

> When one gives up on life, the last remaining human contacts are those you have with shopkeepers. As far as I'm concerned, these are limited to a few words spoken in English. I don't speak Thai, which creates a barrier around me that is suffocating and sad. It is obvious that I will never really understand Asia, and actually it's of no great importance. It's possible to live in the world without understanding it: all you need is to be able to get food, caresses and love. In Pattaya, food and caresses are cheap by Western, and even by Asian, standards. As for love, it's difficult for me to say. I am now convinced that, for me, Valerie was simply a radiant exception. She was one of those

creatures who are capable of devoting their lives to someone else's happiness, of making that alone their goal. This phenomenon is a mystery. Happiness, simplicity and joy lies within them; but I still do not know how or why it occurs. And if I haven't understood love, what use is it to me to have understood the rest? / To the end, I will remain a child of Europe, of worry and of shame; I have no message of hope to deliver. For the West, I do not feel hatred; at most I feel a great contempt. I know only that every single one of us reeks of selfishness, masochism and death. We have created a system in which it has simply become impossible to live; and what's more, we continue to export it. (Houellebecq, 2002: 360–361)

There is consequently no real flight for Houellebecq's protagonists, but besides the dislike of the culture with which they have grown up, there is a sort of joy about a globalized culture that does not belong to anyone, and which can provide a sort of epicurean shelter, in which a philosophy of less identification with one's self and the surrounding culture can be lived out.

Houellebecq's notorious precursor in French literature, Louis-Ferdinand Céline, finds, in *Journey to the End of the Night*, when his alter ego Bardamu has lived in New York City for a while, that there is a certain period when the migrant has shaken off the habits of his former country without quite having adopted those of his new. This is a happy state of being, but also an unstable one that either leads to a new conformity, or to another migration, with all the initial problems of settling that this entails, at least in Céline's description of his journeys to Africa and America (Céline, 1988: 194).

But even though Houellebecq's conclusions and overall narrative are disillusioned, there is also a recurrent meeting between the angry, lonely protagonist and a woman who proves the initial cynicism wrong. However, she has to die or disappear, so the negative atmosphere can be re-established, only more bitterly. Houellebecq thus references a long history of writers who have explored the tragic potential of the lonely male who is in conflict with society, but finds a short-lived comfort with a woman.

It is still premature to project whether Houellebecq will be a writer in the class of Céline and Camus, although his ability to provoke and integrate observations of his world is on the level of Céline, and his presentations of existential nausea are on par with those of Sartre and Camus, written in what Olivier Bardolle calls a 'hostile style' (Bardolle, 2004: 57). Furthermore, his work integrates a number of the complicated issues in the modern world, from the status of religions in world society, to the consequences of genetic research; issues that deal with the idea of what it means to be human, and how pressure from the outside transforms that notion. The end of humanity is a recurrent theme that is also presented with some joy at the conclusion of *The Elementary Particles*:

All across the surface of the globe, a weary, exhausted humanity, filled with self-doubt and uncertain of its history, prepared itself as best it could to enter a new millennium. (Houellebecq, 2000: 245)

In the postscript to the novel, set in the middle of the twenty-first century, mankind is presented as something of the past and a new kind of human has taken over. Made by mankind itself through genetic manipulation, it is presented as having overcome many of the flaws of man, such as vanity and greed. The new humans have kept the ability to love, and that seems to be the positive side of all Houellebecq's works, that love still exists, even if often tragic at some point. The desire for migrancy could then be seen as an attempt to overcome the differences that customs have created.

To conclude, the modernists and the contemporary migrant writers constitute two important clusters of writers in world literature, while at the same time their differences in expression, content, circulation and canonization reflect and clarify a number of changes in the world, which will be addressed here. First, the world has changed, although the internationalism of 1920s that followed the First World War shares features with the globalization that took off fully after the end of the Cold War. Second, there is a changed pace in the circulation of books across borders and continents, and a changed and expanded readership for advanced literature. Third, the literature of the contemporary migrants seems to be less unhappy about lost essences, having found ways to enjoy this loss in a literature that has also, fourth, stylistically mediated these losses, and has found new narrative modes that integrate Aristotelian and non-Aristotelian principles, and which have a strong affinity for the essayistic mode that also goes along with the post-essentialist attitude. Finally, there is the question of negotiating individuality and collectivity, which seems to be a stronger issue to the contemporary migrants than it was to the modernists.

Both the 1920s and the 1990s could be seen as decades of a new openness that followed serious international conflicts, and offered visions of a more international and worldly attitude, although without quite fulfilling the potential of those visions. The difference is that the world of the 1920s still was an imperialistic world, and that it was followed by severe conflicts that altered the climate for international exchange, whereas the focus on, and the effects of globalization have only gained more momentum in the new millennium, and on a much larger and more truly world-wide scale. Globalization is still an ongoing process, something that in a few decades could stop being a topic because it will have become so internalized in the general mindset, that the mixing of local and global cultural phenomena will seem like a natural thing. The local will still be a strong part of people's lives, but woven into a web whose elements come from other parts of the world. This will also be the situation for authors and the environment in which they write, and the migrant writers will, more than they could in the modernist period, be able to function as mediators and critics of cultural diversity, simply juxtaposing what is strange and what is familiar in a double and interchangeable perspective.

The migrant writers of today also differ in being situated in a changed literary market and culture, which, for instance, pushes for very rapid translations of works, sometimes even providing simultaneous releases of the same work in a number of different languages. To a large degree, the modernist writers sought to free themselves of the market forces by being funded by benefactors, day jobs, inheritances or other means, and this has sparked the interest of the new economic criticism of who paid for Modernism (Osteen and Woodmansee, 1999). The contemporary migrant writers have almost all been part of the commercial circuits, but these are also circuits where the academic readership and fairly well-educated people have grown to become a mass of their own. Although the distinctions between 'high-', 'middle-' and 'low-brow' still apply, it has become increasingly difficult to categorize authors as one or the other, as some, such as Salman Rushdie or Milan Kundera, have moved from 'high-brow' to more widely read and appreciated work. Another consequence of this is that it is difficult to envision a breakthrough for a literature as ambitious as that of High Modernism.

Thematically, it is noteworthy that migrancy plays a greater role in contemporary migrant writing. The nation is less of a project, less of a nostalgic thing, and the very idea of being a migrant is often presented as a valuable experience. Contemporary migrant literature is also distinguished by more political exiles who have had an international reception. There have been writers who were forced to leave their countries at other periods, but few have had an international impact. It is noteworthy, for example, that the German exile literature written during the Nazi regime has had little international impact, whereas a number of later exiled writers gained attention.

Stylistically, it is remarkable that a number of migrant novelists have integrated an essayistic element as an important part of their narratives, which allows for the use of multiple perspectives, both in time and in order to shift between specific stories and general observations. Differences can also be significant, as, for example, when Milan Kundera pursues an economy of expression and clear composition, it is almost the opposite of that which Salman Rushdie has come to represent.

Finally, the conflict between individuality and solidarity is highlighted by migrant writers, because they carry with them a sense of having abandoned one place in order to pursue their own path, but since their place in the world is so much determined by themselves, their engagement in political matters in the widest sense will also have a sense of being less of necessity, and more out of deliberate choice. In philosophy, the balancing of self-creation and solidarity has been a recurrent theme in which the idea of pursuing both sides of this distinction to the fullest stands in opposition to the widespread ideal of the human being as an integrated and organically coherent entity in whom the private and the public spheres are integrated. It is significant that a number of migrant writers have exposed their visions of a complex inner life, which is certainly not on the politically correct side, along with an engagement in politics that is more idealistic. This goes back to James Joyce, and has had strong proponents in contemporary literature in Salman Rushdie and Gao Xingjian.

The contributions of contemporary migrant writers are important, not just as works of art, but also in the ways that they have affected literature as such, and in the ways that they present highly relevant experiences. As long as the idea of the migrant writer exists, it is an indication that the world is still in the process of globalization, rather than having left it behind; however, the most widely shared properties of the ideas of culture have changed so drastically over the past decades, that a similar change could happen in other domains.

How strange should it be?

Literature by migrant writers brings a certain strangeness to something familiar. 'Strangeness' has a long history as a positive term in literary criticism, being connected with the idea of gaining access to new and different layers – of the mind, of the world or of different experiences of reality. Furthermore, the concept of 'defamiliarization' introduced by the Russian formalists is still an important implicit or explicit aspect of definitions of literary technique and experience, although not the only one (Bann and Bowlt, 1973). Strangeness is not enough, though. Making things incomprehensible is easy, but has historically it has proven to be futile. There seems to be a limit to the degree of strangeness that can function in a literary work, and literary history shows that there must be something that mixes the strange with the familiar, regardless of whether that distance is of a historic or cultural nature.

In this respect, literary forms provide something to hold on to: a narrative by a Russian or an African writer that emulates the modes of the Western novel bridges some of the gaps presented by the difference in cultural horizons. Considering what has made it into the Western canon or the Western idea of world literature, the extent to which these works and the authors behind them are involved in Western culture and literature is striking.

There may be different reasons for the two-fold success of migrant writing, in particular some formal aspects of which it can take advantage. First, migrant and bicultural writers relate very well to the phenomenon of globalization, which is changing the way we think about the world and how people experience their own worlds, whether by means of the increased spectrum of globalized media or the ever more diversified food culture influenced by local traditions from around the world. Second, the literature of migrants presents a certain double perspective on things by someone who is both at home and away at the same time. This is not just a quality of the content of this literature, but also, and third, a formal quality that creates the opportunity to create a particular narrative voice.

This becomes clear when trying to apply Moretti's model of foreign form, local form and local content, to the literature of migrant and bicultural writers. What is foreign and what local in Salman Rushdie's work? Where does his voice belong to, or come from? Once again, migrant writers deliver a particular twin outlook on things as they write from a place where they are strangers and at home, at one and the same time. The double perspective is not only very interesting with respect to the themes these writers address, the way their observations are coloured by not taking circumstances and norms for granted, as a non-migrant would; the double perspective also opens up a space for experimenting with the form of the novel, following the idea of tacit knowledge of positions and their transfer, in the vein of Bourdieu's theory of the field of art.

As argued previously, the Western canon is relatively closed, and it is characteristic that its openness to literature from other continents and cultures seems to continue to be dominated by writing that has some affiliation with the Western tradition, both when it comes to critical appreciation and to market-wise success. The importance of migrant and cosmopolitan literature already has some empirical support in the form of circulation and recognition, and as has been put forward here, there are also many indications of an ongoing contribution. There are also many good reasons for this from a theoretical point of view, as has been discussed above. In an age of cultural transformation, bicultural writers have important experiences of culture which can make their works valuable, as Richard Rorty has argued (Rorty, 1998: 211–212). They serve as agents of transformation and proponents of a changing view on culture and identity, and the theories of Bourdieu, Beck and Bhabha, discussed here, make important points regarding this.

Although Bourdieu's theory revaluates the importance of the nation as a field with a relative autonomy, it is also apparent that the importance of generating new positions within the field is an important element in the evolution of literature, and it is historically evident, as argued in the examples from modernist and contemporary migrant writing, that these writers have been able to create new positions both through the substance of their hybrid cultures and through the renewal of genres and techniques within an already established field. While the idea of an overrepresentation of migrant writers in the international canon, and more specifically among those who have propelled the evolution of genres, is difficult to transform into exact numbers, there are strong indications that their role is unusually significant.

To Ulrich Beck, a cosmopolitan attitude is both a desirable project and a result of changes in the world. The migrant and cosmopolitan writers are thus located at the centre of an international cultural shift that is tied to numerous other smaller changes in humans' interactions with the world; however, there are no other media as reflective as literature, or as dense in the experiences it carries with it. Migrant writing is thus the writing of a world wherein the ideas of place, nation and identity are more complex than ever, and as such reveal how the strange and the familiar can and will mix in peoples' lives.

This element is also important to Homi Bhabha, who stresses that hybrid objects, of which migrant writing is historically the most evolved, complex and influential, provide models for a complex mode of identification, which both confirms the multifaceted way of generating identity in the contemporary world, and has critical potential and aspects, by speaking from a position between cultures, without affirming or taking either side (Bhabha, 1994: x).

In world literature, migrant writing stands out and forms a constellation of its own, due to the simple fact that the writers have a different relation to languages and book markets than most other writers. That they also share a number of common interests cannot surprise, either, but what is interesting is how they have combined their basic themes, that, with formal solutions which give a particular voice to their material, make them interesting, regardless of whether one reads for the artistic, or the cultural or historic aspect of literature. By focusing on migrant writing with an international reception, it is also evident that these writers have been able to create a space of their own in world literature, rather than generating a compilation of nationally based literatures that need to be understood within a specific frame of reference. This is not to say that the specific and historical are not relevant, but that it must be supplemented by an adherence to the international literary system, and that is a system which has also favoured certain themes, not only for their historic importance, but also for their ability to evolve literature.

In his article 'Geographies of modernism in a globalizing world', Andreas Huyssen makes seven suggestions intended to help the emergence from what he sees as a current deadend to the idea of global literature, as well as cultural studies. There are several distinctions that he wants to abandon, such as the distinction between 'high' and 'low' in the views on elite and popular culture, just as media should not automatically be viewed on such a vertical scale. Furthermore, he does not believe in the power of elite culture to make social transformation, so he instead wants critics to describe the function and role of cultural phenomena, just as he does not want to do away with the aesthetic analyses which should balance the political overload that cultural studies often bring with them. Finally, there are distinctions he does want to maintain, although in a more complex way than that in which they are often used:

> The issue of hierarchy, however, must not disappear entirely from analysis. Hierarchical value relations remain inscribed into all cultural practices, but they operate more subtly depending on stratifications of production and reception, of genres and of media. Cultural hierarchy is a key issue for alternative modernisms, which are inevitably shaped by the power relations between the metropolis and the periphery. In the colonial world, the influx of Western modernism did not automatically gain the status of high in comparison with local classical traditions (for example, India in the post-liberation period), and Western mass culture is often resisted not because it is 'low', but because it is Western (for example, China today). Western hierarchies are thus multiply refracted and transformed by local hierarchies of value. It remains to be analysed how such refractions affected the various alternative modernisms,

where they found fertile ground (as in Latin America) and where they were resisted either by nativism or by official cultural policies (as in the Soviet Union). (Huyssen, 2005: 14)

Huyssen's suggestions are much inspired by Bourdieu's analyses of the literary field. What is most striking is that the core value behind the suggestions is the idea of transnational phenomena, which inspire new forms to arise locally, and thus add to the diversity of the world's cultures while also bearing witness to objects of global fascination, and which cannot be ascribed to a dominant centre, but only add to the importance of breaches created by transnational literatures, in the reflection of what world literature is (Huyssen, 2005: 15).

Chapter 4

Ethics and aesthetics in traumatic literature

Writing that addresses some of the worst horrors and crimes of humankind, genocide and war, has a particular position in world literature, especially since the Second World War and the Holocaust. The theme of mass killing, among which some natural disasters may also be counted, has the potential to engage readers from all cultural contexts, and make them forget the contingent local interests on which much literature otherwise thrives. The Holocaust itself, argue Daniel Levy and Nathan Sznaider in *Erinnerung im globalen Zeitalter: Der Holocaust*, is the first object of historical memory that is truly cosmopolitan and has become a concern even to people who have no direct connection to it (Levy and Sznaider, 2001). In the same vein, Alvin Rosenfeld has pointed out, in *A Double Dying: Reflections on Holocaust Literature*, that the literature on the Holocaust is the first literature that, from the outset, could only be understood in an international context, where the different contributions belong more to the subject than to the national literary scenes of the authors (Rosenfeld, 1980: 34). There is a bitter irony, but perhaps also a portion of hope, in the fact that a nationalistic, racist movement sparked an international consciousness that has been given expression in a range of works that deal with the denial of the right to life, caused by war, genocideand disaster, and that it has become a significant part of world literature. The ways that this literature is linked beyond the confines of the nation and has become a transnational literature, and the ways in which it makes use of its thematic and formal potential form the core of this chapter.

The twentieth century was marked by a substantial number of global events in which people lost their lives without being combatants in a conflict, but were merely unfortunate enough to live in a certain place, or belong to a certain group. In *Final Solutions: Mass Killings and Genocide in the 20th Century*, Benjamin A. Valentino distinguishes three basic categories of mass killings as communist, ethnic and counter-guerrilla, thereby reflecting the most significant crimes in the history of the century. Although the distinctions could be said to be somewhat rough and initially problematic, as 'counter-guerrilla' could invoke the notion of a justified mass killing, the three categories comprise the larger part of the mass killings in the twentieth century. Foremost among the ethnic mass killings are those of the Nazi regime in Germany, in which six million people where killed, the majority being Jews, although the Roma, mentally challenged people and political opponents were also killed as groups. Two other large genocides took place at each end of the twentieth century, the first being the genocide of the Armenian population in Turkey, which began in 1915 and continued in the following years, while the Hutu killing of Tutsis in Rwanda lasted only a few months in 1994, but both genocides resulted in the death of about a million people. The immense killings in the last phases of brutal imperialism, particularly in the Congo at the end of the nineteenth century, are also a events that have received more and more attention over the years, countering a problematic forgetfulness in Western consciousness (Hochschild, 1999).

The communist mass killings, sometimes carried out indirectly through famine, took place under a number of regimes, most notably in the Soviet Union in the 1920s, in China in the 1950s, and in Cambodia in the 1970s, and on a scale that, like the genocides, defies belief and imagination. In the name of fighting guerrilla activity, Soviet troops in Afghanistan, the Indonesian Sukartu government and the government of Guatemala have carried out some of the worst killings of this kind (Valentino, 2004: 91–96). Valentino also lists a series of events in twentieth century warfare that can be classified as terrorist because they affected civilians more than an opposing army or infrastructure, including Allied bombings on German cities such as Dresden during the Second World War, as well as terrorist activity in African civil wars (Valentino, 2004: 88).

All in all, the twentieth century witnessed a number of civilian losses in wars on a scale that was unheard of before, although history is filled with mass killings, not least during the European colonization of the Americas. What is perhaps specific to the twentieth century mass killings is the involvement of people who could be recognized as one's neighbour, but who were nevertheless singled out, with fatal consequences.

The universality of its theme, with regard to both its extension as a global phenomenon and as subject that arouses great empathy, is not the only defining property of this literature. The main argument of this chapter is that there is also a series of intricately related consequences of the theme, which provide special conditions for the accounts of the historical material and for the formal properties of this literature. It is important to stress that literature, especially that of the Holocaust, is an area in which any interest in the subject can easily seem irrelevant and trivial, compared to the endless suffering and tragedy that lie behind it. Daniel R. Schwarz consequently opens his book, *Imagining the Holocaust*, by considering a series of questions about who has the right to write about the Holocaust, and how (Schwarz, 1999: 3–4); he defends the formalist interest in Holocaust literature, as it is also evident from the analyses he makes of a variety of works that have explored new genres and modes of representation.

Others, like David Patterson, co-editor of the *Encyclopedia of Holocaust Literature*, dismiss those who are interested in the representation of the Holocaust for not being interested in the history of the Jews, and hence fundamentally wrong in their scope. This contrasts with the views of Naomi Mandel and Berel Lang, for example, who argue at length against the rhetoric of the unspeakable that surrounds Holocaust discourse.[1] Imre Kertész suggests a position fostered by the dilemma of the Holocaust survivors' desire to be remembered, but not to be stylized or made into industrial kitsch:

> I regard as kitsch any representation of the Holocaust that is incapable of understanding or unwilling to understand the organic connection between our own deformed mode of life (whether in the private sphere or on the level of 'civilization' as such) and the very possibility of the Holocaust. Here I have in mind those representations that seek to establish the Holocaust once and for all as something foreign to human nature; that seek to drive the Holocaust out of the realm of human experience. I would also use the term kitsch to describe those works where Auschwitz is regarded as simply a matter concerning Germans and Jews, and thereby reduced to something like the fatal incompatibility of two groups; when the political and psychological anatomy of modern totalitarianism more generally is disregarded; when Auschwitz is not seen as a universal experience, but reduced to whatever immediately 'hits the eye.' Apart from this, of course, I regard anything that *is* kitsch, as kitsch. (Kertész, 2001: 270)

Kertész' ambitions are high, as he wants to unite historical analysis with such abstract categories as 'human nature' and 'universal experience', but he is also very much to the point when explaining why this literature is both challenging and authentic. The literature of genocide, war and disaster is both historical testimony and work of art, and there is a reason that the artistic effort to apply forms and words to aspects of history is a valuable supplement to the accounts of witnesses and the cold statistical figures, and why this literature can be taken seriously as literature, and therefore also criticized from an aesthetic point of view. History has been made into literature, but it is a literature that could have failed artistically and could have failed as the object of a wider interest, but nevertheless it has become one of the most meaningful literature of our time. The testimonies could have been sufficient, historically and rhetorically, leaving no place for a literature of the denial of life, but there seems to be a need and justification for this literature, when its importance in world literature is considered.

Combining history with aesthetics can seen as ethically problematic, but it is not the ethics of the field that is the reason for dealing with it here, but instead its undeniable presence in emergent international canonization, which is dependent both on ethics and aesthetics, in the sense of the ways in which experience is given a literary form. A criticism of this could be that one should not produce aesthetic artefacts out of the horrors of history, even if literature on genocide is also a literature of the beauty of compassion and poise amidst horror, and of rescue in a desperate situation. The latter, however, could just as well be criticized for romanticizing what is the absolute opposite of romance.

On the other hand, it is untenable to suggest that the impact of this literature should only be accounted for by the weight of history, and part of the proof of why it should not, is that an interest in the Holocaust and genocide has only emerged over the years, in a gradual and complex process that also involves artistic contributions.[2] The literature on war and genocide is also a valuable contribution to the literary field, which this chapter aims to show. So, despite the absolutes surrounding this literature, it is hard to deny that it serves multiple functions. It is not just about recollection, but also how to deal with trauma, warn the future, understand contemporary misdeeds; it is literature that demonstrates a need for confronting the past in certain ways which are about more than the past – literature about the denial of the right to life is also about what it means to be human, now.

Global memory

Alvin Rosenfeld, and Daniel Levy and Nathan Sznaider have contributed important points concerning the international dimension of Holocaust memories, most importantly in that they see them as an almost unique example of a genuine transnational object of memory. Where Rosenfeld is specifically concerned with the nature of the literary field, Levy and Sznaider are focused on the wide-spread consequences of the general cultural importance of the Holocaust, but they agree on the fundamentally new situation of a global object of remembrance.

Rosenfeld makes a series of arguments regarding how Holocaust literature should be read and historicized, claiming that there has been a lack of a phenomenology in the reading of Holocaust literature (Rosenfeld, 1980: 19). The most important of his conceptual suggestions is that Holocaust literature is an amalgamated literature, which was both transnational from its very outset and has created an autonomous field in world literature. He argues that these literary works can be understood on an individual basis, yet always as voices addressing a collective fate:

> The individual cry is always recognizable, but as it echoes across a continent it is the assemblage of pain and rebellion that impresses itself upon us more than anything else. To hear it otherwise is in this instance to hear falsely. (Rosenfeld, 1980: 34)

Rosenfeld further argues that a distinction should be made between the literature addressing the Holocaust and the literature addressing general warfare. It is not that the horrors of war, as experienced in The First World War, for example, cannot be compared to those of the Holocaust, but the Holocaust was extreme in its racism, its attack on civilians, and its determined plan. While stating these differences, he also points to a number of prefigurations of the fundamental features of the Holocaust, most importantly Franz Kafka's prison camp, which uncannily predicts the tattoos of the concentration camps, even though it also differs radically, because there can be no mythological or metaphorical meaning to the Holocaust, as Elie Wiesel has stated, which is a possibility that the allegorical tale always carries with it (Rosenfeld, 1980: 18–25).[3]

Rosenfeld also makes a point of reading all kinds of literature, whether fiction, documentary or multi-authored memoir. He does not privilege fiction over non-fiction, or vice versa, and it is noteworthy that both Rosenfeld, and Levy and Sznaider recognize Anne Frank's *The Diary of a Young Girl* as a defining work of Holocaust literature and general recollection, due to its international impact. It is a work which is a testimony about life in an Amsterdam hideout, but it is also a testimony which was carefully rewritten with a literary consciousness by Anne Frank herself, thus placing it between pure testimony and the literary work that is aware of its own form.

The way in which Rosenfeld argues for the relative autonomy of a range of works, based on thematic and formal criteria, is not unlike the idea of constellations that was presented previously, and which also claims that the appropriate contexts for certain works are not necessarily those closer to it in genre and origin, but rather ones that have been canonized based on the existence of common challenges of certain problems of representation. This is also the case within Holocaust literature, which has its own canon, ranging from poems through novels, to memoirs and recorded testimonies. Furthermore, Rosenfeld's argument is that this field gives strength to the individual works, which can thrive on the multitude of expressions and representations connected to the Holocaust, and to the shared experience. This last point makes Holocaust literature different, because of the density of its historical concentration in time and space. Whereas other genocides are comparable to one another, they lack the unifying context of the Holocaust, and also the immediate transnational context that spanned more than twenty nations and a comparable number of languages.

Although most of what Rosenfeld writes is apt, he could have gone a step further in recognizing the attributes of the most important and canonized Holocaust literature, to determine what it is that makes it differ from the less defining works, whose worth as testimonies remains uncontested. He could also have given more consideration to the sometimes closed nature of the field of Holocaust literature. As other critics of Holocaust literature tend to do, Rosenfeld ultimately resorts to labelling the Holocaust as more or less unique, a gesture that annuls the attempt to draw on the literature addressing other events in history, and their means of representation. It is an open question whether focus will be lost or maintained when trying to find similar problems in related literatures, and arguing for the existence of a transnational field of genocide literature. This is a difficult issue, because the Holocaust is unique in some respects, not least in involving so many nationalities (see also Rosenbaum, 2001).

Where Rosenfeld focuses on the literature of the Holocaust, Levy and Sznaider analyse the memory of the Holocaust as a cultural phenomenon that has evolved considerably, especially in the past twenty years, from a problematic subject of guilt and trauma, to a universal memory that belongs to mankind (Levy and Sznaider, 2002). This development has had a number of defining events, from the success of *The Diary of a Young Girl* in the 1950s, through the trial against Adolf Eichmann in 1960s in Israel, to the 1970s television series, *Holocaust* (Novick, 1999: 127–130). Alongside a growing interest in the Holocaust, there has been a tragic re-actualization of it, in the contemporary ethnic conflicts in Kosovo and Rwanda, with the intense international political attention to genocides and the Holocaust culminating in the Stockholm declaration of 2000, which makes an explicit commitment to the recollection of the Holocaust, and places it in an international context. The opening in 2005 of the Memorial to the Murdered Jews of Europe, at the centre of Berlin, embodied the importance of this recollection, as well as the importance for it to be a part of public awareness.

The story of this development from a somewhat overlooked, and, to many, highly problematic topic, not just on the German side, but also that of those Allies who were aware of the existence of 'ethnic cleansing' programs, to a universally known and highly profiled memory, demonstrates at least two things: that there are many contingencies involved in the process leading to a situation in which the historical and cultural meaning of the Holocaust has become so important and institutionalized to guarantee its future; and that the Holocaust's overwhelming position in history and culture should be explained with a change in culture that envisions past and identity in new ways, creating the need for new functions of memory.

Levy and Sznaider see the interest in the Holocaust as connected to globalization. While collective memory was usually nation-based, the Holocaust could never be an exclusive national remembrance, and it paves the way for a globalized recollection, which is all the more interesting in connection with the fact that, from the outset, Holocaust literature formed a distinctive group of works across national borders. Levy and Sznaider's central thesis is thus that:

> alongside nationally bounded memories a new form of memory emerges which we call 'cosmopolitan memory'. The study of collective memory usually considers these memory structures as being bound by tight social and political groups like the 'nation' or 'ethnos'. (Levy and Sznaider, 2002: 88)

Levy and Sznaider go on to ask what will happen when an increasing number of people in Western societies define themselves less and less with reference to their national or ethnic affiliation, and whether it is possible to imagine collective memories that transcend national and ethnic boundaries. Their affirmative answer and suggestion is, that the:

> shared memories of the Holocaust, the term used to describe the destruction of European Jewry by Nazi Germany between 1941 and 1945, a formative event of the twentieth century, provide the foundations for a new cosmopolitan memory, a memory transcending ethnic and national boundaries. . . . But recently this memory has continued to exist on a global level. Its strength as a global collective memory has been powered and maintained precisely through the fiery interaction between the local and the global. We argue that this dual process of particularization and universalization has produced a symbol of transnational solidarity that is based on a cosmopolitanized memory – one that does not replace national collective memories but exists as their horizon. (Levy and Sznaider, 2002: 88 and 93)

While generally correct in their analysis of the importance of the Holocaust as an emerging global memory, both Rosenfeld, and Levy and Sznaider could be criticized for presenting the idea of the global memory of the Holocaust as too unique. For example, both Marxist theory and the Communist movement could also be said to be a global historical narrative about the change of society from a feudal exploitation of the peasants, to an industrial, capitalist exploitation of the worker. In the same vein, the memory of the colonial past is a unifying memory that also addresses the atrocities of a no longer acceptable ideology, across a wide range of nations and cultures. These memories are more complicated, due to their longer history, geographical diversity and fortunate lack of extermination as the primary object, as instead is the case with genocide, but the global aspects of these histories has also been presented as unified. This is most notable in *The Black Book of Communism* and *The Black Book of Colonialism*, both of which have, with considerable success, documented and contributed to the transnational memory of the historical footprints of these ideologies, although not with the same degree of universal recognition and interest as is expressed in the Holocaust (Courtois et al., 1999; Ferro, 2003).

Levy and Sznaider identify four ways in which the Holocaust can be presented, leading up to its current universalization:

> as far as the victims are concerned in the past (was it the Jews plus a supporting cast, or many different peoples who suffered?); as far as the victims are concerned in the future (is the lesson Never Again for the Jews, or Never Again for Anyone?); as far as the perpetrators are concerned in the past (were the Nazis uniquely evil, or were they only different in quantity from other mass murderers?); and as far as the subjects in the present are concerned (who remembers? i.e. who has the right to pronounce the truth of the Holocaust?). In a newly European 'cosmopolitan' memory, the Holocaust future (and not the past) is now considered in absolutely universal terms: it can happen to anyone, at anytime, and everyone is responsible. (Levy and Sznaider, 2002: 101)

The important shift for Levy and Sznaider follows from distinction, made by Ulrich Beck, between a First and a Second Modernity. In the First Modernity, there was a sharp opposition between perpetrator and victim, which, according to Levy and Sznaider, provided the basis for mutual disdain and misunderstanding. This attitude has, in the Second Modernity, been succeeded by a more general understanding of the 'Other' as a generalized suffering subject, which provides the basis for a shared understanding of the past, and of what can be called a global memory (Levy and Sznaider, 2002: 103). Yet Levy and Sznaider do not provide the phenomenology of literature and of cultural understanding that Rosenfeld calls for, that is, the explanation of how forms arise out of necessity and combine with memories of the past in this transnational literary field.

Five theses on the ethics and aesthetics in traumatic literature

As acknowledged earlier, discussing the literary qualities and potential of a field that refers to real and terrifying events can be problematic, yet the thematic and formal potential in the field of war, genocide and the Holocaust also serve to keep the memory vivid and to make historical distance seem irrelevant. In *Caught by History: Holocaust Effects in Contemporary Art, Literature, & Theory*, Ernst van Alphen argues for a cross-aesthetic understanding of Holocaust memories, claiming that the testimonies themselves have representational problems that legitimatize other kinds of representations, and a wider interest in the forms of representation. One problem with the testimonies is not so much accounting for the horrors that took place, but that the experience had no symbolic order within which it might be understood, and the links between a frame of reference, a discursive understanding and the actual events are missing. This lack of framework, and the consequences of retelling the events in a meaningful way was also experienced by many German soldiers who took part in the Holocaust, although the experiences are otherwise beyond comparison. Another problem is the inevitable employment of testimony, which works against the desire for objective transmission of historical events, since the framing of the events will also be part of a discursive mode (Alphen, 1997: 55–64). Alphen's argument is thus on par with Rosenfeld's claim that Holocaust literature must be seen as a field in which the individual voices complement one another. Even though Alphen makes a series of interesting analyses of representations of the Holocaust, particularly in visual art, he seems somewhat hesitant to explore the representational structures used in literature.

Robert Eaglestone has gone deeper into this aspect in *The Holocaust and the Postmodern*, in which he notes that testimony is the fundamental form of Auschwitz literature, while he simultaneously lists a number of reasons why the testimony is neither a pure form, nor one that can stand alone (Eaglestone, 2004: 28–34). Testimonies use a series of literary devices to tell their story, and their perspective leads to, as Alphen also emphasizes, discursive, historical considerations of truth, evil, meaning, identity and so on. Importantly, Eaglestone describes how Holocaust literature produces a desire to stop reading, and literature concerning a radical denial of life is perhaps unique in this sense, as it leads to reading which is fascinating, but not pleasurable (Eaglestone, 2004: 15). When reading Primo Levi's accounts, for example, the reader literally wishes to put down the book and stop reading, because of the immense painfulness of the events described. However, instead of exploring the reading of the literature, Eaglestone devotes the larger part of his book to an investigation of the testimony and the discursive meta-representations and considerations of the Holocaust in the aftermath of post-structuralist theory. This decision to emphasize the ethics of history, rather than the specific coupling of aesthetics and ethics in literature, omits large parts of the literature.[4]

In contrast to this, Daniel R. Schwarz' *Imagining the Holocaust* presents a series of close readings of seminal works in Holocaust literature that has the great virtue of differentiating between its modes of expression. Schwarz operates with four clusters of genres which also represent a historical progression. The first is the memoir, such as those of Elie Wiesel, Anne Frank and Primo Levi. After that comes the fiction of realism, such as Thomas Keneally's *Schindler's List*, which is followed by a turning away from meticulous registration, to the modes of the fable. Finally, there is a literature of the Holocaust which makes use of fantasy and the comic grotesque, for example Art Spiegelman's cartoon, *Maus;* modes that might potentially seem to mock the original memoirs, but which Schwarz shows can be both artistically successful and true to history (Schwarz, 1999: 288). Schwarz thus traces a development from the relatively simple referentially, although often sophisticatedly narrated, memoirs, to an increasingly innovative way of presenting the past. This is a development that is also based on the rise of new generations of writers who were not first-hand witnesses to the Holocaust, but who write to commemorate the loss of their ancestors, or the events themselves, without having been personally involved.

What will be presented here is not so much a development of the literature as a group of characteristics in the form of five theses on what separates this literature from other kinds of literature, thereby attempting to give a part of the explanation of the artistic and international impact and success of these works. Some of the theses apply more directly to the theme of traumatic literature and the denial of the right to life, whereas others can be seen as part of a more general development in aesthetics and literature, but together they form a unique constellation of properties.

In short, the theses address 1) the metaphysical absolutes of the field, primarily the ideas of absolute evil, of fate and of not being considered an individual but a member of a group. On a contextual level, the field is marked by 2) a corresponding emptying of all contextual significance, reducing the basic desires to that of escaping death. From that follow two important representational questions. The first 3) concerns the representation of the incomprehensible masses that are victimized, vis-à-vis the presentation of the individual stories, while another 4) concerns the problem of finding meaning when facing the absolutes of evil and death. Finally, 5) this literary field is marked by a close relationship with history, making it what Timothy Garton Ash has called a 'literature of fact', or what could be described as literature's return to the real.

1. The specific metaphysical aspect of the literature of denial of life is its ability to evoke the idea of absolutes in an otherwise contingent world, something that other literature most often cannot provide. The *Endlösung*, the genocide in Rwanda, the deliberate starvation of rural populations in the Ukraine and many other historical events have all come to represent absolute or radical evil, in their total disregard of the rights of both individuals and groups; an evil which usually cannot be ascribed to the evil of any individual, but stems from the sum of the events. This aspect is only reinforced by the often bureaucratic behaviour of those carrying out the deeds, as here, in Elie Wiesel's presentation of disinterestedness and horror side by side:

> The lorries drove toward a forest. The Jews were made to get out. They were made to dig huge graves. And when they had finished their work, the Gestapo began theirs. Without passion, without haste, they slaughtered their prisoners. Each one had to go up to the hole and present his neck. Babies were thrown into the air and the machine gunners used them as targets. (Wiesel, 1974: 3)

From the perceived absoluteness of the evil, the adjoining metaphysical properties also attain an aura of being absolute. The incomprehensible and cumulative horror of the killings becomes absolute horror, but so does the compassion that can be shown under such circumstances. In an otherwise secular and relativistic world, there are few things that give access to metaphysical absolutes in the way that these historical events permit a gaze into incomprehensible evil.

There is a cathartic effect to the literature of genocide, war and disaster, but it is also very different from the effect of the classic dramas. In the tradition of Aristotle's *Poetics*, catharsis is the result of witnessing human beings' unsuccessful attempts to avoid the fate decreed by the gods. This produces a cleansing effect of feeling, which involves compassion for the human characters (Aristotle, 1973: 677), while recognizing the fundamental laws of the universe and its balance of *hubris* and *nemesis*. But in this literature there are no gods to instigate the law, only humans who act as gods, whether it is in the name of historical justice to their people, or the necessary arrangement to bring forward the dialectics of history faster. This order is false, if human life is held to be valuable, so while the literature of denial of life produces an effect similar to that of catharsis, it simultaneously creates a very different feeling, since those who represent absolute power have no right to it, so there cannot be a true confirmation of a universal order.

If there is anything that could be seen as a substitute for this order, it would be the very existence of the testimony, the survival, the change of regime and the general condemnation of a past that points to a history beyond the reign of evil, just as George Orwell, in *Nineteen Eighty-Four*, placed an appendix written in the past tense, after the death of the protagonist, Winston Smith, to suggest that there would be a different time after the rule of Big Brother (Orwell, 1949: 299–302).

The function of the literature on war and genocide could be the renunciation of the evil 'other', in a universal humanistic view of the world order that, in many cases, has replaced a religious view. The validity of this interpretation is supported by historical responses to mass destructions which have also been regarded as almost absolute, but without human beings being responsible. The most obvious example is Voltaire's depiction of the earthquake in Lisbon, both in his 'Poem on the Lisbon Disaster; Or an Examination of the Axiom, "All is Well"', and in *Candide*. To Voltaire, the horror of this event raised the question of theodicy, and ultimately questioned the existence of an almighty god who would allow the mass destruction of man by nature. The metaphysical system came under pressure to explain what fate and justice can mean under such circumstances, eventually acting as a catalyst for the process of secularization. The strong memories and use of the Holocaust and genocides in general as warnings to the future, contrasted with the far less potent problems of finding a metaphysical dimension of modern day catastrophes, such as the tsunami in East Asia on 26 December 2004, make it clear that there is an active metaphysics of evil and of the human which can be grasped in concrete narratives. Theodor W. Adorno was also aware of this shift from the natural to the social as the dominant mode, in the representation of evil in *Negative Dialectics*:

> The earthquake of Lisbon sufficed to cure Voltaire of the theodicy of Leibniz, and the visible disaster of the first nature was insignificant in comparison with the second, social one, which defies human imagination as it distils a real hell from human evil. Our metaphysical faculty is paralyzed because actual events have shattered the basis on which speculative metaphysical thought could be reconciled with experience. (Adorno, 2000: 361)

2. In contrast to the metaphysical absolutes, this literature also conjures up scenarios wherein the key questions are reduced to a matter of life, death and survival. The metaphysical right to one's life is matched by the sheer need to survive as a biological entity, which produces a series of conflicts between individual and group, as Primo Levi, among many others, has depicted in his writings on Auschwitz.

The problem of contextual knowledge as a prerequisite for understanding literature, which was investigated in the previous chapter, is diminished here, because the basic division between life and death is dominant. Unlike the social context, with its distribution of power, money and love, and which is usually the essence of much other literature, there is no societal context that can be meaningfully navigated in war and genocide literature, because it is the literature of a state of emergency, in which everything comes down to the fundamentals. There are social codifications everywhere, even in concentration camps, but they are unstable and always refer back to the fundamental quest for survival. This is unique to this literature, and is part of the explanation for its potential as a truly international literature, since the basics of life place the contingent historical and social conditions in another light, although they are still relevant to the further understanding of the literature. Death establishes a framework which would otherwise be difficult to conceive, as when it is merely a question of a better life which is at stake.

Moreover, the literature concerned with genocides in particular demonstrates the hard choices of saving one's own life or the life of a larger group, such as family, relatives, comrades, countrymen and so on. These are choices that are bewildering, because it is impossible to know whether a sacrifice will be in vain, since the essence of the situation is that there often is no certain rescue. All variations of the Prisoner's dilemma are brought forward, but with uncertain rules, because the nature of genocide and war is a state of emergency, where the most powerful make and change the rules. All the emotions attached to other suffering human beings are thereby conjured up, together with a sense of helplessness.

3. The third thesis is that this literature concerns massive loss of human life and that it therefore struggles to find an adequate representation: how can the individual fates of six million Jews or a million Armenian or Rwandan people be represented in a meaningful way? Through this effort, the literature of denial of life brings into play a representational problem that is linked to the fascination of the social sublime. The idea of the overwhelming masses that cannot be represented as a whole, even though they can be thought of as such, has a significant, yet somewhat overlooked presence in a number of seminal literary works, and is also important in a number of cultural phenomena. The unrepresentable masses, in particular, have sparked the development and canonization of specific literary techniques, and not only within the literature on war and genocide. The social sublime can thus be defined as *the attempt to represent an overwhelming mass of people that cannot be represented as a whole, even though it can be thought of as such*. This is an extension of Immanuel Kant's definitions of the mathematical sublime, where it is possible to have an idea of an object without being able to make an adequate representation (Kant, 1987: 106–113).

Modernist literature, in particular, strongly expresses the desire for the social sublime in works by James Joyce, Virginia Woolf, Ezra Pound, T. S. Eliot, Marcel Proust, William Carlos Williams, Jorge Luis Borges and Giuseppe Ungaretti (Borges, 1999; Eliot, 1971; Pound, 1949; Proust, 1954; Ungaretti, 1969; Williams, 1923; Woolf, 1976). They each dealt with the problem of finding an expression for this feeling or thought, but Dante, William Wordsworth, Honoré de Balzac and Walt Whitman have also given form to this theme (Balzac, 1972; Dante, 1995; Whitman, 1965; Wordsworth, 1975), and, just as the above-mentioned authors, they have done it in a way that produced a comparatively high interest in those works or passages dealing with the social sublime. The social sublime has become a powerful motif in literature, with even more significance after the decline of the divine and the natural sublime. It is also in evidence in the literature of war and genocide, where individual fates are linked to the fates of an incomprehensible number of individuals.

The French filmmaker Claude Lanzmann started a controversy in a reaction to the American director and producer Steven Spielberg's film, *Schindler's List* (Lanzmann, 1994). Lanzmann argued that the Jewish Holocaust during the Nazi regime could not and should not be retold in film scenes reconstructing particular events. In Lanzmann's opinion, the Holocaust cannot be represented, and in his own nine-hour documentary *Shoah*, the strategy is to interview survivors of the Holocaust as well as those who took part in its execution. They bear testimony to the Holocaust while representing just a few among the many. The film thus consists of different attempts to give an impression of the vast number of victims tortured and killed.

It is difficult to ultimately deem Lanzmann or Spielberg right or wrong, since both filmmakers made complex and insightful contributions, but the controversy shows that, concerning the social sublime and its representations, there is much at stake. Confronted with the memory of, and vain attempts to imagine the full scale of suffering in mass killings and genocides, the social sublime presents its most horrible and provoking side, with the task of finding the most adequate representations possible.

In 'Against Holocaust-Sublime: Naive Reference and the Generation of Memory' Zachary Braiterman has argued that the idea of the sublime does not apply to the Holocaust, and presents a subtle argument that does not make use of the most obvious objection to the term, namely its positive connotations of joy and ecstasy. Instead, Braiterman first shows how the Kantian concepts of the mathematical and dynamic sublime do not apply to the historical situation of the Holocaust, and that the neutral position of the observer presupposed by Kant cannot exist, when it comes to the Holocaust. From there he draws attention to Friedrich Schiller's overlooked concept of the pathetically sublime; a term that emphasizes a compassionate aspect, and holds that world history is a sublime object. As such, it is not far from the idea of the social sublime, even though this concept also refers to smaller entities than the world, it too is laden with emotion and empathy, and the pathetic and the social sublime both overcome distances, rather than being dependent on them for enjoyment. Yet Braiterman has difficulties in presenting the vast differences between those who witnessed the Holocaust, and those who merely remember it:

Physical safety represents a critical condition by which one can judge sublime objects of enormous size, objects that threaten by their power, and the sight of human suffering. This safety necessitates spatial and/or temporal distance from the threatening object. It requires that the subject does not actually suffer. In Kant's description, the

object judged sublime never really threatens. We can 'consider an object *fearful* without being afraid *of* it.' The subject feels overwhelmed by '*amazement* bordering on
terror, by horror and a sacred thrill; but since he knows he is safe, this is not actual
fear.' Schiller, for whom moral sublimity trumps physical threat, also knew that people
do not judge their own suffering sublime. Aesthetic judgment is finished when the
subject finds itself in danger. Schiller noted: 'As sublime as a storm at sea may be when
viewed from the shore, those who find themselves on the ship devastated by the storm
are just as little disposed to pass this aesthetic judgment on it.' (Braiterman, 2001: 10)

Even though Braiterman's reading of Schiller is interesting, he misses the point
that almost all readers of Holocaust narratives have not experienced it; some
still deal with personal loss, some have heard first-hand accounts of the events,
but they are not in danger now, yet they share the memory of an unrepresentable loss, a sum of people whose magnitude is present even when the most
personal narratives are told. Hence there is the need for an idea of the sublime,
and the problems of representing the overwhelming.

4. The historical reference to the suffering of overwhelming masses of
people separates literature on war and genocide from the wider field of literature on trauma, which can address both collective and individual traumas,
but which naturally give ample attention to the former (see for example Miller
and Tougaw, 2002). These fields have in common their efforts to give form and
expression to something which may be possible to retell at the level of events,
but whose deeper effects, of emotions and understanding, are problematic
and traumatic. This literature is, therefore, often as much about the cause of
the trauma as the after-effects, as shown, for example, in the work of Imre
Kertész.

Facing the incomprehensible is traditionally one of the *raisons d'être* of literature, and it comes into its own when absolute evil and collective persecution
are at its centre, providing therapeutic ways of integrating memories in a mixture of what can be understood and what will always be hauntingly elusive.
Aside from these functions, there is also a productive tension between the
unbearable memory and the will to put it into words and find a literary form
to express it. Thus, the fourth thesis is that the tension between that to which
literature cannot do justice, and that which only literature can communicate, is
vital to the literature of genocide, war and disaster. This paradoxical division is
emblematically presented by Theodor W. Adorno's dictum on the impossibility
of writing after Auschwitz, and Paul Celan's response in the form of poetry, but
it is also a tension that is reflected in the form and content of the works of this
literature (Adorno, 1975: 66).

5. The discrepancy between event and memory, and, to some extent, between
fact and fiction, is also connected to the fifth thesis, namely that the literature
of denial of life is a literature of fact, whose connection to real references
is important, not only to the ethical validity of the literature, but also for its

aesthetic capabilities. The importance of the factual background to this literature is obvious, if one imagines how outrageous a detailed novel on a fictitious
genocide would be. The historical validity is also important to the experience of
the literature, even though an element of fiction, analogy and allegory can exist
without upsetting the claim to truth. The allegorical strategy can be advanced
further to become the primary strategy of a text, but is then dependent on less
detailed description, and quasi-historical anchoring of the narrative, as is the
case in Franz Kafka's works, where the anonymity of the settings anticipates and
counters any questions of the real reference behind the narrative. Concerning
the uses of analogy, Alvin Rosenfeld refers to Elie Wiesel's refusal to accept
Holocaust literature as literature, because it is or should be a literature of fact,
and not of analogy or of some intertextual relation to antecedents in the literary canon (Rosenfeld, 1980: 22). Although Rosenfeld does not wholly agree
with Wiesel, the point about the aesthetic and moral implications of this literature is underlined, and a cautiousness towards the way in which historical facts
should be handled is evident.

Timothy Garton Ash has made the distinction between facticity and veracity
in literature, where the former deals with facts that can be established with
some certainty, for example the date of a certain battle, the existence of a particular concentration camp, etc. Although facts can be hard to establish, this is
something that historians can do, making cumulative assessments of what is,
beyond any reasonable doubt, the truth about the past. Things get more complicated, Garton Ash argues, when it comes to events which people, often an
author, have witnessed. The most outrageously invented stories can be countered with facts that question their validity, but the finer details of life during a
time of war and persecution often depends on singular witnesses.[5] Garton Ash
admits that there is often no certain way to tell true from false, however he
argues that the aesthetics of the text can reveal something about its relationship
to the truth:

> Veracity is revealed in tone, style, voice. It takes us back to the artistic reasons for
> defending this line. You can often tell just from internal, stylistic evidence when a
> writer has strayed. Take a now notorious example: the book published in 1995 as
> *Bruchstücke* (in English, *Fragments*) by Benjamin Wilkomirski, which purported to be
> the memories of a man who survived the Nazi death camps as a Polish Jewish child.
> It is now established beyond reasonable doubt that the author was a Swiss musician of
> troubled past and disturbed mind, originally called Bruno Grosjean, who had never
> been near a Nazi death camp – but had imagined himself into that past, that other self.
> Reading *Fragments* now, one is amazed that it could ever have been hailed as it was. The
> wooden irony ('Majdanek is no playground'), the hackneyed images (silences broken
> by the sound of cracking skulls), the crude, hectoring melodrama (his father squashed
> against the wall by a transporter, dead women with rats crawling on their stomachs).
> Material which, once you know it is fraudulent, is truly obscene. But even before one
> knew that, all the aesthetic alarms should have sounded. For every page has the

authentic ring of falsehood. / Compare this with the great books of true witness. Of course there are large variations in tone and style between these works. Many none-theless have a certain voice in common: one of pained, sober, yet often ironical or even sarcastic veracity, which speaks from the very first line. Take, for example, and contrast with Wilkomirski, the first line of Levi's *If This Is a Man*: 'It was my good fortune to be deported to Auschwitz only in 1944, that is, after the German government had decided, owing to the growing scarcity of labour, to lengthen the average life-span of the prisoners destined for elimination; it conceded noticeable improvements in the camp routine and temporarily suspended killings at the whim of individuals.' How could we not believe this? (Garton Ash, 2002: 66–67)

This linking of the aesthetic consequences of the real and the true is important to the idea of realism, but it has also been explored further by modern avant-garde movements, described most pertinently by Hal Foster in terms of 'the return of the real', a return that refers to a non-metaphorical expression in art, where the idea of meaning is not as important as the very presence of certain objects, and the effects this presence has (Foster, 1996; Gumbrecht, 2004). The literature of the denial of life follows a parallel track, because the objective may not always be to explain and find meaning, but simply to present. Whether the artistic success of the literature of the denial of life is connected to the move-ments in avant-garde art is an impossible question to answer, but it should be clear that there is a shared aesthetic, as well as shared fascinations and a need for expression.

The dependence on references to 'the real' of much of the literature of the denial of life underlines how this literature must viewed as a larger field of works wherein the singular works always relate to other texts, much more than is the case with other fields, although effects of realism have a widespread importance in literature in general. As Rosenfeld argues, the literature of the Holocaust is a literature where novels, testimonies and documents are inter-twined, and form a larger whole held together by a common historical referent (Rosenfeld, 1980: 34), while acknowledging that Holocaust literature has had to respond to general developments in literature, and its ways of representing the past.

To sum up, some of the defining properties presented apply to many texts, others are more specifically related to the field, but it is the connection of these elements that is unique. As mentioned, this is a complicated field, because there is so much suffering and historical emotion at stake in this literature, and because the whole question of reading this literature aesthetically can be problematic. It is remarkable that the works that stand out as literary achieve-ments dominate both the specific field of genocide and war literature, as well as having yielded works which have entered a wider international canon. Once this is acknowledged, the specific aesthetic possibilities of this literature should also be investigated, and taken seriously as contributions to the development of literature. The combination of metaphysical absolutes and biological funda-mentals as constitutive parts of the text, with otherwise much canonized elements such as the social sublime, and the integration of traumatic experi-ence with a high dependence on references to the real, makes this literature unique. It provides a frame of reference for the unique and strong inner coher-ence of the field, and hence the necessity of reading across it, to see how the diverse works add to this transnational literature.

Genocides

Imre Kertész has pointed out that there has not been much truly great litera-ture written on the experience of the Holocaust, modestly leaving himself out, but mentioning Paul Celan, Tadeusz Borowski, Primo Levi, Jean Améry, Ruth Klüger, Claude Lanzmann and Miklós Radóti as some of the ten or so writers whom he thinks qualify (Kertész, 2001: 268). Certainly, he is being too critical, but there is a vast difference between the numerous testimonies that have been published in various forms, valuable in other ways, and the few authors who have also made an impact as writers who have written about the Holocaust. However, as has been shown, some of these works have had remarkable impor-tance to the general perception of the Holocaust, proving that literary attributes matter to the way in which it is recollected.

The internationally canonized literature on other twentieth century geno-cides is also scarce. Kurt Vonnegut has written on the Armenian genocide which took place during the First World War, in *Bluebeard*, while Philip Gourevitch received praise for his book on the genocide in Rwanda, *We Wish To Inform You That Tomorrow We Will Be Killed With Our Families*. Regarding communist mass killings and suppression, the writers who have received the most international exposure are Alexander Solzhenitsyn and Gao Xingjian, but they are only a few of many writers who have dealt with this, just as other kinds of systematized suppression are recounted by numerous authors, such as that in South Africa by writers such as Nadine Gordimer and J. M. Coetzee, in Chile by Isabel Allende, in South America, generally, by Gabriel García Márquez and Eduardo Galeano, and recently Aleksandar Hemon on Bosnia. Edward Quinn has, in *History in Literature*, given a comprehensive overview of the impact of historical events on literature, as well as the lack of monumental works on a number of seminal events in history (Quinn, 2004).

This section takes particular interest in works by Primo Levi, Georges Perec, Kurt Vonnegut, Philip Gourevitch, Aleksandar Hemon and Philip Roth. Apart from their international recognition, one reason for focusing on these authors is their divergence of experience. Levi was deported to Auschwitz, Perec's mother died in a concentration camp, and Kurt Vonnegut was born after the

Armenian genocide, but had been a prisoner of war and witness to the bombing of Dresden in 1945. Philip Gourevitch witnesses the aftermath of the Rwandan genocide, although he was not present during the genocide itself, whereas Aleksandar Hemon became a refugee, as the war in Bosnia evolved. Finally, Philip Roth has written a counterfactual history of the United States during the Second World War. Another reason for analysing these writers is the great divergence in their formal approaches to writing on traumatic experiences, which will be at the centre of attention in the following.

Primo Levi is the most internationally canonized Holocaust survivor, together with Imre Kertész, who emerged later. It both seems unlikely and is very telling of the gradual development of a consciousness of the Holocaust that Levi's central work, *If This Is a Man*, was published in Italy in 1947, without getting a fraction of the attention it would later receive. It was only in 1958 that the book was republished, and then quickly became an internationally acclaimed book.

Levi's narrative is marked by a sobriety of style, where revenge or forgiveness are not issues. Instead, the detailed facts of life in the camp speak for themselves, and produce a moving and often unbearable reading:

> Then for the first time we became aware that our language lacks words to express this offence, the demolition of a man. In a moment, with almost prophetic intuition, the reality was revealed to us: we had reached the bottom. It is not possible to sink lower than this; no human condition is more miserable than this, nor could it conceivably be so. Nothing belongs to us anymore; they have taken away our clothes, our shoes, even our hair; if we speak, they will not listen to us, and if they listen, they will not understand. (Levi, 1979: 32–33)

Levi's survival is a tragic survival, because it is not at all representative of what went on. Almost all the deported Italians died, and Italians died in higher numbers than other groups because they understood less of the German language in which commands were given, and they found it more difficult to communicate with other detainees. Levi writes that the railway cart that transported him to Auschwitz was by far the 'luckiest', with four survivors out of forty-five, thereby quietly illustrating the unlikelihood of survival (Levi, 1979: 23–24). Levi is very cautious about bringing attention to all the lost lives, and by making smaller groups very concrete – the people in a certain transport, the people in a certain cart, the people left behind at the infirmary when the Germans abandoned Auschwitz and began the death marches – he makes it very clear how impossible it is to grasp the individuality of these people, although each of their lives deserves it, as much as those who lived to tell about the horrors. In this way Levi very subtly gives the social sublime a presence in his autobiographical testimony.

As Levi stresses the lack of linguistic skills among the Italian prisoners as one of the main reasons for their extremely low survival rate, the necessity of learning new rules in order to survive is also a constant feature of Levi's narrative, and the way in which the rules of the outside were replaced by a new set of rules that were never quite transparent to the prisoners. All they knew was that failing to live up to the rules could be fatal, and they always lived in anxiety of not living up to the rules, or of simply being victims of the random use of power. The intertwining between death and the distortion of social knowledge that used to govern exchange and communication is, here more than in any other literature, dominant in the narrative.

If reference in Holocaust literature should be non-allegoric, Levi attains this objective, but makes it complex at the same time, by inserting such details that underscore the absolute horror and effectiveness of the killing machines that the camps were, contrasted with the daily life in the camp and all the problems in it, and the efforts to maintain hope and health. Dalay M. Sachs has identified two major ways of making the narrative complex. The most important trait lies in Levi's use of shifting points of view and shifting temporalities. Even though *If This Is a Man* seems to read like a straight-forward story with one protagonist and a linear progression in time, it is in fact more complicated. Besides being highly reflexive regarding his experiences and the responses of people to the many horrible situations in which they found themselves, Levi shifts between singular and plural voices, which is an obvious choice, given the shared conditions, but not the shared survival and way of living through the hell of the camp. But even more sophisticated are the temporal changes in the narration, which to Sachs:

> de-fictionalizes the text whose diary-like tone of narration captures us precisely with the authority of its storytelling voice, but thereby risks suggesting a false genre, i.e., fiction, for the events here recorded. The interruption of a voice which can explain events that were indecipherable to Levi at the time he was first deported to Auschwitz lets us know the simple, but crucial, detail that he survived. (Sachs, 2001: 759)

Second, it is important to Levi that his Auschwitz experiences are not constructed as the ultimate Other, but understood within the cultural canon and framework that Levi carried with him. Sachs calls this an intellectual resistance to the experience (Sachs, 1995: 769), but it is also an important aspect of avoiding the kitsch to which Kertész refers, when discussing authors who lend credence to the idea of the unspeakable and absolute Other in contrast to normal civilization. The absolute evil must mix with the historically contingent, in order to present this.

The very length of Levi's testimony is also not to be overlooked as an important aspect. This is not just in order to record the extent of the atrocities, but also to present himself as a multi-facetted person who tries to make sense of the events within a larger context. If there is a certain function that the modes of fiction and style of literature can contribute to this subject, it is not least the ability to narrate not only about the atrocities, but also about the ordinary lives and desires of the victims, and to see them in a larger framework.

The sobriety of style and the meticulous depiction of the daily life in the camp are also the central traits of Aleksandar Solzhenitsyn's *One Day in the Life of Ivan Denisovich*. In an interview, Levi acknowledges the kinship with Solzhenitsyn when it comes to the descriptions of life in the camps, but otherwise he thought of himself as a very different writer with different material, principally because the Soviet camps were not killing camps, although the hard labour took its toll. The almost metaphysical evil behind the plan of the death camps was of a different order. Levi also agrees that, at a formal level, Solzhenitsyn is not a great writer, although he thinks his legacy is secured by *One Day in the Life of Ivan Denisovich* (Camon, 1989: 48).

Levi was one of relatively few survivors of one of the worst of the German camps, a fact that limits the number of first-hand literature that there can be about the subject. However, taking a stance in a difficult debate and defending director Roberto Benigni's *Life is Beautiful*, Imre Kertész has recognized that there can be no absolute ownership to the memory:

> Holocaust survivors will have to face the facts: as they grow weaker with age, Auschwitz is slipping out of their hands. But to whom will it belong? Obviously, to the next generation, and to the one after that – as long as they continue to lay claim to it, of course. (Kertész, 2001: 267)

There is thus a younger group of writers, who were not directly in touch with the labour and killing camps, but who were the children left behind, growing up with only few memories of their parents. To these belong the French writer Georges Perec, whose father died as a soldier in the French army in the first days of the invasion in May 1940, and whose mother were deported by the Germans and died in a concentration camp, while Perec grew up in relative safety among family members in Vichy-France.

Perec is particularly interesting in this context, because his authorship contrasts strongly with that of Primo Levi. He was involved in radical formal experiments as a member of the avant-garde group OuLiPo, where he excelled at making experiments such as a detective novel without the letter 'e', or in the construction of large palindromes. Perec broke through as young writer with the short novel *Things: A Story from the Sixties* in the early 1960s, that described the boredom of a materialistic society, but he was generally unknown to a wider audience until the 1970s, with the publication of his *Life – A User's Manual*, in 1978, which was soon established as an instant classic. It is in *W, Or the Memory of a Childhood*, from 1974, that he most directly addresses his traumatic past, in a novel which is full of formal experiments, but also has a thematic imperative that complements it. One could argue that this narrative is even more heartbreaking than the tale of a survivor, since the loss of his parents and the void that follows is not a story of survival despite all sufferings, which would have injected some optimism.

Perec's authorship is an unlikely combination of formal experiment and historical recollection, and his canonization could also be said to be unlikely, yet he now stands as the most eminent French writer of the 1970s. Heralded for his formal experiments, it is probably equally important that he incorporated his own persona, and his personal dreams and ambitions, into his literature, which in both its form and content pay homage to a inquisitive, multi-facetted way of approaching the world, while maintaining a central fascination with the complexity of life. To Perec, writing was obviously central, but he also composed a much too lengthy and humorous list of 'Things to do before I die' (Perec, 1996: 124–126). Much in the same vein, some of central characters in *Life – A User's Manual* have designated passions, while the novel as such is a catalogue of stories of different ways of life, many of them involving the idea of an intense focus on some activity, whether it is racing, meditation or puzzles. In other works there are different examples of a futile restlessness, such as his debut, *Things*, which criticizes consumer society, and *A Man Who Sleeps*, in which the protagonist is a student whose spleen renders him incapable of taking action. The attitude of Perec's work and its themes are thus split between two ideals: being focused or being manifold.

But whereas these three basic attitudes of being inactive, focused or endlessly curious present themselves as options to the protagonists in most of Perec's work, the world of the island W in *W, Or the Memory of a Childhood* is an allegory about a concentration camp, combined with overtones of antique athletic culture in which privileges are earned on the basis of performance, and severe, often fatal, punishments are distributed on the same basis. Discipline and violence rule on W; instead of the ennui of modern living, survival is all that matters.

The allegory of the concentration camps that killed Perec's mother and millions more is intertwined with recollections from his childhood, in which his attempts to remember being with his mother and father yield only vague, if emotionally laden fragments. Joanna Spiro sees this vagueness as both a consequence of Perec's situation, and as something that has important consequences for the effects of the narrative:

> Perec's memoir sets itself apart from other accounts of Holocaust events in its emphasis on the scarcity and unreliability of his memories and in its use of fantasy. With these two elements Perec provocatively differentiates *W* from testimonies of both the survivors of the Nazi death camps and the children of the survivors (the 'second generation'). Primo Levi, for instance, sees his imperative to testify as a survivor as following from the clarity and intensity of his memories: 'At Auschwitz, and on the long road returning home, I had seen and experienced things that appeared important not only for me, things that imperiously demanded to be told . . . I have not forgotten a single thing . . . not a detail was lost.' Perec, in contrast, directs our attention to the gaps and falsehoods that riddle the few memories of the wartime years he retains. On the question of the reliability of memory, historically and ethically crucial to accounts of

the Holocaust, Perec gives way before he can even be questioned. (Spiro, 2001: 116; see also Bellos, 1995: 545–555)

In *W*, Perec tells of the few pictures he still has of his father and mother, and of the vague memories he has, and how they have changed. This aspect is made particularly clear by including a text, set in bold to distinguish it from the rest of the text, written by a then fifteen years younger Perec, in the mid-fifties, about the pictures and the lives of his mother and father, ending with an account of his last view of his mother at the Gare de Lyon in Paris, where she had brought him to the train that would take him south, and into safety. The quotidian nature of this moment, a mother buying her son a magazine and taking him to the train that will carry him to his relatives, combined with the following dry account of the fate of his mother, who stayed in Paris, believing she was safe, but who was eventually deported to a concentration camp, most likely Auschwitz, makes the recollection even more disturbing.

Perec then goes on to correct his notes in a series of twenty-six numbered items, including comments on the misspellings he made, only to end the chapter by stating that these corrections really do not add anything new, and that no matter how much he wishes that he could add something new, or something substantially different from the previous corrections, he is not capable of doing anything but making repetitions in his writing. Yet this repetitive writing is the inscription of the memory of his parents, and the confirmation of Perec's own life (Perec, 1996: 32).

Perec's combination of his real, personal memoirs and the uncertainty of the circumstances of his mother's death, and the allegory of the camps and real personal memoir, produces a very special combination, presenting a singular history enfolded in the larger realm of the Holocaust, intertwined with a generalized allegory that criticizes an element in civilization from the Antique to present, that has produced inhuman societies. The allegory can be seen as a search, to some quite provocative, for the deeper structures that allow a nation that once praised itself for its civilization to transform into a tyranny. By intertwining the much praised ideals of Western culture, the Greek Antiquity in which democracy was born, and the Olympic ideals of fair competition and the striving for the utmost man can attain, with the cultures of discipline, control, inhuman law-obedience and the lack of respect for the lives of others, Perec implicitly claims that these things go together, or rather, that there is a fine balance between the good and evil outcomes of these characteristics within a culture. The reference to the real is central to his narrative, because the allegory could hardly stand alone without being a bewildering unhistorical account, but in the context of the orphan's story, it becomes a powerful sphere of reflection about the evil and violence in culture, making a sublime gesture from the allegory to all the sufferings down through the centuries, not least by letting his book end with a reference to the camps of the Pinochet regime in Chile, which were co-incidentally situated on islands much like those on which the young Perec had envisioned his story taking place.

Kurt Vonnegut's novel, *Bluebeard*, is about the Armenian genocide that began in 1915, The Second World War and modern art, brought together in a way that highlights several problems of representation. The novel is the meta-autobiography of Rabo Karabekian, born in 1916 in America, the son of Armenian genocide survivors. He writes it after being influenced by meeting a popular author, Circe Berman, who has unexpectedly entered his life, and constantly questions his views and way of life.[6] The book switches back and forth between the present and the past, beginning with the parents' rescue from the genocide, through the protagonist's adventures as a young commercial artist in an advertising agency, his the experiences of the Second World War, and his career as an abstract expressionist after the war (Vonnegut, 1988).

The representational challenge of the autobiography is to represent the life of a human being in all its complexity, whereas the suffering of genocide and war present the problems of giving expression to a mass of people, and convey the magnitude of their accumulated pain and loss. The identity as an abstract expressionist, to which Karabekian clings at the beginning of the book, is also an evasion of the issue of representing, his most famous painting being three huge monochrome canvasses. But during the novel he returns to figurative painting, and works on a secret project which is revealed over two chapters at the end of the book, namely that the once monochrome paintings have been turned into a large and detailed tableau that represents figures of the Second World War, both real and allegorical (Vonnegut, 1988: 241–253).

The conflict between the abstract and the figurative had been thematized earlier in the book, when Karabekian discovers that Berman has replaced the abstract expressionist masterpieces by Jackson Pollock and others in his foyer, with Victorian pictures of girls playing. Karabekian is furious, and insists that the abstract paintings are negations of art that work as 'black holes' for anyone who sees them. Berman replies that it seems like a lot for these little paintings to do, and in return she dismisses the idea that her Victorian paintings are kitsch:

'Try thinking what the Victorians thought when they looked at them, which was how sick and unhappy so many of these happy, innocent little girls would be in just a little while – diphtheria, pneumonia, smallpox, miscarriages, violent husbands, poverty, widowhood, prostitution – death and burial in potter's field.' (Vonnegut, 1988: 116)

This narrative mode is not dissimilar to the way that Anne Frank's *The Diary of a Young Girl* works, with its balancing of hope and despair, of her dreams of American movie stars and the reality of the hideout, but not a description of the destiny that was to overtake her, which is ever present to the reader. It is the same technique Georges Perec develops in *W*, by not telling or guessing too much about the details of his parents' deaths, but instead presenting a picture of the trajectories of lives that were broken.

Vonnegut does not promote any ideal mode of representation, but what *Bluebeard* achieves is the highlighting of how different strategies can work together in a such a way that even abstract expressionism becomes of value: its utter lack of meaning and symbolism serve as reminders of the impossibility of fully representing or comprehending both the Armenian genocide and the Second World War. However, it is also obvious that the muteness of the abstract canvasses is not enough, and does not do justice to the stories that are almost untold, such as those of the Armenian genocide.[7]

In *Slaughterhouse-Five*, Vonnegut's definite breakthrough work, based on his experiences as a prisoner of war at the time Dresden was, from a military standpoint, needlessly bombed four months before the end of Second World War, the problems of representation are also a central part of the novel's self-reflection and form (Vonnegut, 1969: 10–11). As in *Bluebeard*, the story has multiple levels; after the opening chapter tells of the novel's coming into being, the life of Vonnegut's alter ego, Billy Pilgrim, is told from the perspective of his war experience, his quotidian post-war life and his life as a prisoner of the very fictitious aliens, the Tralfamadorians, who can skip back and forth in time. As in the discussions on monumental realism and abstract expressionism in *Bluebeard*, this incorporation of an element of science fiction and of middle class life provide contrasts to the events of the war. Middle class life underlines how unbelievable these events are, or how surreal it is that the same person who experiences the chaos of the war and of the bombed city, can also live a relatively carefree mid-Western suburban life, while the Tralfamadorians in all their improbability seem just as likely as some of the events in the war and provide a non-human perspective on the strange behaviour of the people of Earth (Vonnegut, 1969: 83). Thus the fictive and unrealistic framework reflects the unlikelihood of the historical events, and mocks the attempts to understand them fully.

The Tralfamadorians' ability to travel in time, which Billy Pilgrim is also given after being captured, is unlimited, but only to what will happen historically. There is a strange balance between freedom and determinism in this way of experiencing time; even though the aliens can witness their own Armageddon, they cannot prevent it, but only concentrate on experiencing happier times, hence they have distinct levels of freedom and determinism, in strong contrast to human beings. But to make history seem more pre-determined is also to give it more meaning, which is impossible, when one is faced with the mass destruction of human beings, and the contradictory logic of the Tralfamadorian universe is thus an extrapolation of the human universe, wherein the struggle between finding meanings and causes conflicts with the desire to claim that there can be none.

Vonnegut's technique of mixing representations of both war and genocide with the modes of comedy and science fiction has proved to be successful in the international literary system, not least because it possesses a humour that is not offensive, but has a function in portraying the experiences. As in Georges Perec's authorship, it shows how mixed modes and highly inventive strategies can work without distorting the seriousness of the reference to historical events.

The early 1990s witnessed two genocides that seemed, to the world public, to come out of the blue. One was of great magnitude, namely the Hutu killings of Tutsis in Rwanda in 1994, in which a million people were killed in a matter of months, on the basis of their ethnicity. The war in Bosnia was more complicated, as Croats, Serbs and Bosnian Muslims were at war with one another other and crimes of war were committed by all sides, but there were also events that could be characterized as ethnic cleansings, and thus attempts to carry out a genocide, such as the mass killings in Srebrenica, in July 1995.

One of the few related narratives that has had an international reception is *Nowhere Man*, written in English by Aleksandar Hemon. He left Bosnia just before the war broke out, and quickly established himself, with the publication of two books, as an innovative and profound writer. *Nowhere Man* is a complex narrative that deals more with his alter ego's experiences as an immigrant to the United States than with the war in Bosnia. Yet the war is the pivotal theme, which is thematized both by the protagonist's problems of explaining to the Americans what the war is about, and what he has left behind (Hemon, 2002: 178). The most direct representation of the situation in Bosnia comes in the form of a letter sent to the protagonist, Josef, by his friend Mirza, who is still in Bosnia and in constant danger of being the victim of a sniper. In a chapter of its own, the four pages, written in a deliberately less than perfect English to reflect the translation that Jozef Pronek has made, give a moving expression of the new situation, of the loneliness and the horror that people experience. One passage is about how snipers seem to just toy with the frightened people in the city, but also how they are merciless, and the evil of their warfare is exemplified by their killing of a young couple in love. The snipers create a shared condition for the people in the city, making the simplest movement outdoors a matter of life and death. Another passage in the letter shows how the war cripples the capacity for empathy, when the sight of a dead man means less than that of a dead horse:

> I saw a horse kill himself on Treskavica. We carried this man which had to hold his stomach with hand so it doesn't fall out. He was screaming all the time, and we must run. But we ran by one unite, they had camp nearby the edge of one cliff – you look down, and it is just one big deep hole in the earth. This man died finally, so we stop to have little water and we are sitting there, we cannot breath. It is so high there is not air. We see their horse, who carried their munition, very skinny and hungry and sad The horse goes slowly to the edge, we think he wants some grass there. Some soldiers yell, Come back! But he walks slowly and then he stops on the edge. We watch him three meters away. He turns around, looks at us directly in our eyes, like person, big, wet eyes and then just jumps – hop! He just jumps and we can hear remote echo of his body

hitting stones. I never saw anything so much sad. // I am sorry I talk too much. Me in Sarajevo have nobody to talk, just each other, nobody wants to listen to these stories. I cannot talk more. You talk now. I am waiting for your letter. You must write me. Send me one book, I can read little English language, maybe one detective novel, maybe something about children. See I'm little crazy. Write me. (Hemon, 2002: 133–134)

Much as Levi stressed the problems of giving expression to the situation, Hemon's letter addresses the problems of speaking about the war, both for those who are in the middle of it, and for those who try to give an expression of it from a distance, and in this situation, the need for a literary rendering of the events is implicitly given.

Hemon has been rightly praised for his subtle and elegant English prose, both in its own right, and as being particularly impressive, considering that he had taken up writing in English only a few years prior to his debut. At the same time, he also experiments with the inclusion of incorrect English as a stylistic feature. Pronek, the protagonist of *Nowhere Man*, makes several mistakes which are often corrected by other characters in the novel, and more radically, the important letter from his friend Mirza which is translated by Pronek, about his experiences during the war in Bosnia, is, as mentioned, written in a more broken English. The use of incorrect language in large passages is a deliberate narrative device that can also be found in works such as Mark Twain's *Huckleberry Finn* and William Faulkner's *The Sound and the Fury*, as well as in Sam Selvon's *The Lonely Londeners*, Don DeLillo's *The Names*, which actually incorporated parts of the writing of a ten-year-old and lately in the novels of Jonathan Safran Foer, *Everything Is Illuminated* and *Extremely Close and Incredibly Loud*, which also address the mass destruction of people (DeLillo, 1982; Faulkner, 1990; Foer, 2002 and 2005; Selvon, 1956; Twain, 1977: 3). The incorrect dialogue in Hemon's writings is more wide-spread, yet less radical, but both modes provide the text with some interesting elements. First, the passages differentiate themselves from the rest of the narrative and suggest a naïve, less calculating voice that struggles to tell something honestly and straightforwardly, delivering a message which is anti-authoritarian and democratic in the sense that those who cannot speak eloquently are given a voice anyway. Second, the liberation from the norms of proper writing and speech makes way for play with the language that can be joyful through both the sound and the rhythm of the words, and the gliding into other, unintended meanings. The migrant author has the advantage of being able to present such writing with the pathos of someone who has experienced something like this, and in many ways this kind of experience is a prerequisite. Hemon's use is particularly convincing, although in the final analysis it is very difficult for an outsider to validate the realism of such speech.

Hemon's narrative runs parallel to his own history as a man who became a refugee by chance, being abroad while things developed in Bosnia, and he uses that situation to create a portrait of a man who is out of step with history; a tragicomic figure who is caught between a longing for less identity and less history, and for taking history upon him as an individual who actually has a choice in the middle of a war. This very much echoes the situation that Milan Kundera's protagonists face, where the dilemma between collective engagement and individual desires is played out as two valid problems set against each other, precisely because collective identity does not present itself as supreme to the individual's own creation of identity and pursuit of happiness. As in Kundera's novels, this also leads to a complex narration in Hemon's novel, with an undecided outcome to the dilemma.

The last major genocide of the twentieth century took place in Rwanda in 1994, and it has been recounted in Philip Gourevitch's *We Wish To Inform You That Tomorrow We Will Be Killed With Our Families*, which draws on both journalistic traditions for research and novelistic descriptions and dialogue (Gourevitch, 1998). Like many other testimonies written shortly after the events, Gourevitch's is sober and factual, and lets the events and testimonies speak for themselves. Gourevitch was not a first-hand witness to the genocide, but he travelled extensively in Rwanda in 1995, and it is clearly an ambition of his to give a voice to people's stories, not least because, especially in the West, the Rwandan genocide is at risk of being less remembered than it should be, given the magnitude of the crimes. This also means that Gourevitch has to include a substantial amount of background material about both the people and state of Rwanda, and about the international political dimensions, such as the geography and history of the country, as well as the problematic role of the United Nations.

Gourevitch's position as a journalistic researcher rather than a first-hand witness allows for some special perspectives. He can give voice to several witness accounts, often with an extensive representation that conjures up a feeling of witnessing the events, and orchestrated into a composition that does not follow the linear form of the memoir or personal testimony. He can also tell about his impressions of Rwanda a year after the genocide, from a completely different position than that of those who experienced the months of terror. It is worth noticing at least two things about his strategies for presenting this: First, Gourevitch often comments on the beauty of things, from skeletons to the landscapes of Rwanda. The first type of observation, in particular, could be controversial and offensive, but Gourevitch argues that the human skeleton simply is beautiful, just as nobody would argue that a landscape where genocide had taken place would, per se, have to be ugly. Gourevitch's impressions help to enhance the incomprehensible fact of the genocide, just as when he cannot tell if one of the few dead bodies he sees is a person asleep, or a corpse. Second, Gourevitch repeatedly quotes classics from the Western canon, on human nature and power, as epitaphs to the chapters or in the text. This prevents the reader from writing off the genocide as an expression of a certain tribal logic, and instead brings attention to the elements of modernity in the genocide: the use of mass media, the fabrication of propaganda, the organization of small squads that spread terror but which are not a part of government controlled forces, and the use of disinformation to pacify the international community. *We Wish To Inform You That Tomorrow We Will Be Killed With Our Families* is thus an intelligent composition of many elements that are disparate in object and tone, but which come together to form a single strong expression.

Another work on the Rwandan genocide, *A Sunday at the Pool in Kigali* by Gil Courtemanche enters a problematic, yet interesting field, with its use of a protagonist who is fictitious, yet who tells about a real event (Courtemanche, 2003). Courtemanche struggles to find a convincing way of writing, as Phil Clark also notes that Courtemanche should be praised for bringing the subject of the Rwandan genocide to a literary audience, but also that he struggles to find a balance between personal testimony and the outright polemic, and that he is not convincing in either. Clark calls for the angry voice of the Rwandans themselves, and it has come forward in a mediated form in Gourevitch's book, where he draws clear lines by admitting that he is not a witness, but that he can give voice to those who saw what happened (Clark, 2003).

Philip Roth's *The Plot Against America* combines a counterfactual history of what would happen if Charles Lindbergh had run against Franklin D. Roosevelt in the presidential election in 1940 and had won based on a programme of non-interference with the war in Europe, combined with an undercurrent of anti-Semitism that would eventually get out of control (Roth, 2004). Roth's novel ends with a surprising twist that portrays Lindbergh himself as the victim of a plot, leading back to the kidnapping and killing of his child in 1932, which in the novel was a setup by the Nazis that enabled them to control Lindbergh. The Lindbergh child was not killed in Roth's story, but taken to Germany and raised there secretly. At the same time Roth lets history get back on track in 1942 with the reinstallation of Roosevelt in the White House after the death of Lindbergh, and there is war against Japan and Germany. However, the great accomplishment of the novel is that it tells the story of a small Jewish family and their reactions to changes in what they thought was a stable democracy, but would in a short time turn into the site of pogroms. The plot-turn comes at last minute: the United States is about to go to war with Canada, the death of Lindbergh in a flight accident is blamed on a Jewish conspiracy and the equivalent of the Nurnberg laws is about to be imposed. Unable to handle the pressure and the questions of the all too well-informed young Philip Roth, his mother sends him to bed:

> Bed – as though as a place of warmth and comfort, rather than an incubator for dread, bed still existed. / War with Canada was far les of an enigma to me than what Aunt Evelyn was going to use for a toilet during the night. As best I could understand, the United States was at last entering into the worldwide war, not on the side of England and the British Commonwealth, whom everyone had expected we would support while FDR was president, but on the side of Hitler and Hitler's allies. (Roth, 2004: 354)

In the appendix, Roth has reprinted a speech by Lindbergh, to show how the argument for the United States avoiding engagement in Europe is partly based on allegations of a Jewish interest in dragging America into the war. As in any good counterfactual narrative, there were potentials in the real world that could have gained force and become dominant (see also Ferguson, 1997). At the same time, it is also a strong history because it gives an account of how discrimination can accelerate, and how restricted the opportunities for the Jews in Europe were, with respect to migrating and escaping the fate coming from without, since the normal reaction is to maintain hope for a long time, and wait for things to return to normal, especially if it seems like small adaptations are all that are needed. Finally, there is a tragicomic perspective to Roth's novel, namely that one could consider the actual historical outcome as a great fortune, rather than the inevitable result of the struggle between good and evil. If the United States had not gone into the war, if anti-Semitism had somehow spread, things could have been very different and much worse. It makes the well-known history stronger, but more contingent, when it carries a trace of some other potential path.

What also makes Roth's novel interesting is how the limits of the counterfactual present themselves, or at least, the extent to which Roth has decided to limit his narrative. The Holocaust and its magnitude, for example, are introduced very early, to make it clear that this will not be questioned, as the reader quickly has grasped that other historical knowledge is turned upside-down, but also that the Holocaust is part of the narrative no matter what else will happen (Roth, 2004: 4). A counterfactual novel in which the Holocaust is prevented could be imagined, or one where the whole Second World War as such never took place, if, for example, France and England had put their foot down when Germany militarized the Rhineland in 1936, or something similar, yet that would be extremely offensive, not least to the victims of the war. Fiction cannot retract the actual suffering of the world, but only try to give an impression of it. Still, Roth could also have gone further and let the plot continue and have the Nazis triumph, as Robert Harris has done in *Fatherland* (Harris, 1992), but is up to the reader to decide how that would have been. Just as any experiment can be broken off, *The Plot Against America* breaks off at the time where the point has been sufficiently made, without the need for exaggeration.

The contrast between Gourevitch's reliance on witnesses and the sober retelling of events, and Roth's counterfactual description, are very indicative of a more or less natural evolution in the means of expression that, for each event, must begin with a simple retelling, before the story can be rendered in other, more complex modes that incorporate allegory, like Perec, science fiction, like Vonnegut or counterfactual narrative, like Roth. This is much in line with the development sketched by Daniel R. Schwarz in his typology of autobiography, realism, myth, and fable, before ending up with fantasy (Fridman, 2000; Schwarz, 1999: 40–45). The latter genres thrive on the general public knowledge of events, which has also been established by testimonies.

Another and more important aspect of this literature is that it takes part in the discursive features described before, the absolute evil, the basics of survival, the social sublimity, the addressing of trauma and the use of real references, no matter how it tells its story, because it will always be a literature, as Alvin Rosenfeld points out, that should be seen in connection to a larger field, which is a transnational field that has expanded as new wars and genocides have taken place, and where old traumas and fresh memories intersect in this area of world literature.

Disaster, war, and witness literature

Genocides are unsurpassed in their evil planning, but history and literature are filled with natural disasters, wars and civil terrors that sometimes supersede the scale of genocides, or which can be seen as representing the same kind of evil. The number of people who were starved to death during the famine of the 1950s Chinese 'Great Leap Forward', or the number of dead soldiers in the First and Second World Wars, comprises more people than does the Holocaust, and the Russians killed in the wars alone comprise more than three times the number of Holocaust victims. The plague in Europe of 1348–50 was of the same magnitude, relative to the total population at the time, but these events were not planned in the same way as genocides, making the idea of absolute evil less relevant in these instances (Gray and Oliver, 2004; Larsen, 2004). Conversely, the theodicy problems that arose from the earthquake in Lisbon can be said to have generated the same kinds of considerations of the absolute evil involved in the taking of human lives. In the following section, the representation of natural disasters and war in literature will be surveyed, before turning to the more general question of the role of witnesses and testimony in literature. More specifically, it comes from the point of view of authors of contemporary literature who have been honoured by the Nobel committee. This also examines the question of why the literature of denial of life has been very well represented as a prize winning literature.

Natural disasters have not had a great influence on world literature, but there are seminal occurrences of them. One of the most notable uses is by Giovanni Boccaccio in *The Decameron*, where the plague sets the framework for the escape of ten young people into the countryside, who tell their stories while the dangers of the epidemic lessen. There is an interesting double effect to this narrative position: the gravity of history is felt, and the delightful pastime of storytelling is contrasted with the knowledge of people dying in the city. Alternatively, there is also a certain decadent element to this aristocratic escape and playful telling of stories while the plague abates. However, throughout the stories there is great attention paid to dying and suffering. This balancing of the sombre and the playful are part of Boccaccio's strategy, as the narrator reveals in the last paragraph of the book:

> Nor make I any doubt but there are yet others who will say that the said stories are too full of jests and merry conceits, and that it ill beseems a man of weight and gravity to have written on such wise. To these I am bound to render, and do render, my thanks, for that, prompted by well-meant zeal, they have so tender a regard to my reputation. But to that, which they urge against me, I reply after this sort: – That I am of weight I acknowledge, having been often weighed in my time; wherefore, in answer to the fair that have not weighed me, I affirm that I am not of gravity; on the contrary I am so light that I float on the surface of the water; and considering that the sermons which the friars make, when they would chide folk for their sins, are to-day, for the most part, full of jests and merry conceits, and drolleries, I deemed that the like stuff would not ill beseem my stories, written, as they were, to banish women's dumps. However, if thereby they should laugh too much, they may be readily cured thereof by the Lament of Jeremiah, the passion of the Saviour, or the Complaint of the Magdalen. (Boccaccio, 2003: 806)

A more direct description of the plague is found in Daniel Defoe's *A Journal of the Plague Year*, about the plague in 1664. It is not one of Defoe's most canonized works, but it is an interesting book from the perspective of documenting a catastrophe in a narrative written long after the events took place. Defoe's narrative is told from a sensitive point of view with an emphatic narrator who is touched by the suffering. There are meticulous accounts of how villages were affected and how the plague spread from house to house, while at the same time the numbers are overwhelming, often described as 'great' or in the thousands:

> The Number of these miserable Objects were many, and I know so many that perish'd thus, and so exactly where, that I believe I could go to the very Place and dig their Bones up still; . . . great Numbers went out of the World, who were never known, or any Account of them taken, as well within the Bills of Mortality as without. (Defoe, 2003: 97)

The empathy with the unknown victims of the plague is recurrent in the text, and the overwhelming feeling of catastrophe is related with a great many details and many historical references that provoke effects of the social sublime, as well as having access to the historically real. A critique of God's role in this is absent, as he is thanked and prayed to, but not thematized as the omnipotent force that could have prevented this, or that may have inflicted this disease. He is ultimately praised for having saved the people from the disease.

Another interesting aspect of Defoe's authorship is that it also comprises an account of war, *Memoirs of a Cavalier a Military Journal of the Wars in Germany, and the Wars in England. From the Year 1632 to the Year 1648,* which also describes the suffering from man's point of view:

> The Prince of Wales seeing the distress we were in, and loth to fall into the enemy's hands, ships himself on board some vessels at Falmouth, with about 400 lords and gentlemen. And as I had no command here to oblige my attendance, I was once going to make one, but my comrades, whom I had been the principal occasion of bringing hither, began to take it ill, that I would leave them, and so I resolved we would take our fate together. / While thus we had nothing before us but a soldier's death, a fair field, and a strong enemy, and people began to look one upon another, the soldiers asked how their officers looked, and the officers asked how their soldiers looked, and every day we expected to be our last . . . (Defoe, 1972: 263)

Defoe's accounts are historical and not based on his own impressions, even though the plaque memoir is written as if it were created a few years after the event, although in fact published in 1722, just as *Memoirs of a Cavalier* was published in 1720 about events that took place before Defoe's birth. That does not, however, take anything away from the empathy in Defoe's writing or the general perspective he offers, including that of avoiding the theodicy question.

The decisive threshold in this literature was made by Voltaire's literary use of the 1755 earthquake in Lisbon, which work has been highly canonized and holds a remarkable position between the literature of natural disaster and the literature of suffering inflicted by human beings. Voltaire's poem on the Lisbon earthquake formulates the theodicy problem and the argument against Leibniz that is also a central issue in *Candide*:

> Come, ye philosophers, who cry, 'All's well,' / And contemplate this ruin of a world. / Behold these shreds and cinders of your race, / This child and mother heaped in common wreck, / These scattered limbs beneath the marble shafts – / A hundred thousand whom the earth devours, / Who, torn and bloody, palpitating yet, / Entombed beneath their hospitable roofs, / In racking torment end their stricken lives. / To those expiring murmurs of distress, / To that appalling / spectacle of woe, / Will ye reply: 'You do but illustrate / The iron laws that chain / the will of God'? (Voltaire, 2002: 77)

Voltaire combines a simple philosophical question, directed at the philosophers, with a very graphic illustration of the historical events in Portugal. The existence or nature of God is also questioned:

> But how conceive a God supremely good, / Who heaps his favours on the sons he loves, / Yet scatters evil with as large a hand? / What eye can pierce the depth of his designs? (Voltaire, 2002: 80)

Voltaire's poem combines the idea of absolute evil, which is the evil of the force that is supposed to be absolutely good, with the themes of survival, the overwhelming masses, the traumatic aftermath and the exactitude of historical details. The Lisbon earthquake is recurrent in Voltaire's most canonized novel, *Candide*, where it is given a central position in chapters five and six, but this time set in the context of many other atrocities of man, including war, exploitation, etc. *Candide* is a tour de force that shows that there is not a place where people have not behaved inhumanly towards one another (Voltaire, 1947).

It is noteworthy that Voltaire was probably the eighteenth century's most internationally read author. In his work he draws on the experiences of his youthful exile in England, as well as on his knowledge of the world's different countries, and incorporates them into his work. Yet, the thematic properties of the literature of the denial of life are those that seem to have been decisive in the canonization of these portions of his work, bridging the passage from the horrors of natural disaster to a new understanding of war.

The most canonized novel on war from the nineteenth century is Leo Tolstoy's *War and Peace*, in which the fates of many characters living during the Napoleonic wars are woven together, as when the wounded Prince Bolkonski sees Napoleon and hears him comment on his fate, 'That's a fine death', thereby combining an aristocratic and stoic attitude to war with the sheer cruelty evoked by the sight of a bleeding body (Tolstoy, 1998: 305). Another significant element is the almost constant appearance of crowds in one form or another, balancing the portraits of the individual characters with the anonymity of the masses.

In his second epilogue to *War and Peace*, Tolstoy explains his views on history and argues, much in keeping with the comprehensive narrative of the novel, for an understanding that excludes the contingent elements of man, yet also respects the idea of larger formations:

> The movement of nations is caused not by power, nor by intellectual activity, nor even by a combination of the two as historians have supposed, but by the activity of all the people who participate in the events, and who always combine in such a way that those taking the largest direct share in the event take on themselves the least responsibility and vice versa. . . . Speaking of the interaction of heat and electricity and of atoms, we cannot say why this occurs, and we say that it is so because it is inconceivable otherwise, because it must be so and that it is a law. The same applies to historical events. Why war and revolution occur we do not know. We only know that to produce the one or the other action, people combine in a certain formation in which they all take part, and we say that this is so because it is unthinkable otherwise, or in other words that it is a law. (Tolstoy, 1998: 1290)

The quote could also be applied to an understanding of literary history, where canons emerge from the activity of all readers and institutions, where there is also no lawfulness, only the patterns of the formation which can be described and interpreted. More important to the theme, though, in the final paragraphs of *War and Peace*, Tolstoy pays tribute to Voltaire and his attack on those who would not recognize the laws of gravity and the insights to astronomy made by

Copernicus and Newton. He argues that history also contains structures that are not dependent on the free will of the individual, but obeys 'laws' that add a certain element of inevitability to history (Tolstoy, 1998: 1303–1306). By adding compassion to the inevitable and inhuman logic of history, Tolstoy modernizes the pattern of the Greek tragedy on a scale in which the masses have a presence.

In the twentieth century a new sobriety and harsh realism marked literature after the First World War. Ernest Hemingway, John Dos Passos and Louis-Ferdinand Céline were three of the most prominent, albeit very different, authors to write on their experiences of the war in Europe. As mentioned earlier, the poetry of Giuseppe Ungaretti is also highly dependent on war experiences, not least when the canonical status of his poems is considered. Most significantly, perhaps, is the success of Erich Maria Remarque's *All Quiet on the Western Front* all over Europe and in the United States, following its publication in 1928 (Remarque, 1996). The novel was the only foreign work to make the American bestseller lists in the 1920s, lists that, for most part, consisted of now forgotten works. In literature, the literary memoir peaked in the late 1920s, with a number of seminal works by both German and Anglo-American writers (Engdahl, 2002: 49). War as a theme has also been highly successful in movies, where more than a third of the Oscar winning pictures have been about war, including the 1930 adaptation of *All Quiet on the Western Front*.[8]

A major difference between the First and the Second World War was the static front in the First World War, with the massive slaughter of soldiers on the front which persisted, despite the minimal ground gained, and which has left an impression of the generals as equally cynical and stupid. The warfare of the Second World War was, in contrast, mostly dynamic, except for the long sieges of the major Soviet cities. Whereas the underlying reason behind the First World War was the less than noble goal of securing power, in which every nation involved in the war participated, there was an absolutely evil regime to fight in the Second World War. Furthermore, the latter yielded many more civilian losses, which have come to dominate the memory of the war. The sieges, the Holocaust and the bombings of the cities represent the victims of evil, whereas the soldiers of the First World War represent the victims of stupidity and cynicism. This is not to say that there has not been good literature written about the Second World War or the wars that followed, as the works of Kurt Vonnegut, Aleksandar Hemon and many others have proved.

In the collection of articles, *Witness Literature*, with contributions from several Nobel laureates, Horace Engdahl quotes Elie Wiesel as having said that the literature of testimony is the literary invention of our time, and he compares it to the Greek's invention of the tragedy or the invention of the sonnet in the Renaissance (Engdahl, 2002: 5–6). Engdahl believes that Wiesel exaggerates the novelty of the invention, and instead points to the break with Modernism that is inherent to the literature of testimony. This does not privilege experiment, but reality, without relinquishing the formal presentation. The literature thus balances what Timothy Garton Ash calls ornamentation, which undermines the persuasiveness of the literature, and the belief that artistic freedom and the lack of a fixed form for witness literature that, to Nadine Gordimer, is essential for capturing and conveying the meaning of the events (Garton Ash, 2002: 63–64; Gordimer, 2002: 93–96). There is both a purpose to the testimony, and the need to find a form, which will then bring in unforeseen expressions arising from the meeting between form and event, and a structuring of the narrative that also brings about new understandings. Or, in Gao Xingjian's words:

> The writer is continually searching for a unique way of narrating: in other words, what he is searching for is his own path to actual perceptions, even if he has to do this through fabrication. The writing of fiction does not need to adhere rigidly to any particular style. But it is, of course, meaningless to search for a new way of writing unless the aim is to stimulate clearer perceptions, just as it is meaningless to explore new modes of literary narration unless this exploration contributes to the search for truth. (Gao Xingjian, 2002b: 120)

Precisely because traumatic literature deals with complex and incomprehensible events, there is in this literature, more than in any other, a need for those qualities that literary innovation can bring. This is accomplished while finding a balance, not between truth and fiction, because veracity is a given, but between the simple narrative of the eyewitness, and the complexity of history and discursive paradigms that colour history.

Gao Xingjian also points to a very important function of literary testimonies, namely that they can be more profound than history, which is often controlled by those in power, whereas the testimony bears the mark of an individual. The literary form is presented as a whole that cannot be changed in the way that the more fluid telling and re-telling of a series of historical events can be, and therefore it offers a greater resistance to the forgery of history (Gao Xingjian, 2002b: 118).[9]

A critique of this literature could be that it is a too politically correct and obvious a theme for the Nobel committee, rather than a true world theme. It can also be construed as an elitist, narrow, time-bound and political theme. Some of this critique can be dismissed by pointing out the extent of the circulation of this literature, which certainly counters the idea of elitism, whereas the narrowness of the topic and its expressions might be countered by pointing to the diversity of forms that have been explored. As for being time-bound, this is obviously more difficult to predict. Parts of the literature have been established for a long time, whereas the interest in genocide and its emergence as a major cultural phenomenon is of a more recent date, and will probably be important for a long time. The strength of this literature is that it is both political in its insistence on memory, and literary in that it fulfils the potentials of a topic. It is thus appropriate that, in *Farewell to an Idea*, T. J. Clark gives the final word to writers such as Antonio Gramsci, Primo Levi and Samuel Beckett, all anti-fascist writers, unlike a central persona of Modernism, Ezra Pound, highlighting a political dimension of Modernism which was lacking after the First World War, when the whole establishment and world order seemed corrupted (Clark, 2001: 408–409).

This still the begs question, if this literature and its theme of the denial of life is of universal interest, a world theme, what, then, is not a world theme? Anything could potentially be a world theme, but some themes have historically lent themselves better to this than others. War is dramatic and dynamic, whereas peace is not. Religious fiction could have been a world theme, but it is either a literature for minorities or is overshadowed the canonized works of world religions, which themselves make use of narratives that are hard to discern from fictitious storytelling. Georg Brandes thought, as mentioned in his article on world literature in the appendix, that there would be some works that readers could enjoy without too much contextual knowledge, such as books on science, which concerns all humanity, whereas biographies and historical accounts tend to be more locally based, and require a more intimate knowledge of the setting in which the person lived. Yet knowledge about context can be trumped by other factors, as has been argued here, for instance, with respect to the literature of denial of life.

There are also tendencies in international bestsellers that are quite interesting to observe. There is the success of crime fiction, which to some is the most global genre of all, but has had only minor canonical importance in literary history. A recent trend is the combination of historical and philosophical content and the plot of crime fiction, such as in the case of the fiction of Umberto Eco and, much more successfully, but unlikely to be remembered over time, the works of Dan Brown, whose readers seem to live at airports around the world. As Pierre Bourdieu has shown, however, the periods of a work's success are still divided into the contemporary and the longer history of works that speak beyond their own time and place (Bourdieu, 1996: 142–154).

A general theme does not say much about literature, other than giving some indication of where cultures intersect, and they unfortunately do when at war. But when there are a number of works that, through a certain theme, also display related ways of addressing it, a constellation based on international canonization emerges, and reveals several related properties, such as taking an interest in absolute evil, the struggle for survival, the overwhelming and unrepresentable masses, the lack of meaning and existence of trauma and the representation of reality in literature, then it is significant that this is something that has evolved in literary culture and has more dimensions to it than being only a theme, but instead represents a constellation in world literature.

Conclusion: constellations as
facts and experiments

A constellation is a group of stars visibly related to each other in a particular configuration. In three-dimensional space, most of the stars we see have little relation to one another, but can appear to be grouped on the celestial sphere of the night sky. Humans excel at finding patterns and throughout history have grouped stars that appear close to one another into constellations.[1]

The main argument of this book is that seeking and finding constellations based on formal and thematic similarities in international canons is not just an experiment; it also represents facts about a complex, socially based selection. This approach is not without its predecessors. In 'Philologie der Weltliteratur', Erich Auerbach saw the solution to the complexity of world literature in finding *Ansätze* that would have a particular *Strahlkraft*, around which knowledge about literature from diverse parts of the world could be assembled. Much in line with that, David Damrosch has suggested that works are brought together so the less canonical can thrive on the highly canonized (Auerbach, 1992: 94–95; Damrosch, 2003: 298). What separates constellations from these approaches is the insistence on using international canonization as an analytical resource, as has been done here, with lonely canonicals, migrant writers and literature on traumatic events.

The approach to world literature through the paradigm of constellations has at least four significant arguments in its favour: it is realistic, innovative, pluralistic and didactic. These four attributes are seemingly contradictory, as realism could exclude innovation, and the ambition to be pluralistic could interfere with the intent to be didactic, yet this is not the case.

The *realism* of constellations is based on the process of selection, or canonization, whose complexity is overwhelming, but produces results that are very clear at a number of levels: at the level of genres, such as the importance of the novel to modern literature, or poetry to romantic literature; at the level of forms, such as the importance of the sonnet to poetry, or the Haiku to the image of Japanese literature globally; at the level of authors, separating Shakespeare from his contemporaries, just as Dante and Joyce stand out, while at the same time, these are connected to one another across the centuries; at the level of works within authorships, that make *Hamlet* or *Oedipus the King* stand out, as well as very short poems such as William Carlos Williams' 'The Red Wheelbarrow' or Ezra Pound's 'In a Station of the Metro', even though these are not typical of the entire production in their respective works, yet they are widely canonized as central achievements.

It is particularly at the level of single works that the selection reveals which properties have contributed to the canonization of one text and not any other text in the authorship. 'In a Station of the Metro', for example, combines a visual snapshot of a scene in what is likely the Paris metro – 'The apparition of these faces in the crowd;' – followed by a gesture towards a larger whole, which transcends the time and space of the snapshot to a degree of incomprehensibility, here through a metaphoric complex – 'Petals on a wet, black bough' – the petals and the bough implying a tree and thus likening the people in the snapshot to just small leaves on the large tree of a perpetually moving society. A similar use of this combination of snapshot and a gesture towards a larger whole can be found in the most canonized of William Carlos Williams' poems, of Giuseppe Ungaretti and in a number of central passages of works in the international canon, as has been suggested in the previous chapter's considerations of the social sublime (Ungaretti, 1969; Williams, 1923).

When such convergence occurs between a number of texts that have stood out over time, and which share a common feature that has been realized in a number of genres and with different approaches, the importance of formal and thematic traits to the international canonization of works becomes clear, along with the significance of seeing these features as part of a larger structure of the literary system, reflecting an identity that has been built up and evolved over centuries. The basis of constellations is thus empirical. Themes and forms can be described and defined, sought after and found, just as the international impact of a work can be traced in translations and sales, inclusion in literary histories, anthologies and in the general valuation it receives in critical works. This type of analysis can also differentiate between the importance of a certain form or theme at different times and in different areas, without losing focus on the particular defining properties of the works.

The *innovative* dimension of constellations lies in their capacity for finding similarities in works that are usually not thought of as belonging together, but which will have a greater chance of being connected, because the canonical imperative directs the gaze towards a limited body of works, and because the idea of the constellation is not to find an almost complete coherence among works, but to connect central attributes that can also be said to define the work, in contrast to other, less canonical works from the same authors or the same literatures, as in the example of William Carlos Williams, given above.

Finding such points of connection across genres, nations, languages and ages can result in a series of links forming a constellation that appears as an integrated whole. A thematic example of a very evident constellation is the theme of hunger that is so important to works by Knut Hamsun, Franz Kafka and Paul Auster, as well as to new Chinese writers like Mo Yan. The same cluster can also be said to include a remarkable kind of modern narrator, the lonely male standing on a sidetrack of society, who is half-bitter but who also has certain insistence on a more or less self-absorbed project of his own. This is a very distinctive character who can also be found in the work of Fyodor Dostoyevsky, Herman Melville, Louis-Ferdinand Céline, Albert Camus and Georges Perec, and it is characteristic that the works in which he appears have a high ranking, although not necessarily the highest, in the international canonization, compared to other works by the same author. This goes for Dostoyevsky's *Notes from the Underground*, Melville's 'Bartleby the Scrivener', Hamsun's *Hunger*, Kafka's 'A Hunger Artist', Céline's *Journey to the End of the Night*, Camus' *The Stranger*, and *The Fall*, a number of Paul Auster's novels and Perec's *A Man Asleep*, which explicitly connects to Melville's story. The reasons for the success of this narrative voice and character are most likely that they combine a position of being at the edge of society with some hope of being included, alternating with disgust for the general culture and the determination to persist in a futile project that lets the narrative continue to unfold a relatively simple plot, where the condition itself is the narrative content.

Constellations are not platonic and ideal, but on the other hand they are more than mere constructions, and the innovative aspect of constellations therefore lies more in defining a series of properties that can help to find relations to other works. A strong constellation, once found or described, would then seem as if it were a given, whereas constellations that are built on loose descriptions of certain features, and whose canonical impact is varied, would then stand out as constructions, and therefore as weak constellations.

The *pluralism* of constellations lies first and foremost in their ability to connect less circulated literature with the most internationally canonized works, and describe how they belong to the same wave in a certain period, and focus on the evolution of literature in time, as Franco Moretti has demonstrated with the evolution of the technique of stream-of-consciousness (Moretti, 1996: 168–181), or how they have been canonized as an expression of a certain interest in the literary community in the longer process of canonization, to use the example above again, this could be in either hunger as a theme, or in a certain narrative style, or as in the previous chapter's analyses, how the voice of migrant writers display properties that were appealing in the history of twentieth century literature.

Connecting more and less canonized texts could also extend to nationally and internationally canonized texts, if there are homologies in the formal and thematic aspects of a certain constellation. This would at least demonstrate a potential for international canonization, although the actual realization of this is a complex and uncertain affair. The use of constellations that take nationally canonized texts into account in anthologies and in the writing of world literary history would be a reasonable way of showing the far-reaching implications of a certain feature, as well as a presentation of texts with potential, that, for contingent reasons, may not yet have been given a chance to demonstrate their worth to a different audience.

A second aspect of the pluralism of constellations is that they do not claim to find the key to certain works, but only a convincing pattern, and a portion of the explanation for their canonization. A work can be an obvious element of more than one constellation, and the intersecting constellations only add to the understanding of the work when trying to give meaning to the intersecting patterns, such as the traumatic literature did, with respect to both the larger theme of the social sublime and the interest in witness literature.

The *didactic* dimension of constellations is related to their ability to establish a point of view and reduce complexity by the use of international canonization, while at the same time facilitating unlikely meetings of texts across cultures. A simple reproduction of the list of great books is an unimaginative way to teach world literature, but a change to this approach must be backed up by arguments for grouping together diverse texts that are not part of a core canon. The canonical constellations both touch upon the canon and are open to the counter-canon or shadow-canon in world literature.

Teaching world literature by way of constellations thus means to take an interest in the details of literary history and the identity of the international literary system. This kind of sensibility is also proposed by Homi Bhabha:

> If we are seeking a 'worlding' of literature, then perhaps it lies in a critical act that attempts to grasp the sleight of hand with which literature conjures with historical specificity, using the medium of psychic uncertainty, aesthetic distancing, or the obscure signs of the spirit-world, the sublime and the subliminal. As literary creatures and political animals we ought to concern ourselves with the understanding of human action and the social world as a moment when *something is beyond control, but it is not beyond accommodation.* (Bhabha, 1994: 12)

Constellations and canonization can, in this respect, be valuable in revealing the finer web of literature. Like the universe, world literature is infinite, but constellations appear and help connect things near and far in a reflection of interests shared by human beings in the perpetual process of experiencing the world and its words.

Appendix

World Literature[1]

Georg Brandes

The editors of this journal have asked me to express my views on the concept of world literature. I am afraid that I shall be unable to give a satisfactory response. I am aware that the term derives from Goethe, but at the moment the context in which he used it is not clear to me.[2] I dimly recall that he prophesied a world literature in opposition to the previous national literatures.

But if I put to myself the question, 'What is world literature?' without reference to the great inventor of the phrase, it appears to me that one must think in the first place of the works of discoverers and inventors in the natural sciences. The writings of Pasteur, Darwin, Bunsen or Helmholtz certainly belong to world literature; they apply directly to the human race and enrich humanity as a whole. Certain travel narratives like those of Stanley or Nansen also without a doubt make up part of world literature.

The works of historians – even the greatest among them – seem to me not wholly to belong to world literature in this way, since by the nature of their subject they are less final, they necessarily bear a strongly individual stamp and thus are better geared to the analogous personality of the author's compatriots. Despite all the learning and genius of their authors, such exceptional works as Carlyle's *Oliver Cromwell*, Michelet's *History of France*, or Mommsen's *Roman History* are not definitive works of scholarship but can only be regarded as indissoluble wholes to the degree that they are works of art – which does not hinder them from becoming familiar to the main nations of Europe and America, in the original as in translation. For when one speaks of world literature, one thinks primarily and principally of belles-lettres in all their forms.

Time itself has passed judgment on the literature of the past. A few writers out of many thousands, a few works from hundreds of thousands, are part of world literature. Everyone has the names of such writers and works on the tip of the tongue: the *Divine Comedy* belongs not to Italy alone, nor *Don Quixote* to Spain. Alongside the world-famous works, numberless others are preserved, loved and respected – and continuously read – in their countries of origin without being known abroad. Shakespeare is part of world literature, but his great contemporary Marlowe belongs to English literature. In the same way Klopstock is merely German, Coleridge merely English, Slovacky merely Polish. As far as the world is concerned, they do not exist.

Moreover a difference is to be observed between premodern and modern times, since nowadays foreign languages are studied better and more frequently and the activity of translation has gained such an extraordinary momentum; in no other language do translations play so great a role as in German.

Apart from all that is lost in translation, it is incontestable that writers of different countries and languages occupy enormously different positions where their chances of obtaining worldwide fame, or even a moderate degree of recognition, are concerned. The most favourably situated are the French writers, although the French language occupies only the fifth rank in terms of extension. When a writer has succeeded in France, he is known throughout the world. English and Germans, who can count on an immense public if they are successful, take second place. It is only writers from these three nations who can hope to be read in the original by the most educated people of all nations.

Italian and Spanish writers are far less fortunate, though they may be read by a significant number of readers outside their native lands. Such is not the case for Russian writers, although the Russian population with its millions compensates for this.

But whoever writes in Finnish, Hungarian, Swedish, Danish, Dutch, Greek or the like is obviously poorly placed in the universal struggle for fame. In this competition he lacks the major weapon, a language – which is, for a writer, almost everything.

It is impossible to write anything of artistic value in a language other than one's own. On that, everyone agrees. 'But what about translations?' someone may object. I confess to the heresy that sees in them nothing but a lamentable necessity. Translations leave out the linguistic artistry whereby the writer affirms himself, and the better and greater he is in his own language, the more he loses in translation.

The inescapable incompleteness of translations is the reason that an author of the sixth rank who writes in a widely spoken world language can easily become better known than a second-rank author whose language is spoken by no more than a few million. Anyone who knows the literatures of smaller and larger countries will readily concede this point, though the inhabitants of large countries are as a rule slow to believe it.

The only concession to make is this: lyric poems are hard to translate, always lose a great deal by it, and normally the attempt to translate them is abandoned because the results are not worth while. Germans can well conceive that anyone who knows Goethe's poems only through a prose translation must find them unworthy of admiration. A Frenchman is incapable of imagining the verses of Victor Hugo and Leconte de Lisle translated into a foreign language. Most consider that in the case of prose works, not so much is lost in translation; but that is an error. The difficulty is still enormous, immense, even if less apparent than with poetry. The selection and resonance of words, the singularities of linguistic expression, all vanish. Translations are never replicas.

Even someone who, recalling certain artistically executed versions, holds translators in high esteem will not deny that writers of different origins are unequally favoured in the pursuit of worldwide fame.

It has nonetheless been observed that some authors who, like Ibsen, write in a language of small compass have succeeded in making themselves known everywhere – some of them far lesser spirits than Ibsen. Is fame in the present, fame among one's contemporaries, decisive? Are the author and the work therefore likely to endure in world literature? Only an optimist could think so. World fame seems to me too poor a measure to be useful.

In the first place, some win it without deserving it in any way. Where their level coincides with the level of general culture or of common taste, and if they belong to a major people, it is easy for them to become universally known. Georges Ohnet is read everywhere.[3] And to capture general attention, such a writer must not merely be inoffensive, he need not directly cater to dominant prejudices; he can do so indirectly, as when he crudely and superficially counters a banal idea with a banal idea of his own, for example, if he takes up arms against royalist, clerical or aristocratic prejudices. One has seen writers without the least artistic education or sense of craft who became famous for attacking the greatest artists, poets, or thinkers of their time with obstinate smugness and spoke of them condescendingly as empty-headed or insane. This act makes an impression on the greatest mass in most countries, and the fellow-traveler too is received into world literature.

On the other hand, it seems often to be a matter of sheer chance that this or that author of the first rank dies without fame and remains unknown after his death.

I find examples ready to hand from the literature that I know best. Of all the writers of Denmark in the nineteenth century, only one, Hans Christian Andersen, has achieved world fame. This has caused much amazement in Denmark. Among us Andersen is thought of as one among many, nothing more. He does not stand with our greatest; in his own lifetime he was never thought of as belonging to the first or second class. Nor, I might add, even after his death. As a thinker he was inconsequential and never had an intellectual influence. He was viewed as a gifted, childlike creature, and this estimation was not incorrect. But nonetheless he belongs to world literature, for he wrote fairy tales that made their way everywhere through their general comprehensibility.

`At least a dozen of his literary colleagues in Denmark were far more important as individuals and no less well equipped as poets or writers. But they have never been translated. Remaining untranslated, they became local celebrities instead, and were far more cherished, indeed deified, in their home country. Who, outside the Scandinavian North, knows the name of Poul Möller, who in Denmark is revered like a demigod? Who knows Johan Ludvig Heiberg, who defined good taste in Denmark and Norway in near-dictatorial fashion? Who knows Christian Winther, the greatest lyric poet in Denmark between the 1830s and 1850s, and who is still far more beloved, recited and revered than Andersen?

But my intention is to restrict myself to the truly great alone. Søren Kierkegaard, the greatest religious thinker of the Scandinavian North, is unknown in Europe. One would think that every paladin of Christianity in Europe would have to engage with him, as with Pascal some centuries ago; but he has no place in world literature. This is unfortunate for world literature, though it represents no great loss to the dead philosopher. It would be good if a few of his works such as *Sickness Unto Death, Stages on Life's Way*, or *Practice in Christianity*, were known everywhere. No one knows them.

There is no point in closing one's eyes to the fact that most of humanity is dull, ignorant, of limited judgment. The best is inaccessible to them, the finest is incomprehensible. They follow the loud market-crier and the charismatic charlatan. They demand success and obey fashion. What pleases mankind in one's own time will not necessarily become a lasting part of world literature.

At present there are in Europe, as far as I know, no poets and hardly any writers of the first rank. The best are no match for the great dead: neither Kipling in England nor d'Annunzio in Italy. But in all probability they are far more famous than the greatest of their predecessors ever were.

Something unprecedented has arisen in our time, precisely because writers see before them the possibility of being known and read throughout the whole world. People begin to write for an invisible, abstract public, and this does damage to literary production. Emile Zola provides an example. His great series of novels, *Les Rougon-Macquart,* was written for the French and is therefore carefully and concretely executed. His trilogy *Lourdes, Rome, Paris,* composed after he had achieved great fame, was written for the whole world, and for this reason is far more abstract than before. In this trilogy he wrote as Sarah Bernhardt acts – whether she is performing in Peru or in Chicago. If a writer wants to have a powerful effect, he must have his surroundings before his eyes, he must be active there where he was born, he must write for his compatriots, whose stage of development he knows well. Whatever is written for the whole world sacrifices strength and vigour for the sake of universal comprehensibility, it no longer carries the flavour of the soil. If it were not so odious to name them, I could mention several great writers who, in the process of becoming first local, then worldwide celebrities, have done homage to an alien and ordinary taste as they had once embraced the taste of their own people. There is something dangerous in the courting of world fame and world literature.

On the other hand, it is obvious that one should not write for those who live in the same street or the same city as oneself, as polemical writers in particular try to do.

When Goethe coined the term 'world literature,' humanism and cosmopolitanism were still ideas that everyone held in honor. In the last years of the nineteenth century, an ever stronger and more jealous national sentiment has caused these ideas to recede almost everywhere. Today literature is becoming more and more national. But I do not believe that nationality and cosmopolitanism are incompatible. The world literature of the future will be all the more interesting, the more strongly its national stamp is pronounced and the more distinctive it is, even if, as art, it also has its international side; for that which is written directly for the world will hardly appear as a work of art. Truly, the work of art is a fortress, not an open city.[4]

Notes

Introduction

[1] The two terms are sometimes used interchangeably. Postnational suggests a historical movement towards a new epoch, whereas transnational merely reflects the idea of literatures that are rooted outside of a single nation. Settling on the best term is difficult, since there are historical changes that make it plausible to speak about the postnational, but on the other hand, there are no signs that the idea of nationhood is dead. Transnational is therefore the broader and more inclusive term.

[2] See also David Perkins' reflections on the balance between coherence and complexity in *Is Literary History Possible?* (Perkins, 1992: 27).

Chapter 1

[1] Although it can be questioned how important *belles lettres* will be in contrast to educational books and other kinds of non-fiction (Sun Qingguo, 2003: 127).

[2] See also Jürgen Habermas' comments on Rorty's 'frank ethnocentrism' (Habermas, 2001: 150–151).

[3.] By Stephen Mitchell in 2004 and Andrew George in 1999.

[4] Thanks to Theo D'haen for informing me about the early Dutch publication of *Love in the Time of Cholera*.

[5] Fitzgerald wrote in a letter to Edmund Wilson: 'Italy has no one. When Anatole France dies French literature will be a silly jealous rehashing of technical quarrels. They're thru and done. You may have spoken in jest about New York as the capital of culture but in 25 years it will be just as London is now. Culture follows money and all the refinements of aestheticism can't stave off its change of seat (Christ! what a metaphor). We will be the Romans in the next generation as the English are now' (Fitzgerald, 1970: 303–304).

[6] Thanks to Peter Simonsen for directing me to this quote.

[7] See Georg Brandes' essay on this topic, in the appendix. The text appeared in German in 1899 and is here presented in its first English translation (see also Madsen, 2004; Moretti, 2003).

[8] To be fair, Bloom has omitted the list in some of the translations of his book, but there are still striking examples. To a Dane it is somewhat mind-boggling to see works by Martin Andersen Nexø and Karen Blixen as the only Danish authors making the list of modern literature; not that they are not good; they are just not the best or most recognized. Martin Andersen Nexø was a big name in the German Democratic Republic, where he lived in his final years, and where the ideological content of his novels was in good standing with the Communist party. However, both Nexø's and Blixen's works

were made into Oscar-winning films in the late 1980s, respectively, *Pelle the Conqueror*, by Bille August and *Babette's Feast*, by Gabriel Axel.

[9] For a historical overview of the origin of the discipline, see Bassnett (1993).

[10] For a book that tries to counter this tendency and bring diversity to the otherwise Anglophone dominated post-colonial studies, see Charles Forsdick and David Murray (2003).

[11] See also Yingjin Zhang (1998).

[12] That is not to say that Shakespeare is the best by any standard, but that he is unique in terms of influence and universal recognition. Ironically, Ben Jonson was perhaps the first to introduce the idea that Shakespeare would be a poet for all times (Bartolovich, 2002: 36–39).

[13] Walter Blair writes: 'In Denmark, there was really no literature, as we know it, until the sixteenth century. The only things written before that time had been laws, and scientific and technical treatises. There had been a few histories but there is little evidence of more advanced literary forms, such as the drama, before the Reformation' (Blair, 1940: 316).

[14] This estimate and the lack of more exact figures came up in a discussion with Russell Berman in 2004.

Chapter 2

[1] This tendency can also be seen in historical textbooks that tend to adopt a more cosmopolitan view-point (see Schissler and Soysal, 2005).

[2] The works of Charles Dickens and George Eliot could also be considered as rivals to this position, but internationally the edge goes to the Russians.

[3] Steinbeck is not a 1920s writer per se, although he made his debut just within that decade. The gradual exclusion or fading of Dreiser and Lewis, and the rise of the above mentioned are very noticeable in the writing of American literary history when comparing Spiller (1946) and Elliott (1988).

[4] This goes for poetry in general, as opposed to fiction.

[5] As a group they are also very interesting because of the unusual combination of close relationships and high degree of canonization. Pound influenced Eliot, and was a friend of Williams, whereas Williams despised Eliot, but corresponded with Stevens, and everyone knew Stein, from Paris.

[6] Figures such as Ezra Pound and T. S. Eliot would also belong to this group, but differ in coming from extensive literary cultures.

[7] See the next chapter for a discussion of Bourdieu's theory.

[8] As mentioned, the Oscar-winning *Babette's Feast*, and Sidney Pollack's *Out of Africa*.

[9] See http://www.ualberta.ca/~cins/lectures/isak_dinesen.htm

[10] An interesting thesis concerning the success of J. K. Rowling's 'Harry Potter' series is that the English prep-school environment, and British culture as such, have been portrayed in many movies and stories, making it a commonplace of which readers feel they have some knowledge11. Quoted from the appendix of this book.

[12] In the way that Harold Bloom suggests that we are inventions of Shakespeare (Bloom, 1998).

[13] The American Beat Generation generated aspects of the same aura, but were too limited in their production and range to set new standards. Novelists such as

Thomas Pynchon, Georges Perec, Péter Nádas and Péter Esterházy are perhaps a new generation that has had the image of the uncompromising author attached to them, whereas David Foster Wallace is one of those authors from an even younger generation who has written highly ambitious and complex novels, most notably *Infinite Jest*.

14 Digital literature has still not had a breakthrough, despite many interesting attempts to write multimedia fiction. On the other hand, there has been some import of stylistic conventions from computer media to literature, for example in the works of Douglas Coupland, but the synergy is still not overwhelming.

15 Günter Grass is one example, as are many exiled writers.

16 See my review of volume F of *The Longman Anthology of World Literature* (Thomsen, 2005b).

17 In philosophy, the difference between realism and pragmatism is comparable to the problem of how to describe the literatures of the world. This is an ongoing debate spanning from Plato, Aristotle, Kant and Nietzsche to twentieth-century philosophers such as Hilary Putnam and Richard Rorty.

Chapter 3

1 Of the sixteen, some, such as Thomas Mann or Wole Soyinka, migrated late in life due to political situations, whereas others, such as Samuel Beckett, Elias Canetti and V. S. Naipaul, had migrant experience from early on. Another group migrated later in life, but wrote their seminal works as migrants, including Isaac Bashevis Singer and Gao Xingjian. For recent interesting contributions to the study of migrant literature, see Philips (1997), Seyhan (2001), Walkowitz (2006a and 2006b), Sommer (2001), Ette (2005), Smith (2004) and Huyssen (2003).

2 'Migrancy' is not an officially recognized word, but I use it here as a relevant term that designates the condition of being a migrant.

3 Elleke Boehmer's critique of the cosmopolitan migrant will be discussed later in this chapter.

4 On migration in general, see Castles and Miller (1993).

5 Thanks to Wlad Godzich for this metaphor.

6 Source: *Statens offentliga utredningar* 69/1974, 58/1984 and 55/1996, Stockholm.

7 For example, Peter Høeg's *Smilla's Sense of Snow*, the best-selling Danish novel of the 1990s, was an international bestseller in 1993, as well as a best-seller in Denmark. But it only became a Danish best-seller over half a year after its publication in 1992, when news about its possible foreign success provided important feedback.

8 See the obituary in *The Guardian* 28 January 2002.

9 This is, in a way, also the case with some of France's great literary figures of the twentieth century: Albert Camus and Jacques Derrida were both brought up in Algeria, and Georges Perec was descended from Polish Jewish migrants.

10 Beck's views on the universals in a plurality of cosmopolitanism are also discussed in Beck (2002), and is very much in line with Immanuel Wallerstein's argument in 'The National and the Universal: Can There Be Such a Thing as World Culture?,' which does not express belief in a unified world culture but in more mixed cultures sharing a number of universals (Wallerstein, 1991).

11 This is perhaps one of the most untranslatable poems, due to its minimal structure. A rough translation would be: 'Infinity/Enlightens me.'

12 'Soldier: Bosco de Courton, July 1918,' 'They stand/like leaves/on the trees/in autumn.'

13 *Lolita* was published in France in 1954, but was banned in 1956, following pressure from the British government. Initially, American authorities also confiscated copies of the book, but only for a short period, until the book was published in America and became successful.

14 Frank Kermode argues that canonization can be seen as way of 'making modern', and the exploration of the theme of identity and cosmopolitanism, and the status of these writers fits well into that thesis (Kermode, 1988).

15 The Chinese author Mo Yan touches upon something similar: 'I knew I had to write what was natural to me, something clearly different from what other writers, Western and Chinese, were writing. This does not mean that Western writing exerted no influence on me. Quite the contrary: I have been profoundly influenced by some Western writers, and am happy to openly acknowledge that influence. But what sets me apart from other Chinese writers is that I neither copy the narrative techniques of foreign writers nor imitate their story lines; what I am happy to do is closely explore what is embedded in their work in order to understand their observations of life and comprehend how they view the world we live in' (Mo Yan, 2001: xv–xvi).

16 See http://nobelprize.org/literature/laureates/2000

17 I owe this insight to Søren Frank.

Chapter 4

1 Patterson concludes a review article with: 'their subject is not the Holocaust. For in their concern with "representations of the Holocaust," these scholars are unconcerned with those who lie at the core of the Holocaust: the Jews who as Jews were shot and butchered, gassed and burned. Therefore they are unconcerned with the God who defines the Jews and who makes absolute the prohibition against murder. Elie Wiesel is not mistaken when he maintains that when dealing with the Holocaust, one can affirm God or one can deny God, but one cannot ignore God. These scholars are not proof to the contrary; they simply ignore the Holocaust' (Patterson, 2003: 123). Mandel, on the other hand, states that, 'focusing on what has been constructed as "unspeakable" merely reiterates the ethical imperative by which we, as members of post-Holocaust culture, refrain from further wronging the victims of the Holocaust, and, further, avoid the uncomfortable implications of addressing the presence of the Holocaust in a culture that defines itself as the product of the Holocaust in its past. By emphasizing the unspeakability of the victims' experience, its incommensurability to conceptual structures, we absolve the victims of guilt – as if we, nonsurvivors, had the ability or even the right to do so – and distance ourselves from their experience, as if we could determine which aspects of our own history are constitutive and which are unassimilable. Finally, a rhetoric of the unspeakable facilitates the masquerade of rhetorical performance as ethical practice, as eloquent gestures toward the limits of language replace far less comfortable engagement with a painful and morally

ambiguous reality in which there never is, and never has been, a "moral high ground"' (Mandel, 2001: 228; see also Lang, 2000).

2 The literature on the Holocaust is extremely rich, and includes writers such as Paul Celan, Ingeborg Bachmann, W. G. Sebald, Jorge Semprún, George Perec, Peter Weiss, Nelly Sachs, Isaac Bashevis Singer, Elie Wiesel, Primo Levi, Anne Frank and many others. Apart from the already mentioned critical works, see also Adorno (2000), Lang (1988), Köppen (1993), Banner (2000), Engdahl (2002), Dunker (2003) and Eaglestone (2004).

3 In contrast, Shoshana Felman and Dori Laub have argued that Holocaust-memory will always be allegorical (Felman and Laub, 1991)

4. This also applies to Dominick LeCapra's otherwise interesting *Representing the Holocaust: History, Theory, Trauma* (1996).

5 This was the case with Tania Head, who claimed to have been in one of the World Trade Center towers on 9/11 and survived as one of the few from the top floors. She provided details about other victims regardless of the fact that her story was, in all likelihood, made up. See *New York Times* 27 September 2007.

6 On the fictive meta-autobiographical genre, see also Thomsen (2004).

7 The Turkish state still denies that there was a genocide, and in 2005 the nation's most significant international literary voice, Orhan Pamuk, was indicted for referring to the Armenian genocide. The charges were dropped in January 2006, after much international attention and diplomatic pressure on the Turkish state. A resolution from the Congress of the United States of America in 2007 stated that there was a genocide, and sparked loud protests from the Turkish government. The 1933 novel *The Forty Days of Musa Dagh*, by Franz Werfel, is one of the few other literary accounts of the genocide, and thus a demonstration of the relative lack of interest in it, at least until recently.

8 See http://www.oscars.org/awardsdatabase/index.html

9 There is also an interesting parallel to this, in the stories Paul Auster has collected from ordinary Americans, and given voice to in a series of readings on National Public Radio, as part of the National Story Project. A number of these stories, which obviously thrive on their status as true accounts, have been collected by Auster (2002).

Conclusion

1 Source: http://www.redorbit.com/education/reference_library/universe/constellation/179/index.html

Appendix

1 Translated by Haun Saussy from 'Weltliteratur,' in *Das litterarische Echo*, 2:1 (1 October 1899).

2 [Editorial note, 1899:] The manuscript of this essay reached us from Bagnoles de l'Orne (France). We add that Goethe first used the term in 1827 as the title to his epigram 'Wie David königlich zur Harfe sang…'

3 But no longer in 2006. Q.E.D. [HS]

4 The last sentence appears only in the German text of the article, not in the Danish. [HS]

Bibliography

Achebe, C. (1958) *Things Fall Apart*. London: Heinemann.

Adorno, T. W. (1975) *Gesellschaftstheorie und Kulturkritik*. Frankfurt am Main: Suhrkamp.

Adorno, T. W. (2000) *Negative Dialectics*. London: Routledge.

Agamben, G. (2000) *Remnants of Auschwitz: The Witness and the Archive*. New York: Zone Books.

Alphen, E. v. (1997) *Caught by History: Holocaust Effects in Contemporary Art, Literature, & Theory*. Stanford: Stanford University Press.

Annesley, J. (2006) *Fictions of Globalization: Consumption, the Market and the Contemporary American Novel*. London: Continuum.

Appiah, K. A. (2004) *The Ethics of Identity*. Princeton: Princeton University Press.

Apter, E. (2001) 'On Translation in a Global Market', in *Public Culture*, 13:1.

Apter, E. (2006) *The Translation Zone: A New Comparative Literature*. Princeton: Princeton University Press.

Aristotle (1964) *Politics and Poetics*. New York: Heritage.

Auerbach, E. (1992) *Philologie der Weltliteratur*. Frankfurt am Main: Fischer.

Auster, P. (ed.) (2002) *I Thought My Father Was God: And Other True Tales From NPR's National Story Project*. New York: Picador.

Auster, P. (2003) *Oracle Night*. New York: Henry Holt.

Balderston, D. (1986) *The Literary Universe of Jorge Luis Borges: An Index to References and Allusions to Persons, Titles and Places in His Writings*. New York: Greenwood.

Balderston, D. (1993) *Out of Context: Historical Reference and the Representation of Reality in Borges*. Durham: Duke University Press.

Balzac, H. de (1972) *Le père Goriot*. Paris: Gallimard.

Bann, S. and Bowlt, J. E. (eds) (1973) *Russian Formalism: A Collection of Articles and Texts in Translation*. Edinburgh: Scottish Academic Press.

Banner, G. (2000) *Holocaust Literature*. London: Valentine Mitchell.

Bardolle, O. (2004) *La literature à vif (Le cas Houellebecq)*. Paris: L'esprit des péninsules.

Bartolovich, C. (2002) 'Afterlife', in *Shakespeare Studies*, 30.

Bassnett, S. (1993) *Comparative Literature: A Critical Introduction*. Oxford: Blackwell.

Baudelaire, C. (1964) *The Painter of Modern Life and Other Essays*. London: Phaidon.

Beck, U. (2000) 'The Cosmopolitan Perspective: Sociology of the Second Age of Modernity', in *British Journal of Sociology*, 51:1.

Beck, U. (2004) *Der kosmopolitische Blik oder: Krieg ist Frieden*. Frankfurt am Main: Suhrkamp.

Beck, U. (2006) *The Cosmopolitan Vision*. Cambridge: Polity Press.

Beck, U., Sznaider, N. and Winter, R. (eds) (2003) *Global America?* Liverpool: Liverpool University Press.

Beckett, S. (1964) *Waiting for Godot: Tragicomedy in 2 acts.* New York: Grove.

Beckett, S. (1985) *Three Novels: Molloy. Malone Dies. The Unnamable.* New York: Grove.
Behrendt, S. C. (1998) 'The Romantic Reader', in Wu, D. (ed.) *A Companion to Romanticism.* Oxford: Blackwell.

Bellos, D. (1995) *Georges Perec: A Life in Words.* London: Harwill.

Bernheimer, C. (ed.) (1995) *Comparative Literature in the Age of Multiculturalism.* Baltimore: Johns Hopkins University Press.

Bhabha, H. (1994) *The Location of Culture.* London: Routledge.

Bigsby, C. W. E. (2006) *Remembering and Imagining the Holocaust.* Cambridge: Cambridge University Press.

Birus, H. (2000) 'The Goethean Concept of World Literature and Comparative Literature', online at http://clcwebjournal.lib.purdue.edu/clcweb00-4/birus00. html

Blair, W. (1940) *The History of World Literature.* Chicago: University of Knowledge.

Blixen, K. (1934) *Seven Gothic Tales.* New York: Smith and Haas.

Blixen, K. (1987) *Out of Africa.* New York: Crown.

Bloom, H. (1994) *The Western Canon: The Books and Schools of the Ages.* New York: Harcourt Brace.

Bloom, H. (1998) *Shakespeare: The Invention of the Human.* New York: Riverhead Books.

Bloom, H. (2002) *Genius.* New York: Warner Books.

Boccaccio, G. (2003) *The Decameron.* New York: Signet Classic.

Boehmer, E. (1996) *Colonial & Postcolonial Literature.* Oxford: Oxford University Press.

Borges, J. L. (1999) *Collected Fictions.* New York: Penguin.

Borges, J. L. (2000) *Selected Non-Fiction.* New York: Penguin.

Bourdieu, P. (1983) *The Field of Cultural Production.* Cambridge: Polity Press.

Bourdieu, P. (1992) *Distinction: A Social Critique of the Judgement of Taste.* London: Routledge.

Bourdieu, P. (1996) *The Rules of Art.* Cambridge: Polity Press.

Bowers, M. A. (2004) *Magic(al) Realism.* London: Routledge.

Bradbury, M. (ed.) (1996) *The Atlas of Literature.* London: De Agostini.

Bradbury, M. and McFarlane, J. (eds) (1976) *Modernism: 1880–1930.* Harmondsworth: Penguin.

Brah, A. and Coombs, A. E. (eds) (2000) *Hybridity and Its Discontents.* London: Routledge.

Braiterman, Z. (2001) 'Against Holocaust-Sublime: Naive Reference and the Generation of Memory', in *History and Memory,* 12:2.

Brandes, G. (1901) 'The Emigrant Literature', in *Main Currents in Nineteenth Century Literature,* vol. 1. London: Heinemann.

Brandes, G. (1940) 'Brev til Sophus Schandorph, April 1888', in Brandes, E. and Brandes, G. (eds) *Brevveksling mellem nordiske forfattere og videnskabsmænd,* vol. 3. Copenhagen: Gyldendal. Translation online at http://thenietzschechannel. fws1.com/corresp.htm.

Bugge, P. (2003) 'Clementis's Hat; or, Is Kundera a Palimpsest', in *Kosmas,* 16:2.

Butler, J. (1995) 'Collected and Fractured', in Appiah, K. A. and Gates Jr., H. L. (eds) *Identities.* Chicago: University of Chicago Press.

Calvino, I. (1996) *Six Memos for the Next Millennium.* London: Vintage.

Camon, F. (1989) *Conversations with Primo Levi.* Vermont: Marlboro Press.

Camus, A. (1946) *The Stranger.* New York: Knopf.

Camus, A. (1957) *The Fall.* New York: Knopf.

Carnochan, W. B. (1993) *The Battleground of the Curriculum.* Stanford: Stanford University Press.

Casanova, P. (2004) *The World Republic of Letters.* Cambridge: Harvard University Press.

Casanova, P. (2005) 'Literature as a World', in *New Left Review,* 31.

Castles, S. and Miller, M. J. (1993) *The Age of Migration: International Population Movements in the Modern World.* Houndmills: Macmillan.

Caws, M. A. and Prendergast, C. (eds) (1997) *The HarperCollins World Reader.* New York: Harper Collins.

Celan, P. (1963) *Selected Poems.* London: Penguin.

Celan, P. (1995) 'Tenebrae', in Langer, L. L. (ed.) *Art from the Ashes: A Holocaust Anthology.* Oxford: Oxford University Press.

Céline, L.-F. (1988) *Journey to the End of the Night.* London: Calder.

Ceserani, R. (1994) 'Modernity and Postmodernity: A Cultural Change Seen from the Italian Perspective', in *Italica,* 3.

Clark, P. (2003) 'Voices of the Victims: Narrating the Genocide in Rwanda', in *Oxonian Review of Books,* 2:1.

Clark, T. J. (1993) *Farewell to an Idea: Episodes from a History of Modernism.* New Haven: Yale University Press.

Cohen, R. (1997) *Global Diaspora.* London: Routledge.

Connell, J., King, R. and White, P. (eds) (1995) *Writing Across Worlds: Literature and Migration.* London: Routledge.

Conrad, J. (2003) *Heart of Darkness and Other Tales.* New York: Oxford University Press.

Courtemanche, G. (2003) *A Sunday at the Pool in Kigali.* Edinburgh: Canongate.

Courtois, S. (ed.) (1999) *The Black Book of Communism: Crimes, Terror, Repression.* Cambridge: Harvard University Press.

Damrosch, D. (2003) *What Is World Literature?* Princeton: Princeton University Press.

Damrosch, D. (ed.) (2003) *The Longman Anthology of World Literature.* New York: Longman.

Damrosch, D. (2006) 'World Literature in a Postcanonical, Hypercanonical Age', in Saussy, H. (ed.) *Comparative Literature in an Age of Globalization.* Baltimore: Johns Hopkins University Press.

Damrosch, D. (2007) *The Buried Book: The Loss and Rediscovery of the Great Epic of Gilgamesh.* New York: Henry Holt.

Damrosch, D. (ed.) (2008) *Teaching World Literature.* New York: Modern Language Association (in press).

Danius, S. (2002) *The Senses of Modernism.* Durham: Duke University Press.

Dante Alighieri (1995) *The Divine Comedy.* New York: Knopf.

Davis, P., Harrison, G., Johnson, D. M., Smith, P. C., Crawford, J. F. (eds) (2003) *The Bedford Anthology of World Literature.* New York: Bedford/St. Martin's.

De Man, P. (1983) *Blindness and Insight.* London: Routledge.

De Quincey, T. (1854) *Autobiographic Sketches.* Edinburgh: James Hogg.

Defoe, D. (1972) *Memoirs of a Cavalier: A Military Journal of the Wars in Germany, and the Wars in England. From the Year 1632 to the Year 1648.* London: Oxford University Press.

Defoe, D. (2003) *A Journal of the Plague Year.* London: Penguin.

DeLillo, D. (1982) *The Names.* New York: Knopf. DeLillo, D. (2001) *The Body Artist.* New York: Scribner.

Dharwadker, V. (ed.) (2001) *Cosmopolitan Geographies.* London: Routledge.

Dickinson, E. (1960) *Complete Poems.* Boston: Little, Brown.

Dos Passos, J. (1953) *Manhattan Transfer.* Boston: Houghton, Mifflin.

Dos Passos, J. (1996) *U.S.A.* New York: Library of America.

Dostoyevsky, F. (1992) *Notes from the Underground.* New York: Dover.

Dunker, A. (2003) *Die anwesende Abwesenheit. Literatur im Schatten von Auschwitz.* München: Wilhelm Fink.

Eaglestone, R. (2004) *The Holocaust and the Postmodern.* Oxford: Oxford University Press.

Eckermann, J. P. (1998) *Conversations of Goethe.* Oxford: Da Capo.

Eliot, T. S. (1971) *The Waste Land: Facsimile Edition.* New York: Harvest Books.

Elliott, E. (ed.) (1988) *Columbia History of Literature of the United States.* New York: Columbia University Press.

Engdahl, H. (ed.) (2002) *Witness Literature.* Hackensack and Singapore: World Scientific.

Ette, O. (2005) *ZwischenWeltenSchreiben.* Berlin: Kadmos.

Étiemble, R. (1963) *Comparaison n'est pas raison: La crise de la littérature comparée.* Paris: Gallimard.

Etiemble, R. (1974) *Essais de littérature (vraiment) générale.* Paris: Gallimard.

Fanon, F. (1963) *The Wretched of the Earth.* New York: Grove.

Faulkner, W. (1990) *The Sound and the Fury: The Corrected Text.* New York: Vintage.

Felman, S. and Laub, D. (eds) (1991) *Testimony: Crises of Witnessing in Literature, Psychoanalysis, and History.* New York: Routledge.

Ferguson, N. (1997) *Virtual History: Alternatives and Counterfactuals.* London: Picador.

Ferro, M. (ed.) (2003) *Le livre noir du colonialisme.* Paris: Robert Laffont.

Fitzgerald, F. S. (1925) *The Great Gatsby.* New York: Schribner.

Fitzgerald, F. S. (1970) 'History's Most Expensive Orgy', in Baritz, L. (ed.) *The Culture of the Twenties.* Indianapolis: Bobbs-Merill.

Foer, J. F. (2002) *Everything is Illuminated.* New York: Harper.

Foer, J. F. (2005) *Extremely Loud and Incredibly Close.* New York: Houghton Miffin.

Forsdick, C. and Murray, D. (eds) (2003) *Francophone Postcolonial Studies: A Critical Introduction.* London: Arnold.

Foster, H. (1996) *The Return of the Real.* Cambridge: MIT Press.

Foucault, M. (1987) 'What Is an Author?', in Lambropoulos, V. and Miller, D. N. (eds) *Twentieth-Century Literary Theory.* Albany: State University Press of New York.

France, P. (ed.) (2000) *The Oxford Guide to Literature in English Translation.* Oxford: Oxford University Press.

Frank, A. (1997) *The Diary of a Young Girl.* London: Penguin.

Frank, S. (2008) *Migration and Literature: Günter Grass, Milan Kundera, Salman Rushdie and Jan Kjærstad.* New York: Palgrave Macmillan (in press).

Fridman, L. W. (2000) *Words and Witness: Narrative and Aesthetic Strategies in the Representation of the Holocaust.* New York: State University of New York Press.

Friedman, T. L. (2005) *The World Is Flat.* New York: Farrar, Straus and Giroux.

Fuentes, C. (1964) *The Death of Artemio Cruz.* New York: Farrar, Straus and Giroux.

Fukuyama, F. (1992) *The End of History and the Last Man.* New York: Free Press.

Gao Xingjian (2000a) *Soul Mountain.* New York: HarperCollins.

Gao Xingjian (2000b) 'Nobel Prize Lecture', online at http://nobelprize.org/literature/laureates/2000/gao-lecture-e.html.

Gao Xingjian (2002a) *One Man's Bible.* New York: HarperCollins.

Gao Xingjian (2002b) 'Literature as Testimony: The Search for Truth', in Engdahl, H. (ed.) *Witness Literature.* New Jersey: World Scientific.

Gardels, N. (2005) 'Post-National Voices', in *New Perspectives Quarterly*, Summer 2005.

Garton Ash, T. (2002) 'On the Frontier', in Engdahl, H. (ed.) *Witness Literature.* New Jersey: World Scientific.

Gentz, N. and Kramer, S. (eds) (2006) *Globalization, Cultural Identities, and Media Representations.* Albany: State University of New York Press.

George, A. (1999) *The Epic of Gilgamesh.* Oxford: Oxford University Press.

Gervinus, G. G. (1863) *Shakespeare Commentaries.* London: Smith, Elder, and Co.

Gibbon, E. (1960) *The Decline and Fall of the Roman Empire.* New York: Harcourt, Brace.

Gordimer, N. (2002) 'The Inward Testimony', in Engdahl, H. (ed.) *Witness Literature.* New Jersey: World Scientific.

Gourevitch, P. (1998) *We Wish To Inform You That Tomorrow We Will Be Killed With Our Families.* New York: Farrar, Straus and Giroux.

Gray, P. and Oliver, K. (eds) (2004) *The Memory of Catastrophe.* Manchester: Manchester University Press.

Greenblatt, S. (1995) 'Culture', in Lentricchia, F. and McLaughlin, T. (eds) *Critical Terms for Literary Study.* Chicago: University of Chicago Press.

Griese, S., Kerscher, H., Meier, A. and Stockinger, C. (eds) (1994) *Die Leseliste: Kommentierte Empfehlungen.* Stuttgart: Reclam.

Guillory, J. (1993) *Cultural Capital: The Problem of Literary Canon Formation.* Chicago: University of Chicago Press.

Gumbrecht, H. U. (1997) *In 1926: Living at the Edge of Time.* Cambridge: Harvard University Press.

Gumbrecht, H. U. (2004) *The Production of Presence: What Meaning Cannot Convey.* Stanford: Stanford University Press.

Habermas, J. (2001) *The Postnational Constellation: Political Essays.* Cambridge: Polity Press.

Hamsun, K. (1967) *Hunger.* New York: Farrar, Straus and Giroux.

Hardt, M. and Negri, A. (2000) *Empire.* Cambridge: Harvard University Press.

Harris, R. (1992) *Fatherland.* London: Hutchinton.

Haywood, J. A. (1972) *Modern Arabic Literature, 1800–1970: An Introduction, with Extracts in Tsranslation.* New York: St. Martin's Press.

Hemingway, E. (1954) *The Sun Also Rises*. New York: Scribner.

Hemingway, E. (1995) *The Collected Stories*. London: Everyman's Library.

Hemon, A. (2002) *Nowhere Man: The Pronek Fantasies*. New York: Random House.

Heydebrand, R. v. (ed.) (1998) *Kanon – Macht – Kultur*. Stuttgart: Metzler.

Hochschild, A. (1999) *King Leopold's Ghost: A Story of Greed, Terror and Heroism in Colonial Africa*. Boston: Mariner Books.

Hoffman, F. J. (1962) *The Twenties*. New York: Collier Books.

Houellebecq, M. (1998) *Whatever*. London: Serpent's Tail.

Houellebecq, M. (2000) *The Elementary Particles*. New York: Vintage.

Houellebecq, M. (2002) *Platform*. London: Random House.

Huyssen, A. (2003) 'Diaspora and Nation: Migration Into Other Pasts', in *New German Critique*, Winter 2003, 88.

Huyssen, A. (2005) 'Geographies of Modernism in a Globalizing world', in Brooker, P. and Thacker, A. (eds) *Geographies of Modernism: Literatures, Cultures, Spaces*. London: Routledge.

Ibsen, H. (1935) *Eleven Plays of Henrik Ibsen*. New York: Modern Library.

Jenkins, H. and Thorburn, D. (eds) (2003) *Democracy and New Media*. Cambridge: MIT Press.

Joyce, J. (1926) *Dubliners*. New York: Modern Library.

Joyce, J. (1939) *Finnegans Wake*. New York: Viking.

Joyce, J. (1964) *A Portrait of the Artist as a Young Man*. New York: Viking.

Joyce, J. (1992) *Ulysses*. London: Penguin.

Kadir, D. (2004) 'To World, To Globalize', in *Comparative Literature Studies*, 37:1.

Kafka, F. (1957) *The Trial*. New York: Knopf.

Kafka, F. (1971) *The Complete Stories*. New York: Schocken.

Kafka, F. (1992) *The Complete Short Stories of Franz Kafka*. London: Minerva.

Kant, I. (1987) *Critique of Judgment*. Indianapolis: Hackett.

Kermode, F. (1988) *History and Value*. Oxford: Oxford University Press.

Kertész, I. (2001) 'Who Owns Auschwitz?', in *The Yale Journal of Criticism*, 14:1.

King, B. (ed.) (2004) *The Oxford English Literary History*, vol. 13. Oxford: Oxford University Press.

King, R. et al. (eds) (1995) *Writing Across Worlds: Literature and Migration*. London: Routledge.

Kong, S. (2004) *Consuming Literature: Best Sellers and the Commercialization of Literary Production in Contemporary China*. Stanford: Stanford University Press.

Köppen, M. (ed.) (1993) *Kunst und Literatur nach Auschwitz*. Berlin: Erich Schmidt.

Kundera, M. (1980) *The Book of Laughter and Forgetting*. New York: Knopf.

Kundera, M. (1984) *The Unbearable Lightness of Being*. New York: Harper & Row.

Kundera, M. (1987) *Laughable Loves*. New York: Penguin.

Kundera, M. (1988) *The Art of the Novel*. London: Faber and Faber.

Kundera, M. (1991) *Immortality*. New York: Grove.

Kundera, M. (2007) *The Curtain: An Essay in Seven Parts*. London: Faber and Faber.

Lang, B. (2000) *Holocaust Representations: Art within the Limits of History and Ethics*. Baltimore: Johns Hopkins University Press.

Lang, B. (ed.) (1988) *Writing and the Holocaust*. New York: Holmes & Meier.

Lanzmann, C. (1985) *Shoah: An Oral History of the Holocaust: The Complete Text of the Film*. New York: Pantheon.

Lanzmann, C. (1994) 'Holocauste, la représentation impossible', in *Le Monde*, 3 March 1994.

Lanzmann, C. (1995) 'The Obscenity of Understanding: An Evening with Claude Lanzmann', in Caruth, C. (ed.) *Trauma: Explorations in Memory*. Baltimore: Johns Hopkins University Press.

Larsen, S. E. (2004) 'Landscape, Identity, War', in *New Literary History*, 35:3.

Lawall, S. N. and Mack, M. (eds) (2003) *The Norton Anthology of World Literature*, 2nd Edition. New York: Norton.

LeCapra, D. (1996) *Representing the Holocaust: History, Theory, Trauma*. Ithaca: Cornell University Press.

Leitch, Vincent B. (2001) 'Bourdieu Against the Evils of Globalization', in *Symploke*, 9:1-2.

Levi, P. (1979) *If This Is A Man – The Truce*. London: Abacus.

Levy, D. and Sznaider, N. (2001) *Erinnerung im globalen Zeitalter: Der Holocaust*. Suhrkamp: Frankfurt am Main.

Levy, D. and Sznaider, N. (2002) 'Memory Unbound: The Holocaust and the Formation of Cosmopolitan Memory', in *European Journal of Social Theory*, 5:1.

Luhmann, N. (1997) *Die Gesellschaft der Gesellschaft*. Frankfurt am Main: Suhrkamp.

Lukács, G. (1971) *The Theory of the Novel*. London: Merlin.

Madsen, P. (2004) 'World Literature and World Thoughts', in Prendergast, C. (ed.) *Debating World Literature*. London: Verso.

Mandel, N. (2001) 'Rethinking "After Auschwitz": Against a Rhetoric of the Unspeakable in Holocaust Writing', in *Boundary 2*, 28:2.

Manovich, L. (2002) *The Language of New Media*. Cambridge: MIT Press.

Márquez, G. G. (1971) *One Hundred Years of Solitude*. New York: Avon.

Márquez, G. G. (1988) *Love in the Time of Cholera*. New York: Jonathan Cape.

Marx, K. and Engels, F. (1967) *The Communist Manifesto*. New York: The Seabury Press.

McGann, J. (2001) *Radiant Textuality: Literature after the World Wide Web*. New York: Palgrave.

McInturff, K (2001) 'Uses and Abuses of World Literature', in *American Culture*, 9:1.

Melville, H. (1967) *Moby-Dick: An Authorative Text*. New York: Norton.

Melville, H. (1997) *Bartleby the Scrivener: A Story of Wall Street*. New York: Simon & Schuster.

Miller, N. K. and Tougaw, J. (eds) (2002) *Extremities: Trauma, Testimony, and Community*. Urbana: University of Illinois Press.

Mishra, V. and Hodge, B. (2005) 'What was Postcolonialism?', in *New Literary History*, 36:3.

Mitchell, S. (2004) *Gilgamesh: A New English Version*. New York: Free Press.

Møller, P. U. (1989) 'Writing the History of World Literature in the USSR', in *Culture and History*, 5.

Mo Yan (2001) *Shifu, You'll Do Anything For a Laugh*. New York: Arcade.

Moi, T. (2006) *Henrik Ibsen and the Birth of Modernism: Art, Theater, Philosophy*. Oxford: Oxford University Press.

Monteiro, G. (1998) *The Presence of Pessoa*. Lexington: University Press of Kentucky.

Moretti, F. (1983) *Signs Taken for Wonders*. London: Verso.

Moretti, F. (1996) *Modern Epic: The World System from Goethe to García Márquez.* London: Verso.

Moretti, F. (1998) *Atlas of the European Novel 1800–1900.* London: Verso.

Moretti, F. (2000) 'Conjectures on World Literature', in *New Left Review*, 1.

Moretti, F. (2003) 'More Conjectures', in *New Left Review*, 20.

Moretti, F. (2005) *Graphs, Maps, Trees.* London: Verso.

Moretti, F. (2006) 'Evolution, World-Systems, *Weltliteratur*', in Lindberg-Wada, G. (ed.) *Studying Transcultural Literary History.* Berlin: de Gruyter.

Moulton, R. G. (1911) *World Literature and Its Place in General Culture.* London: MacMillan.

Nabokov, V. (1997) *Lolita.* New York: Vintage.

Neruda, P. (1963) *Selected Poems.* New York: Grove.

Nietzsche, F. (1980) *On the Advantage and Disadvantage of History for Life.* Indianapolis: Hackett.

Novick, P (1999) *The Holocaust and Collective Memory.* London: Bloomsbury.

Orwell, G. (1949) *Nineteen Eighty-Four.* London: Secker & Warburg.

Osteen, M. and Woodmansee, M. (eds) (1999) *The New Economic Criticism: Studies at the Intersection of Literature and Economics.* London: Routledge.

Oyeyemi, H. (2005) *The Icarus Girl.* London: Bloomsbury.

Patterson, D. A. (2003) 'Holocaust Studies without the Holocaust', in *Shofar: An Interdisciplinary Journal of Jewish Studies*, 21:4.

Patterson, D., Berger, A. L. and Cargas, S. (eds) (2002) *Encyclopedia of Holocaust literature.* Westport: Oryx Press.

Perec, G. (1967) *Un homme qui dort.* Paris: Denoël.

Perec, G. (1987) *Life, A User's Manual.* Boston: Godine.

Perec, G. (1990) *Things: A Story of the Sixties.* Boston: Godine.

Perec, G. (1996) *W or the Memory of Childhood.* London: Harvill.

Perec, G. (1999) *Things/A Man Asleep.* London: Harvill Press.

Perkins, D. (1992) *Is Literary History Possible?* Baltimore: Johns Hopkins University Press.

Pessoa, F. (1991) *The Book of Disquiet.* New York: Pantheon.

Philips, C. (ed.) (1997) *Extravagant Strangers: A Literature of Belonging.* London: Faber and Faber.

Pizer, J. D. (2006) *The Idea of World Literature: History and Pedagogical Practice.* Baton Rouge: Louisiana State University Press.

Pound, E. (1949) *The Selected Poems of Ezra Pound.* New York: New Directions.

Pound, E. (1970) *The Cantos of Ezra Pound.* New York: New Directions.

Prendergast, C. (ed.) (2004) *Debating World Literature.* London: Verso.

Prendergast, C. (2007) *The Classic: Sainte-Beuve and the Nineteenth-Century Culture Wars.* Oxford: Oxford University Press.

Proust, M. (1954) *A la recherche du temps perdu.* Paris: Pléiade.

Quinn, E. (2004) *History in Literature.* New York: Checkmark Books.

Remarque, E. M. (1996) *All Quiet on the Western Front.* London: Vintage.

Renker, E. (2000) ' "American Literature" in the College Curriculum: Three Case Studies', in *English Literary History*, 3.

Rilke, R. M. (1983) *The Notebooks of Malte Laurids Brigge.* New York: Random House.

Rorty, R. (1998) *Truth and Progress.* Cambridge: Cambridge University Press.

Rosenbaum, A. S. (ed.) (2001) *Is the Holocaust Unique?*, 2nd edition. Boulder: Westview.

Rosenfeld, A. (1980) *A Double Dying: Reflections on Holocaust Literature.* Bloomington: Indiana University Press.

Roth, P. (2004) *The Plot Against America.* London: Jonathan Cape.

Rushdie, S. (1981) *Midnight's Children.* New York: Knopf.

Rushdie, S. (1989) *The Satanic Verses.* New York: Viking.

Rushdie, S. (1991) *Imaginary Homelands.* London: Granta.

Rushdie, S. (1999) *The Ground Beneath Her Feet.* London: Jonathan Cape.

Rushdie, S. and West, E. (eds) (1997) *The Vintage Book of Indian Writing 1947–1997.* London: Vintage.

Sachs, D. M. (2001) 'The Language of Judgment: Primo Levi's *Se questo è un uomo*', in *MLN*, 110:4.

Sachs, J. (2005) *The End of Poverty: Economic Possibilities for Our Time.* New York: Penguin.

Said, E. W. (1978) *Orientalism.* New York: Pantheon Books.

Said, E. W. (2000) *Reflections on Exile and Other Essays.* Cambridge: Harvard University Press.

Sanga, J. C. (2001) *Salman Rushdie's Postcolonial Metaphors: Migration, Translation, Hybridity, Blasphemy, and Globalization.* Westport: Greenwood Press.

Sauerberg, L. O. (2001) *Intercultural Voices in Contemporary British Literature: The Implosion of Empire.* Houndmills: Palgrave.

Saussy, H. (ed.) (2006) *Comparative Literature in an Age of Globalization.* Baltimore: Johns Hopkins University Press.

Schiffrin, A. (2000) *The Business of Books.* London: Verso.

Schissler, H. and Soysal, Y. (eds) (2005) *The Nation, Europe, and the World: Textbooks and Curricula in Transition.* New York: Berghahn.

Schmelling, M. (ed.) (1995) *Weltliterature heute: Konzepte und Perspektiven.* Würzburg: Königshausen & Neumann.

Schrimpf, H. J. (1968) *Goethes Begriff der Weltliteratur.* Stuttgart: Metzler.

Schwarz, D. R. (1999) *Imagining the Holocaust.* Houndmills: Palgrave.

Selvon, S. (1956) *The Lonely Londeners.* London: Wingate.

Seyhan, A. (2001) *Writing outside the Nation.* Princeton: Princeton University Press.

Sinclair, U. (1971) *The Jungle.* New York: Bentley.

Smith, A. (2004) 'Reading Against the Postcolonial Grain: Migrancy and Exile in the Short Stories of Kanchana Ugbabe', in *Research in African Literatures*, 35:3.

Smith, Z. (2000) *White Teeth.* New York: Random House.

Solzhenitsyn, A. (1963) *One Day in the Life of Ivan Denisovich.* London: Victor Gollancz.

Sommer, R. (2001) *Fictions of Migration: Ein Beitrag zur Theorie und Gattungstypologie des zeitgenössischen interkulturellen Romans in Grossbritannien.* Trier: Wissenschaftlicher Verlag.

Sophocles (1978) *Oedipus the King.* New York: Oxford University Press.

Sornette, D., Gilbert, T., Helmstetter, A. and Ageon, Y. (2004) 'Endogenous Versus Exogenous Shocks in Complex Networks: An Empirical Test Using Book Sale Ranking', in *Physics Review Letters*, 93.

Spiller, R. E. (ed.) (1948) *Literary History of the United States.* New York: Macmillan.

Spiro, J. (2001) 'The Testimony of Fantasy in Georges Perec's *W ou le souvenir d'enfance*', in *The Yale Journal of Criticism*, 14:1.

Spivak, G. C. (1999) *A Critique of Postcolonial Reason: Toward a History of the Vanishing Present*. Cambridge: Harvard University Press.

Spivak, G. C. (2005) 'Commonwealth Literature and Comparative Literature', in Duangsamosorn, S. et al. (eds) *Re-imagining Language and Literature for the 21th Century*. Amsterdam: Rodopi.

Stäheli, U. (2000) 'Die Kontingenz des globalen Populären', in *Soziale Systeme*, 6:1.

Starkey, P. (2006) *Modern Arabic Literature*. Edinburgh: Edinburgh University Press.

Steinbeck, J. (1939) *The Grapes of Wrath*. New York: Viking.

Stein, G. (1970) *Tender Buttons*. New York: Haskell.

Steiner, G. (1995) *What is Comparative Literature?* Oxford: Clarendon.Steiner, P. (2000) *The Deserts of Bohemia: Czech Fiction and Its Social Context*. Ithaca: Cornell University Press.

Steinfeld, T. (2001) *Das Phänomen Houellebecq*. Köln: DuMont.

Strindberg, A. (1955) *Six plays*. New York: Doubleday.

Sun Qingguo (2003) 'Economics of the Chinese Book Market', in Baensch, R. E. (ed.) *The Publishing Industry in China*. New Brunswick: Transaction.

Taine, H. (1908) *History of English Literature*. Philadelphia: Altemus.

Thieme, J. (2001) *Post-Colonial Con-texts: Writing Back to the Canon*. London: Continuum.

Thomsen, M. R. (2004) 'Reinventions of the Straight Story: The Novel after Its Extremes', in Simonsen, K. M., Simonsen, K. M., Huang, M. P. and Thomsen, M. R. (eds) *Reinventions of the Novel: Histories and Aesthetics of a Protean Genre*. Amsterdam: Rodopi.

Thomsen, M. R. (2005a) 'Kanonstudien, Literatursystem, Weltliteratur', in *Zeitschrift für Literaturgeschichte und Linguistik*, 139.

Thomsen, M. R. (2005b) 'Review of *The Longman Anthology of World Literature, Volume F*', in *Gramma*, 13.

Tolstoy, L. (1998) *War and Peace*. Oxford: Oxford University Press.

Twain, M. (1977) *Adventures of Huckleberry Finn*. New York: Norton.Tzara, T. (1982) 'Lecture on Dada', in Motherwell, R. (ed.) *Dada Painters and Poets*. New York: Twayne.

Ungaretti, G. (1969) *Vita d'un uomo: Tutte le poesie*. Milano: Mondadori.

Ungaretti, G. (2003) *Selected Poems*. Manchester: Carcanet.

Valdés, M. and Kadir, D. (2004) *Literary Cultures of Latin America: A Comparative History*. New York: Oxford University Press.

Valentino, B. A. (2004) *Final Solutions: Mass Killings and Genocide in the 20th Century*. Ithaca: Cornell University Press.

Vargas Llosa, M. (1968) *The Green House*. New York: Harper & Row.

Verdicchio, P. (1997) *Devils in Paradise: Writings on Post-Emigrant Culture*. Toronto: Guernica.

Vickers, B. (1974) *William Shakespeare: The Critical Heritage*. London: Routledge.

Vico, G. (2000) *New Science*. New York: Penguin.

Voltaire (1947) *Candide*. London: Penguin.

Voltaire (2002) 'Poem on the Destruction of Lisbon', in Hyland, P. (ed.) *The Enlightment Reader*. London: Routledge.

Vonnegut, K. (1969) *Slaugtherhouse-Five*. Boston: Seymour Lawrence.

Vonnegut, K. (1988) *Bluebeard*. London: Grafton.

Walkowitz, R. L. (2006a) *Cosmopolitan Style: Modernism Beyond the Nation*. New York: Columbia University Press.

Walkowitz, R. L. (2006b) 'The Location of Literature: The Transnational Book and the Migrant Writer', in *Contemporary Literature*, 47:4.

Wallace, D. F. (1996) *Infinite Jest: A Novel*. Boston: Little, Brown.

Wallerstein, I. (1991) 'The National and the Universal: Can There be Such a Thing as World Culture?', in King, A.D. (ed.) *Culture, Globalization and the World-System: Contemporary Conditions for the Representation of Identity*. Basingstoke: Macmillan.

Walters, W. W. (2005) *At Home in Diaspora: Black International Writing*. Minneapolis: University of Minnesota Press.

Werfel, F. (1967) *The Forty Days of Musa Dagh*. New York: Viking.

Whitman, W. (1965) *Leaves of Grass*. New York: New York University Press.

Wiesel, E. (1974) *Night, Dawn, The Accident*. London: Robson.

Williams, R. (1973) *The Country and the City*. London: Chatto and Windus.

Williams, R. (1983) *Keywords: A Vocabulary of Culture and Society*. London: Fontana Press.

Williams, W. C. (1923) *Spring and All*. Paris: Contact Publishing.

Wittgenstein, L. (1953) *Philosophical Investigations*. Oxford: Basil Blackwell.

Woolf, V. (1976) *Moments of Being*. Sussex: The University Press.

Woolf, V. (1991) 'Character in Fiction', in McNellie, A. (ed.) *Essays* vol. 3. London: Harcourt.

Wordsworth, W. (1975) *Poetical Works*. Oxford: Oxford University Press.

Yingjin Zhang (ed.) (1998) *China in a Polycentric World: Essays in Chinese Comparative Literature*. Stanford: Stanford University Press.

Young, R. (2001) *Postcolonialism: A Historical Introduction*. Oxford: Blackwell.

Zamora, L. P. and Faris, W. B. (eds) (1995) *Magical Realism: Theory, History, Community*. Durham: Duke University Press.

Zelizer, B. (2001) *Visual Culture and the Holocaust*. New Brunswick: Rutgers University Press.

Index